THE EVOLUTION OF JAPAN'S PARTY SYSTEM: POLITICS AND POLICY IN AN ERA OF INSTITUTIONAL CHANGE

In August 2009, the Democratic Party of Japan (DPJ) won a crushing victory over the Liberal Democratic Party (LDP), thus bringing to an end over fifty years of one-party dominance. Around the world, the victory of the DPJ was seen as a radical break with Japan's past. However, this dramatic political shift was not as sudden as it appeared but rather the culmination of a series of changes first set in motion in the early 1990s.

The Evolution of Japan's Party System analyses the transition by examining both party politics and public policy. Arguing that these political changes were evolutionary rather than revolutionary, the essays in this volume discuss how older parties such as the LDP and the Japan Socialist Party failed to adapt to the new policy environment of the 1990s. Taken as a whole, *The Evolution of Japan's Party System* provides a unique look at party politics in Japan, bringing them into a comparative conversation that usually focuses on Europe and North America.

(Japan and Global Society)

LEONARD J. SCHOPPA is a professor in the Department of Politics at the University of Virginia.

Japan and Global Society

Editors: AKIRA IRIYE, Harvard University; MASATO KIMURA, Shibusawa Eiichi Memorial Foundation; DAVID A. WELCH, Balsillie School of International Affairs, University of Waterloo

How has Japan shaped, and been shaped by, globalization – politically, economically, socially, and culturally? How has its identity, and how have its objectives, changed? *Japan and Global Society* explores Japan's past, present, and future interactions with the Asia Pacific and the world from a wide variety of disciplinary and interdisciplinary perspectives and through diverse paradigmatic lenses. Titles in this series are intended to showcase international scholarship on Japan and its regional neighbours that will appeal to scholars in disciplines both in the humanities and the social sciences.

Japan and Global Society is supported by generous grants from the Shibusawa Eiichi Memorial Foundation and the University of Missouri–St Louis.

EDITED BY LEONARD J. SCHOPPA

The Evolution of Japan's Party System

Politics and Policy in an Era
of Institutional Change

UNIVERSITY OF TORONTO PRESS
Toronto Buffalo London

© University of Toronto Press 2011
Toronto Buffalo London
www.utppublishing.com
Printed in the U.S.A.

Reprinted 2012

ISBN 978-1-4426-4309-3 (cloth)
ISBN 978-1-4426-1167-2 (paper)

Printed on acid-free paper.

Library and Archives Canada Cataloguing in Publication

The evolution of Japan's party system : politics and policy in an era of
institutional change / edited by Leonard J. Schoppa.

(Japan and global society series)
Includes bibliographical references and index.
ISBN 978-1-4426-4309-3 (bound). – ISBN 978-1-4426-1167-2 (pbk.)

1. Political parties – Japan. 2. Political planning – Japan. 3. Japan – Politics
and government – 1945–. I. Schoppa, Leonard J. (Leonard James), 1962–
II. Series: Japan and global society series

JQ1698.A1E96 2011   324.0952   C2011-904228-2

University of Toronto Press acknowledges the financial assistance to its
publishing program of the Canada Council for the Arts and the Ontario
Arts Council.

University of Toronto Press acknowledges the financial support of the
Government of Canada through the Canada Book Fund for its publishing
activities.

Contents

Preface

University of Toronto Press, in cooperation with the University of Missouri–St Louis and the Shibusawa Eiichi Memorial Foundation of Tokyo, is launching an ambitious new series, 'Japan and Global Society.' The volumes in the series will explore how Japan has defined its identities and objectives in the larger region of Asia and the Pacific and, at the same time, how the global community has been shaped by Japan and its interactions with other countries.

The dual focus on Japan and on global society reflects the series editors' and publishers' commitment to globalizing national studies. Scholars and readers have become increasingly aware that it makes little sense to treat a country in isolation. All countries are interdependent and shaped by cross-national forces so that mono-national studies, those that examine a country's past and present in isolation, are never satisfactory. Such awareness has grown during the past few decades when global, transnational phenomena and forces have gained prominence. In the age of globalization, no country retains complete autonomy or freedom of action. Yet nations continue to act in pursuit of their respective national interests, which frequently results in international tensions. Financial, social, and educational policies continue to be defined domestically, with national communities as units. But transnational economic, environmental, and cultural forces always infringe upon national entities, transforming them in subtle and sometimes even violent ways. Global society, consisting of billions of individuals and their organizations, evolves and shapes national communities even as the latter contribute to defining the overall human community.

Japan provides a particularly pertinent instance of such interaction, but this series is not limited to studies of that country alone. Indeed, the books published in the series will show that there is little unique about Japan, whose history has been shaped by interactions with China, Korea, the United States, and many other countries. For this reason, forthcoming volumes will deal with countries in the Asia-Pacific region and compare their respective developments and shared destinies. At the same time, some studies in the series will transcend national frameworks and discuss more transnational themes, such as humanitarianism, migration, and diseases, documenting how these phenomena affect Japan and other countries and how, at the same time, they contribute to the making of a more interdependent global society.

Lastly, we hope these studies will help to promote an understanding of non-national entities, such as regions, religions, and civilizations. Modern history continues to be examined in terms of nations as the key units of analysis, and yet these other entities have their own vibrant histories, which do not necessarily coincide with nation-centred narratives. To look at Japan, or for that matter any other country, and to examine its past and present in these alternative frameworks will enrich our understanding of modern world history and of the contemporary global civilization.

Akira Iriye

THE EVOLUTION OF JAPAN'S PARTY SYSTEM:
POLITICS AND POLICY IN AN ERA
OF INSTITUTIONAL CHANGE

1 Introduction: From the 1955 System to the '2000 System'

LEONARD J. SCHOPPA

In Japan's national election on 30 August 2009, the Democratic Party of Japan (DPJ) won a landslide victory over the Liberal Democratic Party (LDP). The DPJ did not merely eke out a bare-majority victory; it crushed its rival by winning 308 seats to the LDP's 119, just four years after the LDP had won almost 300 seats in its own landslide win. After fifty-four years of one-party dominance under the LDP, the DPJ had finally delivered a 'change of government' (*seiken koutai*) – the slogan under which it fought the 2009 campaign.

Around the world, the Democrats' victory was hailed as a radical break with the past: Japan's entrenched political system had finally delivered *change*. A group of politicians – most of whom had never been 'in government' – were suddenly in, and the old men of the LDP (those who had not lost their seats) were suddenly out. This dramatic change of government was not, however, as sudden as it appeared to observers newly tuning into Japanese politics. It was merely the culmination of a series of changes – a process of evolution – that had been set in motion when the LDP split back in 1993.

From 1955 until 1993 – a period of almost four decades – Japanese politics revolved around the competition between the dominant LDP and the always-losing but resilient Japan Socialist Party (JSP). Political scientists who studied Japan spent a lot of time trying to explain how the LDP could win election after election, but Japan was not at all unusual in the degree to which the same two parties would win the bulk of a nation's votes over a period of many decades. In a pattern that has been likened to 'party cartels' (Katz and Mair 1995), a stable set of political parties has tended to dominate politics over extended periods of time in virtually all democratic systems.

In Japan, the stability of party competition over nearly forty years led the party system to be named for the date of its birth: the '1955 System.' Over this time, the party system was not the only thing that was stable. Electoral competition revolved around the question of whether Japan should be allied with the United States in the Cold War, expand its military role, and put aside its post-war defeatism and celebrate symbols of Japanese nationalism, such as the flag and the anthem. The LDP favoured all of these policies. For the full duration of the 1955 System, the JSP made its disagreement with the LDP over this set of issues its main rallying point, calling for neutrality in the Cold War and vocally opposing rearmament and nationalist symbols.

In the realm of economic policy, party positions were also stable over this period, but here the LDP and JSP collaborated in constructing a system of 'convoy capitalism,' in which the state played a dominant role in the economy, steering capital towards targeted sectors during the 'miracle' years while using trade protection, subsidies, and regulations to spread the benefits of growth to lagging sectors. Facing international calls for Japan to open its rice market and subject its farmers to world market prices, politicians from *both* parties objected and kept such liberalizing reforms from being adopted. Whenever recession threatened to topple large companies, both parties called for policies to prop them up and buy time for them to adjust. In this respect, too, Japan was not unusual: as T.J. Pempel (1998) has argued, other advanced industrialized nations have 'regimes' based on a stable coalition of social groups and offer a stable output of public policies.

Although pushed out of power for a brief, eight-month period in 1993–94, the LDP thereafter resumed its position of dominance in the party system and extended its run in power for another fifteen years. Meanwhile, however, virtually all other aspects of the old party system continued to change. In 1996, the other pole of the 1955 System, the JSP, simply *disappeared,* collapsing one end of the old 'cartel.' After losing almost half its seats in the 1993 election, the JSP had tried desperately to reinvent itself for the post–Cold War era, renouncing its support for unilateral disarmament and adopting a new name – the Social Democratic Party of Japan. This experiment – an effort to paper over the party's differences with the LDP in a 1994–96 coalition of the two – has cost it dearly in the elections since, and the party is winning a dwindling number of seats (see Figure 1.1).

While there was significant instability in Japan's party system in the period right after 1993, it is now clear that the JSP's place as the primary

Figure 1.1: Lower House Election Results, 1990–2009

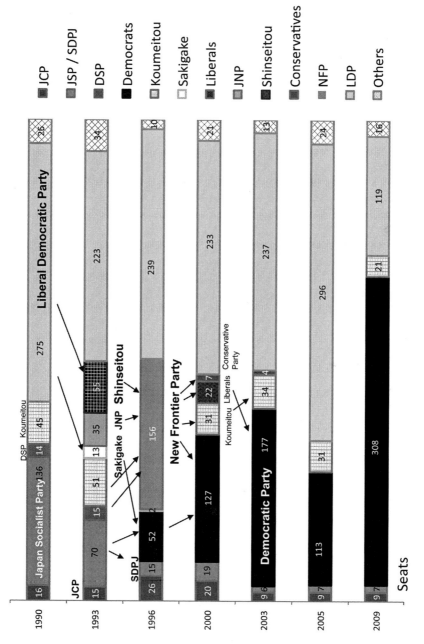

Source: Based on data in various editions of *Seikan Youran* (Tokyo: Seisaku Jihousha, semiannual).

rival to the LDP has been taken by a political party that began contesting elections only in 1996 and emerged in 2000 as the second-largest party: the Democratic Party of Japan. Through the 2003 election, the DPJ steadily expanded its share of lower house seats, from 52 to 127 to 177. Even in the face of a major defeat in 2005, when it fell to 113 seats, it avoided splitting.[1] Then, in the 2007 upper house election, the DPJ managed to win more seats than the combined total of the LDP and its coalition partner, the New Koumeitou Party. Finally, in 2009, the DPJ confirmed that an era of competitive two-party politics had arrived by performing a similar feat in the lower house election.

While it is tempting to mark this DPJ achievement by calling the new party system the '2009 System,' I favour dating the shift to 2000, since that is when the DPJ emerged as the leading alternative to the LDP. The 2000 System also would recognize that, while other components of the old regime have been changing steadily since 1993, momentum picked up in the early 2000s when Koizumi Jun'ichirou took over as unconventional leader of the LDP. Instead of collaborating to construct and preserve the old system of 'convoy capitalism,' as the LDP and JSP did in the years before 1993, the LDP and DPJ have spent most of the past decade competing to see which can outdo the other in favouring 'economic reform.'

The competition got started in 1998, almost immediately after the DPJ emerged on the scene, when that party played a key role in formulating bank bailout legislation in response to the collapse of the Long-Term Credit Bank. By refusing to prop up one of the nation's largest banks with more taxpayer money, legislators essentially ended the 'convoy system' of bank regulation that had protected banks (and their borrowers) from the risk of collapse since the 1950s. The DPJ thus established its credentials as a party that favoured forcing banks to start worrying about the consequences of failure. Having to pay more attention to market forces, banks henceforth would face growing pressure to cut off corporate borrowers who were delinquent in paying back their loans and had no hope of revival – and their employees.

Koizumi's LDP then presided over the next phase of financial reform, which pressured banks to write off bad loans and began to shrink the flow of state-controlled capital from the postal savings system through government financial institutions to favoured clients. Throughout the early 2000s, the LDP and the DPJ thus competed to see which could propose deeper cuts in public works spending and deeper reductions in the number of public employees. Instead of competing over which party could do more for the 'little guy,' as the LDP and JSP had done for decades under the 1955 System, the two leading parties spent most of a decade competing over which could do more to restore economic growth by *reducing* social protection.

Faced with the deepest recession in the post-war period, the two parties abandoned much of their economic reform rhetoric in the year before the 2009 election. The DPJ, in particular, played up support for social safety net programs much more than it had in the past, calling for a dramatic increase in child allowances, the elimination of public high school fees, an increase in university scholarships, the restoration of the pension system to financial sustainability, and the reversal of social insurance cutbacks that the LDP had implemented. It remains to be seen how the DPJ and LDP will position themselves in the typical Left and Right locations in policy space – perhaps the DPJ as a party of the Left that is moderate on security policy and social democratic on economic policy, and the LDP as party of the Right that is hawkish on security policy and neoliberal on economic policy. But it is clear that the old LDP-Socialist consensus in favour of a 'convoy' system of social protection has broken down completely.

A number of recent volumes have focused on either *party politics* or *public policy* in Japan. Reed (2003, 2009), Scheiner (2006), and Martin and Steel (2008), among others, have focused on the electoral and party politics of the period since 1993, while Pempel (1998), Amyx (2004), Schoppa (2006b), and Vogel (2006) have examined trends in policy and political economy since that critical year. This volume, in contrast, sets out to help readers understand the transition from the 1955 System to the 2000 System by focusing on both dimensions of Japanese politics. While the number of scholars who study Japanese politics is relatively small, we somehow still manage to specialize in one or the other of these two dimensions – even though they are clearly intertwined. Here, scholars from both sides of the divide come together to consider the roles that party politics and public policy play in driving the process of 'regime shift.' Party politics, in our view, is inherently connected to the making of public policy. Parties frequently appeal for votes by staking out differing positions on policy, so election results help drive policy in new directions. Even when they take the same position on a given policy, or fudge their differences, parties' decisions *not* to contest a policy position have the effect of locking in that policy line.

At the same time, policy has feedback effects on party politics. When economic structures established as a result of policy give a party, through the levers of state power, the ability to influence the allocation of capital, direct subsidies to clients, and regulatory favours to donors, they also give that party a tremendous advantage over its rivals (Scheiner 2006). When neoliberal economic reforms begin to eliminate some of these options, they remove a major source of incumbent advantage and encourage parties to compete for votes in different ways. The most far-sighted political leaders, including several who have influenced developments in Japan since 1993, are fully aware of the political consequences of policy, and so set out to shape policy – electoral reform, administrative reform, banking reform, postal reform – with the specific aim of locking in political advantages or destroying a source of advantage enjoyed by rivals.

The main argument expressed in this volume, therefore, is that regime change in Japan is an *evolutionary* process that began when changes in the policy environment disadvantaged the old parties, the LDP and the JSP. When these parties could not adapt quickly enough, new parties came into the game. Of course, the metaphor of evolution cannot capture the fact that parties (unlike biological organisms) can react and strategize and even attempt to reshape their environment to survive. Indeed, both the LDP and the new parties attempted to gain advantage during the 1990s by changing the rules of the electoral and economic systems. Nevertheless, they continued to be governed by Darwinian logic, which determined which two survived.

More specifically, the contributors argue that one cannot understand the shift from the 1955 System to the 2000 System without taking into account how developments in party politics – the collapse of the JSP, the rise of the DPJ, machinations within the LDP – have interacted with the shift towards neoliberalism in Japanese economic policy. As long as the nation operated under 'convoy capitalism,' the LDP had a lock on power. It sold itself to farmers, small businesses, and salaried workers who valued lifetime employment, as the party that would protect their livelihood and give them peace and prosperity. At the same time, it marketed itself to big business and to salaried workers who valued low tax rates as the party of 'small government' that could deliver on economic security without raising taxes or moving towards socialism. How could the JSP compete with that? No wonder it continued trying to win votes based on its pacifist platform, which enjoyed much more support than its outdated promises of rule by the proletariat.

The collapse of the bubble economy and the end of the Cold War at the start of the 1990s upset this stable equilibrium. For reasons I explore in more detail in Chapter 2, neither the JSP nor the old LDP was able to adapt to these twin challenges. The JSP continued to offer pacifism and socialism in an era when these prescriptions were fast losing their appeal. Meanwhile, the LDP continued to defend 'convoy capitalism' even as weaker members of the convoy began falling away despite the party's efforts to spend large sums of taxpayer money to keep the system going. These failures opened the door to a challenge from the neoliberal direction by new parties. Once the LDP was challenged from this direction, it became increasingly difficult to be all things to all voters. Was the LDP the party of livelihood protection, helping farmers and small businesses and keeping large employers afloat to preserve jobs? That is what it looked like for several years in the late 1990s as the party spent heavily on public works and few-strings-attached bank bailouts. Or was the LDP what Koizumi was selling from 2001 to 2006: the party of small government, insisting on the discipline of the market as it forced banks to write off bad loans and reduced spending on public works projects? Only by looking at these interactions between party politics and economic policy change, we argue, can one understand how Japan's political system has evolved from a dominant party presiding over 'convoy capitalism' into a two-party competition.

In the next chapter, I elaborate on the model of evolutionary regime change summarized above. I offer some of the historical background needed to make sense of the developments between 1993 and 2009 by focusing, first, on the positive feedback loops that made the LDP and JSP the dominant parties of the 1955 System for 38 years. I then look at how the environment changed in the early 1990s in ways that caused these feedback loops to malfunction, prevented the two parties from adapting quickly to the end of the Cold War and the collapse of the bubble economy. Finally, I sketch out the logic of 'survival of the fittest' that led the DPJ and the LDP to emerge from this struggle as the dominant parties of the new 2000 System.

In Chapter 3, Steve Reed focuses on the LDP's response since 1993 to its new environment – in particular, how it has met the challenge of winning over 'floating' voters (*fudou-hyou*) or 'unaffiliated' voters (*mutouhasou*) by adopting policies to appeal to them and by using the leverage available under new electoral rules to force reluctant members of the old guard to unify behind the new platform. Under the 1955 System, Japan's floating voters were not committed to the LDP in the way farmers and small businesses were, but they also were smaller than other groups of voters (about 20 per cent of the electorate in the 1980s), and many cast their votes for the LDP anyway because they did not like the impractical policies offered by the JSP. The emergence of new parties in 1993 gave this group new voting options and left others who had previously supported the JSP in a similar quandary. Refusing to commit to any party, unaffiliated voters grew to half the electorate by the turn of the century (Tanaka and Martin 2003).

At the same time, electoral rules adopted in 1994 increased the importance of winning the votes of the floating and the unaffiliated – by making the old organized vote on which the LDP had relied insufficient to win single-member districts. Prime ministers also obtained the ability to use their control of nominations to single-member districts to unify the party behind reformist policies that would appeal to these voters. Reed looks at how the LDP has adapted to this new environment, focusing in particular on Koizumi's success in using the new electoral rules to appeal to win the votes of the unaffiliated in 2005. As Reed argues, however, this episode was in fact an exception. It took several elections before Koizumi demonstrated the value of party reform, and there has been a great deal of backsliding since 2005. Reed concludes that it will take two defeats for the party to lock in these adaptations.

In Chapter 4, Robert Weiner shifts the focus to the new party on the block, the DPJ. This party was born and grew through a series of mergers and defections from other parties, so it has long been known as a hodgepodge of opportunists. Since it had never attained power (prior to 2009) and often seemed on the verge of splitting, few scholars have devoted much attention to it. And yet, since 2000, it has been the largest opposition party and in 2009 it became the ruling party with a landslide victory in the lower house election. Weiner analyses election returns to show us what the DPJ is about, where it is strongest, and what kinds of candidates it has been recruiting. He also looks at its membership to see if it is vulnerable to a schism between groups with ties to former socialist and conservative parties. Contrary to the conventional wisdom, Weiner argues, the party is not overly concentrated in the most urban areas, it has made some progress in recruiting 'quality' candidates, and it is not vulnerable to a split caused by former Socialists. Ironically, he concludes, the DPJ has become much more similar to the LDP in its make-up as it has become more electorally successful.

Sherry Martin focuses in Chapter 5 squarely on the nexus between party politics and public policy. Japan's electoral reforms of the 1990s were designed to foster more issue-based competition among parties, but examinations of the first elections held under the rules failed to find any evidence that parties had offered the electorate a choice among issue-positions. Instead, campaigns tended to focus on 'valence' issues such as pension reform (where all voters favour a more secure system), and parties competed to convince voters theirs was the best approach to achieve this aim. In such an environment, both parties and voters had difficulty establishing firm positions in policy space that would structure the vote.

While Martin reports similar findings about the issues that voters say are most important to them (social welfare, inequality), she presents evidence that, by 2005, national security policy had re-emerged for the first time since the 1960s as a divisive issue, and that voters in that year actually chose how to cast their ballots based on positions the DPJ and LDP took on this issue. She argues, based on these findings, that electoral reform has indeed increased the potential for issues to structure voters' choice. The challenge for the parties is to offer voters competing positions on the socio-economic issues that matter most to them.

In the latter half of the volume, the focus shifts to economic policy and its connections with party politics. In Chapter 6, Patti Maclachlan examines Koizumi's signature policy achievement: the privatization of the postal system, including the postal savings and insurance components. Comparing this initiative with earlier privatization campaigns under the 1955 System, she argues that Koizumi was able to achieve victory under circumstances that would certainly have stymied earlier prime ministers by making full use of new institutions that helped him isolate and defeat a formidable alliance of bureaucratic and political foes. Nevertheless, Maclachlan cautions, Koizumi's victory was compromised in the implementation process and rolled back to a certain degree. Unlike some other contributors to this volume, she is not yet ready to write the obituary of 'state-led capitalism' in Japan.

In Chapter 7, Maria Toyoda complements Maclachlan's analysis by focusing on recent reforms to a system that had long funnelled money collected by postal savings and insurance through the Fiscal Investment and Loan Program (FILP) to government financial institutions. Funnelling money to favoured clients through this system of policy-based finance, Toyoda argues, was at the centre of the LDP's dominance in the era when it was able to win election after election. She looks at how party politics evolved during the 1990s in such a way as to enable reform of this system. It was not just the privatization of postal savings, she argues, that broke this web of vested interests; also critical were reforms in the FILP system initiated under Prime Minister Hashimoto Ryuutarou during the 1996–98 period and reforms of government financial institutions that merged several of these behemoths and put others on the path to privatization. Unlike Maclachlan, Toyoda sees the reforms already in place as locking in a move away from 'convoy capitalism.' Although she, too, recognizes that Koizumi's reforms have been rolled back to some degree, she argues that the policy changes currently in place have reinforced the equilibrium of the new 2000 System.

Mari Miura, in Chapter 8, shifts the focus to the effect of public policies on labour. Here, too, she argues, party politics and institutional reforms have empowered interests that favour neoliberal policies. Contrasting the record of labour market policy under the 1955 System with the record of the past decade, she finds that labour has lost its position under the earlier system as a beneficiary of efforts by the LDP and big business to use economic growth to support the system of lifetime employment. The collapse of the bubble economy and growing international competition in the 1990s prompted employers to shift preferences: instead of viewing Japan's labour protections as a source of Japanese firms' competitive advantage, they began calling for reforms that would make the labour market more flexible. While employers have not won all of their legislative battles, in part because the DPJ has emerged as an advocate on issues affecting salaried workers, Miura argues that the new party system and political structures have enabled a shift in labour market rules that has increased inequality and left many more workers vulnerable to layoffs in an economic downturn – as we are seeing today.

This volume arrives just as the DPJ is getting its own first crack at reshaping the policy environment. It is likely to favour labour more than does the LDP, and it has promised a significant expansion of social welfare programs. It has already rolled back, to some degree, Koizumi's reform of the postal system. The DPJ's arrival in office clearly is not the end of the process of evolution we describe here. The changes it makes in policy might lock in the equilibrium we have seen emerging since 1993, but they could also drive a further realignment of the party system and more policy change. What we are sure to see, regardless, is a continuation of the evolutionary dance of party politics and public policy.

NOTE

1 A few years earlier, the New Frontier Party split into several small parts
   after it failed to win a majority in the 1996 election, and the LDP saw defections after it lost badly in 2009. While party splits are rare in most political
   systems, Japan lately has seen quite a few of them, making the DPJ's ability
   to hold together after its 2005 defeat a real achievement.

2 Path Dependence in the Evolution of Japan's Party System since 1993

LEONARD J. SCHOPPA

Japan's party system in the period after 1993 was a picture of instability. Parties were splitting, forming, merging, and dissolving in such rapid succession that the game of musical chairs seemed to describe what was going on better than any known theory of political science. The dominant dynamic was one in which politicians from sinking parties scrambled aboard whatever new party looked likely to float, suggesting that short-term electoral survival of individuals – more than the rational response of parties to fundamental shifts in the preferences of voters – was guiding the process of party system change.

Now, we are in a much better position to make sense of what happened. The parties of the mid-1990s – the Japan New Party, Shinseitou, Shintou Sakigake, the New Frontier Party, Minseitou, Taiyoutou, the Liberal Party, the New Conservative Party – proved transient. In contrast, the Democratic Party of Japan (DPJ) has held its own as the leading opposition party through three lower house election cycles (2000, 2003, and 2005), and in the 2007 upper house election demonstrated that it could win more seats than the two ruling parties combined. Although the DPJ became a ruling party for the first time only in 2009, it has had a full decade to establish its policy positions in published manifestos.

The fact that the DPJ survived the new party shakeout of the 1990s to become a new pole of the '2000 System' suggests that its emergence might have been the product of something more than a game of musical chairs, explained by the survival instincts of individual Diet members eager to be part of some party – *any* party – that would be large enough to survive the brutal 'mechanical effects' of the new electoral rules on single-member districts adopted in 1994. Still, while there was certainly much opportunistic scrambling of this kind in the 1990s, we can see in the aggregate behaviour of many politicians over several election cycles a dynamic that reflects the influence of changing social cleavages and voter preferences. Looking back at the events of the mid-1990s, it is now clear that the party-switching muddle marked a *critical juncture* at which an entrenched party system, out of synch with the changing preferences of voters, gave way, allowing a new system more in line with the underlying structure of social cleavages to take shape. If we are right, that would certainly be reassuring for democratic theory. It would suggest that party systems are not dominated by unbeatable party 'cartels' (Katz and Mair 1995) but instead are subject to change as a result of fundamental shifts in the social structure and policy preferences of voters.

In this chapter, I argue that, while changes in the structure of cleavages and voter preferences help to account for the DPJ's emergence as a new pole of the 2000 System, the *path-dependent* nature of change has prevented the new system from giving Japanese voters a clear choice between options on a cleavage over economic policy that matters a great deal to them and that structures party systems in almost every other democracy. A 2003 survey of experts to map out the 'policy space' that structures Japanese politics found that, 'despite the fact that [it] is seen as a party of the centre-left, the [DPJ] occupies a more right-ist position (fiscal conservatism-support tax increases to reduce deficit bonds) than the [Liberal Democratic Party]' (Kato and Laver 2003, 131). By 2005, when updated results of the survey were presented, the LDP and the DPJ occupied virtually identical positions on economic issues such as 'deregulation' (scoring 12.7 and 12.9, respectively, on a twenty-point scale) and 'taxes vs. spending' (10.6 and 10.1, respectively) (Laver and Benoit 2005, 209). By the time of the 2009 election, both the DPJ and the LDP had moved away from embracing economic reform and now were advocating large new spending increases on social insurance programs. How is it that, after the turmoil of the 1990s, a new party system has emerged in a form that still leaves Japanese voters without a clear choice on economic policy?

To answer this question, and to explain the broader pattern of political change in Japan since 1993, I develop a model of path-dependent party system evolution that emphasizes how, even during 'earthquake' periods of electoral volatility, change is shaped by the way *remaining components* of the party system are tied to specific positions in policy space. When electoral earthquakes destroy one pole of the system (the Social Democratic Party of Japan, SDPJ) but not the other (the LDP), new parties seeking to establish themselves as significant players in the new system are forced to orient themselves vis-à-vis the remnants of the old system. The new system does not take shape *de novo* to reflect the current structure of social cleavages. Instead, it reflects both the old social structure that left remnant parties in particular places in policy space and the new social structure that creates opportunities for new parties to gain strategic advantage over their rivals. These choices can produce a disconnect between social structure and the party system – so that, even after a critical juncture, the new system might not fit neatly with the structure of voter preferences and social cleavages.

The 'Frozen' Party System in Place before 1993

A great deal of theorizing has gone into explaining the endurance of the established 1955 System that structured politics in Japan from the year it took shape until 1993. Figure 2.1 shows the striking continuity of the system. The LDP was the predominant party throughout the entire period, forming governments by itself after all elections – except for a brief period after the 1983 election when the New Liberal Club joined it in a pseudo-coalition – and supplying every prime minister. Throughout, the Japan Socialist Party (JSP) was the main opposition party. While new centrist parties such as the Democratic Socialist Party and Koumeitou emerged and won as many as 58 seats in some elections, none was able to displace the JSP as the dominant pole of opposition to the LDP.

Japan's 1955 System was not unusual in its endurance. As Lipset and Rokkan famously noted in 1967 (50), most democracies had party systems that essentially were *frozen*: 'the party systems of the 1960's reflect, with few but significant exceptions, the cleavage structures of the 1920's.' The pattern of continuity was noted as well by Peter Mair in his 1997 book, written in large part to explain why voters in the 1990s continued to choose among parties, or blocs, that grew up in an era when societies were very different. As recently as 2003, Matt Golder found the continuity enduring across thirteen Western democracies that had held competitive elections without interruption since 1930. These nations saw a total of 385 new parties contest elections, but only eight – including the Gaullists in France and the Freedom Party in Austria – were able to win more than 15 per cent of the vote. Aside from France, *none* of the thirteen had seen a new party win a significant share of the vote, enter government, and endure as a major pole of its party system.

Figure 2.1: Lower House Election Results, 1958–90

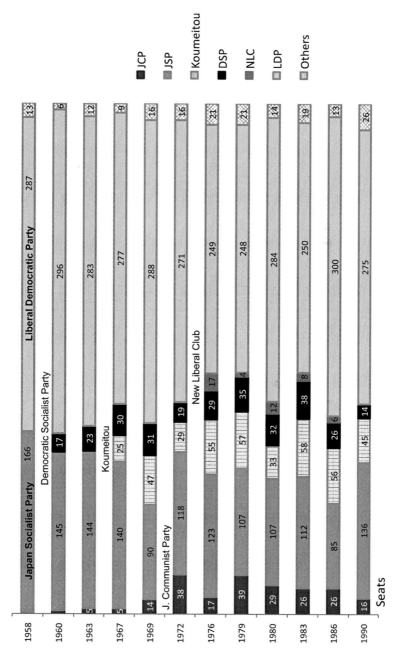

Source: Based on data in *About Japan Series 13: The Diet, Elections, and Political Parties* (Tokyo: Foreign Press Center of Japan, 1995), p. 145.

This striking continuity in party systems – over a period in which nations have evolved into the post-industrial societies of today – has motivated a variety of scholars to identify the mechanisms that allow established parties to retain their dominant positions in mature democracies. In order to understand how the Japanese party system broke out of its pattern of continuity in 1993 and how it has evolved since then, it is therefore necessary to reflect first on how these mechanisms worked to perpetuate the 1955 System for almost four decades.

Lipset and Rokkan, who first offered the 'freezing' hypothesis, argued that the paucity of party system change after the 1920s had a great deal to do with the Western democracies having opened up the voting process to universal suffrage, including the working class. Until that time, party systems had been vulnerable to disruption by the emergence of new parties that catered to disenfranchised groups. As these groups were brought into the voting process, however, established parties were able to create a rough equilibrium that reflected the balance of class, religious, and ethnic cleavages of the time. Incumbent parties, Lipset and Rokkan argued, also were in a position to use the resources at their disposal and their ties to particular groups of voters to perpetuate their dominant positions in the system. As Mair put it, 'Once an equilibrium had been established, however crudely defined, the system could simply generate its own momentum: the structure of competition was more or less defined, the terms of reference were given, and there ensued . . . "the mobilization of bias." The party system "freezes" itself, as it were' (1997, 87). In other words, party systems tend to endure because established parties have incentives and opportunities to keep alive the cleavages that convinced voters to support them in the past.

This process of self-preservation is characterized by a variety of positive feedback loops. Parties founded on a particular line of cleavage have an incentive to continue playing up conflicts with rivals on the other side of the cleavage line in order to mobilize their supporters to vote for them at election time. As they do so, politicians, activists, and voters come to identify with and join the party of those who share these attitudes, and they use their influence over party policy to keep the party faithful to its founding purpose. Once a party develops a particular brand identity for fighting for a specific cause, it discovers that it is much cheaper, because of sunk costs, to continue fighting for votes according to the old script – 'vote for us because we have always stood on the side of (name the group)' – than to appeal for votes on grounds that are unfamiliar to voters and the media.

These feedback loops were much at work in perpetuating the 1955 System. The two parties that emerged from Japan's early post-war elections as the dominant players, the JSP and LDP, were born out of the Cold War struggle between the United States and the communists in China and the Soviet Union. After imposing the pacifist constitutional 'Article 9' on Japan during the Occupation, the Americans reversed course and pushed Japan to rearm and join its efforts to contain the communists. The JSP established itself as a major force in Japanese politics by tapping into opposition to this policy from progressives and unionists who had embraced the pacifist Constitution and preferred a neutralism that they believed would keep Japan out of World War Three. For more than three decades, the leading planks in the JSP platform called for Japan to end its Security Treaty with the United States and abolish the Self-Defense Forces.

The LDP stood squarely on the opposite side of the cleavage over Japan's defence and foreign policies. It was formed in 1955 through a merger of feuding conservative parties brought together by their common fear of what might happen if the newly unified JSP ever came to power and attempted to implement its campaign platform. The LDP included urbane technocrats eager to industrialize the country and rural populists eager to bring roads, rails, dams, and bridges to poor farming communities cut off from the thriving Pacific Coast cities by mountains and seas. To counter the JSP's positions, the leading planks in the LDP platform called for supporting the United States-Japan alliance and revising Article 9 to allow Japan to play a larger military role.

In the 1950s and 1960s, the divide over these issues was wide and emotions ran hot. Hundreds of thousands of citizens marched in the streets in the 1960 Security Treaty Crisis, and in the late 1960s many college campuses were forced to shut down under the pressure of continuous protests. An entire generation of politicians, activists, and voters chose political sides on the basis of this divide, and kept their parties faithful to the cause even when – in the case of the JSP – it became obvious that the party could not win with a platform that called for unarmed neutrality (Curtis 1988, 117–56).

In succeeding years, as the Cold War became less worrisome by most objective measures, Japan and the United States normalized relations with China and signed treaties of commerce and friendship, while the Soviet Union and the United States signed a series of arms control agreements. Nevertheless, the two parties born of the heated struggle over military and foreign policy continued to 'mobilize bias' in such a way as to perpetuate the conflict and keep their voting bases loyal. The LDP warned at election time that the JSP would lead the country into the Soviet bloc. The JSP warned that Japan risked a 'return to pre-war militarism' if the LDP remained in power. The degree to which the two parties succeeded in entrenching this cleavage can be seen in the continuing tendency of experts, politicians, and voters to describe the party system in 'Left-Right' terms according to where each party stood on issues of defence and foreign policy, even after the end of the Cold War (Kato and Laver 2003). As long as the international environment was threatening enough to make voters susceptible to electoral appeals based on the Cold War script, the established parties were best able to exploit that fear to boost their vote totals.

Another mechanism that scholars have identified to explain party system continuity is a product of the well-known collective action problem: the difficulty of organizing individuals with diffuse interests. Parties themselves are organizations in which large numbers of individuals must work together – paying dues, making donations, devoting time to voter mobilization – to achieve electoral success. Established parties that have built the structures that collect dues, gather contributions, and organize local chapters to fight elections have a huge advantage over new parties that must organize collective action from scratch. The advantages of established parties are enhanced still further if they are able to gain office and use tax revenues to support their interests (Shefter 1977; Mair 1997). Some systems provide tax-funded subsidies to parties based on their share of seats or votes; most give parties in power at the central or local level the opportunity to reward supporters by influencing the geographic distribution of public works projects or the choice of government contractors. Either way, incumbent parties have a big advantage over new parties that seek to disrupt the established party system.

Established parties also tend to benefit from long-standing ties to intermediate associations such as unions, business groups, and farm groups. In many cases, the cleavages that drove parties to align in certain ways in the past also drove interest groups to form along similar lines. Once workers and business groups are organized one way (say, to fight each other), they are unlikely to disband and reform along different lines (say, workers and firms in traded sectors versus those in non-traded sectors). The organizational space tends to 'fill up' (Pierson 2004, 71) in ways that make it difficult for new interest groups to form. Established parties naturally have an advantage in building relationships with interest groups, for the reasons enumerated above, allowing them to tap these groups for votes and campaign contributions and depriving new parties of a handy shortcut to growth.

In the 1955 System, these organizational feedback loops allowed the LDP to use its perpetual hold on power to build the party and lock up support from organized groups, especially business groups dependent on government regulatory support, construction contractors dependent on public works, and farmers dependent on rice price subsidies (Scheiner 2006). The same process also kept the JSP as the leading opposition party through its close ties to the only large group not part of the LDP support coalition: unions. While the JSP made foreign policy the primary basis for its appeal for votes, it also catered to its union supporters by fighting for labour rights. With most interest groups aligned with one or the other of the two leading parties and the rest with fringe parties, the only hope for a new party was to appeal to voters who were unorganized and unaffiliated – a notoriously fickle and disparate group.

A third way established parties make it hard for newcomers to gain a foothold is by professionalizing to gain autonomy from their original voting base and by adapting to changes in society (Mair 1997, 10–11). Parties have an incentive to become 'catch-all' parties that appeal to as many groups and causes as possible. As long as the party can appeal to new groups without antagonizing its base, it can add them to its support coalition. This process allows established parties to avoid shrinking as the proportion of their core supporters in society (farmers, unionized workers) declines, and to market themselves across a wide spectrum – the party of workers *and* environmentalists or the party of business *and* traditional values.

The LDP's predominance under the 1955 System can be credited in large measure to its adaptability. Its original support coalition of farmers, small business, and big business included two sectors of society that were in secular decline as Japan urbanized and industrialized. The LDP was able to hold onto power in the face of these headwinds by adapting with surprising versatility to social change (Calder 1988). To appeal to urban voters, the party, after some delay, embraced pollution controls and expanded social welfare programs. It even reached out to private sector unions by including their representatives on government advisory councils and supporting the system of lifetime employment (Kume 1998). T.J. Pempel subtitled his 1982 book 'creative conservatism' in tribute to the LDP's adaptability. By the 1980s, the LDP was enjoying vote- and money-rich connections with farmers, heavy industry, high-tech industry, small business, doctors, pharmaceutical companies, construction firms, banks, postmasters, certain religious groups, and old people – to mention just the largest of its voting blocks.

The JSP had much more difficulty adding constituencies to make up for the fall in unionized workers as a proportion of all voters. Starting in the 1970s, however, it attempted to reach out to environmentalists and citizens' movements, calling for greater transparency in government, consumer protection, and an end to money politics, adding value-based appeals to these groups to its traditional appeals based on workers' rights and unarmed neutralism. While some citizen activists preferred to keep their distance from the hidebound old JSP, the party's ability to win at least some votes from voters with these sympathies prevented any new party from challenging the established 1955 System from this angle.

To these three positive feedback mechanisms working at the societal level to perpetuate established party systems, many political scientists would add at least one institutional factor: *electoral* systems. One reason Democrats and Republicans have dominated U.S. politics for so many decades, the logic goes, is that the combination of a first-past-the-post electoral system for the legislature and a presidential system makes it virtually impossible for new parties to convert votes into political power.[1]

The rules of Japan's old electoral system were much more permissive than those used in the United States, allowing parties to gain representation in the lower house if they had support of at least 15 per cent in some districts. But even this threshold remained a formidable barrier to the emergence of a significant new player in the Japanese party system. Only the LDP and the JSP were able to surpass the 15 per cent threshold nationally prior to 1996, giving both a seat bonus at the expense of smaller parties. In the late 1970s and early 1980s, the system allowed the LDP to convert popular vote in the 41–45 per cent range into a majority of seats; proportional representation, in contrast, would have forced it to share power with at least one centrist party. The JSP, too, enjoyed an advantage – a four percentage point seat bonus in many election years – that made it difficult for centrist parties to displace it as the major opposition party.

A Theory of Path-Dependent Party System Change

Given the mechanisms that 'freeze' party systems, a number of questions present themselves. Is there any room within social and institutional structures for party systems to change? What can account for the case of a party system – Japan's – in which one pole has been replaced completely? Can the literature on 'path dependence' tell us anything about the process of party system change?

Looking at the combination of 'freezing' mechanisms, it is possible to identify a source of vulnerability in the *cleavage structure* of society. Not every change in the structure of the cleavage can disrupt the positive feedback loops, but one type of social change that threatens established party systems is the emergence of a new cleavage that does not correlate with any of the old. In this section, I describe how this change disrupts many of the social and institutional feedback loops that freeze party systems, and show how it creates an opportunity for a new party to overcome the inertia in the system and establish itself as a major player. I also describe how the outcome of this process is likely to be a new party system that reflects a combination of old and new cleavages – one that still might not offer choices on issues that are of the greatest concern to voters.

Paul Pierson, in his influential book *Politics in Time,* cites many of the positive feedback loops that contribute to the freezing of party systems as evidence in favour of a path-dependent approach to political phenomena. He argues that, in politics even more than in other realms such as the economy or sports, the organization that arrives first will use its control over resources and rules to stack the game in its favour, making it virtually impossible for newcomers to join in as equal competitors (2004, 73–4).[2] Nevertheless, Pierson does hint at where an analyst ought to look to see if established structures are vulnerable to change. He notes that institutions are likely to change only when exogenous shocks 'disrupt or overwhelm the specific mechanisms that previously reproduced the existing path' (52). In *How Institutions Evolve* (2004), Kathleen Thelen offers the key insight that institutions reflect a 'layering' that results when old institutions become dysfunctional in a new environment and lead those in power to modify them to better fit the new circumstances.

So which feedback mechanism is the most vulnerable to being 'disrupted,' 'overwhelmed,' or turned into something 'dysfunctional'? Since the work on path dependence places so much emphasis on the advantages that first-movers enjoy because of their prior investment in overcoming collective action problems, we should begin looking for suspects among the range of factors that have the potential to suddenly lower incumbent parties' advantages in this area.

One possibility is that the collective action advantages of incumbent parties can be erased by the emergence of a technology – the Internet, for example – that lowers the costs of communication, making it easier for groups and parties to organize from scratch. Perhaps a change of this kind explains how the DPJ was able to replace the JSP.

A second possibility is that generational and social change shrinks the proportion of society that is organized to support incumbent parties – a process known as 'dealignment' (see Dalton and Wattenberg 2000). Incumbent parties in some Western democracies that invested in organizing, say, farmers or Catholics have seen their advantages eroded by the shrinkage in the proportion of farmers and devout Catholics in the electorate. Likewise, parties that invested in 'clientelistic' modes of organizing voters (Kitschelt 2000) have seen the value of their investment eroded by growing prosperity and urbanization that makes at least some segment of the electorate come to regard public works projects as a nuisance rather than as a reason to vote for the politician who brought home the bacon. As the proportion of the electorate tied to established parties shrinks, newcomer parties find themselves on a much more level playing field in the competition for the votes of unaffiliated voters.

Electoral system change represents a third possible way to lower collective action costs. Pierson's logic suggests incumbent parties that benefit from the established rules never support changes that would level the playing field for upstarts. But politicians sometimes find themselves in uncomfortable situations where they feel they must vote for electoral reforms in order to improve their chances of short-term survival – even if the rules open the door wider to newcomers in the long run (Reed and Thies 2001). In France in 1986, for example, the socialists pushed through a change to proportional representation rules that looked likely to help them in the short term – even though they were one of the larger parties and had long benefited from France's two-ballot majoritarian system. In Italy in the early 1990s, the *voters* overruled politicians and changed the electoral system on their own through a referendum.

As we will see, all three of these factors played at least some role in facilitating party system change in Japan. Collective action advantages of incumbent parties are so great and multifaceted, however, that even the Internet, dealignment, and electoral reform are not enough, on their own, to allow new parties to displace dominant old ones unless they are accompanied by an exogenous shock of another type. Incumbent parties, too, usually are able to adapt to the new environment – using the Internet, appealing to dealigned voters, modifying tactics to deal with new electoral rules – and often more quickly than new parties can take advantage of these changes. Party system change thus remains a rare event – even in an era in which dealignment and the Internet are affecting politics in all the mature democracies and electoral reform has become more common.

A series of exogenous shocks that affect *social cleavages,* in contrast, can disrupt feedback mechanisms so much that, for the dominant parties in the established system, they become negative rather than positive. Although political parties have an incentive to keep old cleavages alive and can expend considerable resources on the effort, an exogenous shock might be sufficiently strong to reduce dramatically the material salience of the most important issues around which the party system is structured, and efforts by the established parties to use the old issues to mobilize their old voting base will be unsuccessful. If this destabilization of the old cleavage structure is accompanied by the rise of a new one, the established parties (and the party system as a whole) are vulnerable to attack from a new direction.

Of course, old issues decline in salience and new issues arise in all political systems all the time. The vulnerability of a party system, therefore, depends on two variable conditions: the speed with which the old cleavage loses salience, and whether an exogenous shock produces a new issue that not only is salient but cuts sharply *across* a party's voting base.

If an issue's loss of salience happens gradually, parties usually are adaptable enough (and enjoy enough of an advantage over newcomers) to find a new issue on which to build their voting base. Thus, for example, in Europe most parties of the Left have managed to adapt successfully to the lessening of importance of labour union issues by adding postmodern issues such as gender rights and environmental protection – although, if issues of concern to labour unions had disappeared completely, these parties might have had difficulty handling a challenge from a nimble New Left party.

The flexibility of a political party and its continuing ability to appeal to voters also depend, however, on whether an exogenous shock produces an issue dimension that is suddenly salient and cuts sharply across the party's base. The relationship between the new cleavage and the old is critical here: if the new issue correlates closely enough with the old that a sizable majority of the party's voters falls on one side, the party will have little difficulty adjusting to the emergence of the new line of cleavage. The Left's embrace of gender rights and environmental issues shows how parties can adapt even when issues cut across their base to some degree. In Sweden and the United Kingdom, for example, some supporters of Old Left parties opposed extending privileges to women or environmental regulations that threatened to hurt the industry in which they worked, but the overlap between those concerned about labour issues and those worried about the environment and women's rights was close enough that traditional labour parties were able to tack towards the constituencies of the New Left without losing too much of their old voting base.[3]

If, however, a new issue splits voting bases neatly in half, dominant parties will find it difficult to adapt. Unwilling to offend a substantial segment of its base by choosing one side in the emerging debate, a party is likely to attempt to ignore the issue or straddle the divide to avoid splitting its supporters apart, and to fall back on appeals to voters based on the tried and true strategies of the past that still unite the party. At this point, social cleavage positive feedback mechanisms start working against the party as politicians and groups drawn to the party by its stand on the old issue use their clout to insist that the party continue focusing on the old fight.

If all the major parties of the old system are caught in the same trap, it might be that none of them reaches out to voters and interest groups concerned about the new issue – creating an opening for a new party to wedge its way into the system. Figure 2.2 shows the strategically optimal location for a new party seeking to take advantage of this confluence of events. Faced with a pair of parties pitted against each other on an old dimension but unable to shift positions on a new dimension (because the voting bases of both parties are split), the new party should locate itself in the centre of the old dimension and on the reformist side of the new dimension. By locating itself in a centrist position on an old dimension that is losing salience, the party will attract voters from both sides of the old divide who share its reformist stand on the new issue that the old parties are ignoring. These voters will be joined by politicians who share the new party's reformist position and defect from the established parties and by aspiring politicians who share reformist views and have centrist positions on the old dimension. Within a short time, the old established parties will have to respond to the challenge of a major new competitor.

What happens next depends on whether the reformist party draws more votes and defecting politicians away from the Old Left or the Old

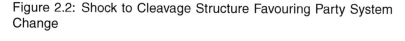

Figure 2.2: Shock to Cleavage Structure Favouring Party System Change

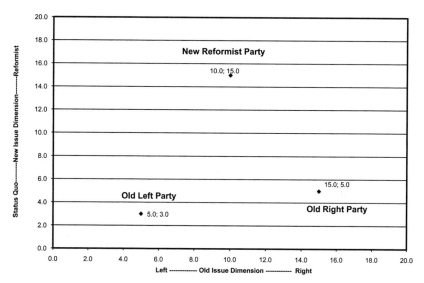

Note: Scores on the x- and y-axes represent possible values for a party's policy platform on a 20-point scale where 0 and 20 represent the extremes. For an example of expert surveys locating parties in 'policy space' in this manner, see Katou and Laver (1998).

Right and on how the two old parties respond. Several permutations are possible. Rather than working through them all, consider the likely results if: 1) the reformist party draws more votes away from the Old Left than from the Old Right; and 2) the Old Right decides to compete for votes with its new leading rival by trying to outflank it on the reform issue. The result, as we will see when we focus next on the story of party system change in Japan, will be a system in which there is no true party of the Left – at least for awhile.

Path Dependence in the Emergence of the 2000 System

We are now ready to look closely at the dissolution of the 1955 System in the 1990s – the collapse of the JSP and the rise of the DPJ – to see whether the model of path-dependent party system change outlined above can help us understand what happened. If the model is correct, the LDP and the JSP should have adjusted relatively smoothly to the declining salience of the dominant cleavage over security policy as long as the process was gradual. They also should have adapted without difficulty to the emergence of new cleavages as long as they overlapped significantly with the old Left-Right divide. The trigger for the collapse of the old system should have been a sudden exogenous shock that affected the old cleavage and the emergence of a new cleavage that cut across the two parties' voting bases. The model suggests that declining costs of communication – for example, the emergence of the Internet – partisan dealignment, and electoral reform should have been part of the story, but posits that the critical combination of shifts in cleavage lines should have been the most important causal factor.

In the years after the LDP and JSP established themselves on opposite sides of the conflict over security policy, the leading parties of the 1955 System encountered and adjusted to a number of new issue cleavages. As in Europe, the Left in Japan had to deal with conflicts over environmental regulation, gender rights, and citizens' rights, but the JSP was able to adapt to and take some advantage of all these new issues from the 1960s through the 1980s. Its support of local environmental regulations, at a time when the LDP was still holding out against such measures at the national level, helped the JSP win top offices in Tokyo, Osaka, and many other large cities in the 1960s. As late as 1990, the party was able to rebound from a gradual loss of seats by tapping into voter support for more progressive gender policies. Under its female leader, Doi Takako, the JSP rode a 'Madonna Boom' to a first-place finish in the upper house in 1989 and gained a significant increase in its lower house representation in 1990.

The JSP was able to adapt in this way because voters and politicians tended to divide into Left and Right on environmental and gender issues along roughly the same lines as over the security conflict. Polls in 1996 and again in 2000, in which experts on Japanese politics were asked to locate parties on a twenty-point scale on these three issues, found that the correlation in the Left-Right placement of parties across the three issues was extremely close. In 2000, party positions on defence and environmental policy correlated at a rate of 0.977, while those on defence and gender policy correlated at a rate of 0.949 (Kato and Laver 2003, 126).[4] Given this degree of overlap, it was not difficult for the JSP to reach out to voters who were motivated by environmental and gender concerns while holding onto voters whose primary concern continued to centre on security policy.

The LDP, meanwhile, adapted to a gradual waning of the intensity of the divide over security policy and the emergence of new concerns about the costs and risks of modern capitalism by embracing policies designed to protect economically vulnerable segments of the population (Calder 1988). In the 1970s, it supported a dramatic expansion of public pensions for the self-employed, along with 'free health care' for the elderly. It also boosted spending on public works projects in rural areas so that the construction industry could serve as a social safety net in areas lacking vibrant private sector employment opportunities. After progressive local officials won some local elections by offering 'no collateral loans' to small businesses having trouble getting loans from private banks, the LDP one-upped the progressives. It created national programs channelling private savings deposited with postal financial services into public financial institutions tasked with providing subsidized loans to small and medium-sized firms. These public financial institutions were just a part of what became an LDP-supported policy of 'convoy capitalism,' designed to cushion firms from market forces and allow them to live up to their lifetime employment commitments to their workers (Schoppa 2006b, 49–61; see also Toyoda, in this volume).

As a result of this decision by the LDP to support a Japanese version of the welfare state, by the 1980s neither the LDP nor the JSP had much reason to campaign against each other on economic or welfare issues (Kabashima and Takenaka 1996; Otake 2000, 128). Both supported protection of farmers and aid to small businesses. Both favoured expanded social welfare services for the elderly. Both supported the lifetime employment system and regulations that protected banks from market forces so that they could continue making loans to troubled sectors of the economy. The JSP did not even object to public works projects pushed by LDP leaders; the opposition party recognized that construction spending served a welfare function, especially when it was designed to counteract an economic slowdown.

Nevertheless, an expanding segment of the Japanese electorate was growing frustrated by the sums of money going to rural public works, tax policies that allowed small businesses and farmers to avoid paying taxes at the rate salaried workers paid, subsidized rice prices, and the corrupt money ties between interest groups and the long-dominant LDP. This group of mostly urban and suburban voters, dubbed the 'new middle mass,' occasionally rebelled when the LDP proposed new taxes or was caught in blatant acts of corruption, turning away for one or two elections to support the latest 'new party' that promised to pay more attention to taxpayer and consumer concerns. As long as the economy boomed, however, no new party that targeted these voters – such as the New Liberal Club, which broke away from the LDP in 1976 – could establish much traction (Otake 2000, 130).

In the early 1990s, a confluence of two exogenous shocks dramatically changed the cleavage structure in which Japanese parties competed. The first was the sudden end to the Cold War, which had kept the security policy issue at the forefront of party politics since the 1950s. As recently as the mid-1980s, the LDP had been able to point to the Soviet military build-up in areas near Japan and mobilize voters with fears of how the JSP might deal with this challenge. The JSP, too, had been able to mobilize its old base by pointing to LDP Prime Minister Nakasone Yasuhiro's declaration that Japan would serve as an 'unsinkable aircraft carrier' for the United States and warning of the risks this entailed. By 1992, however, the world had completely changed. The Soviet Union had broken up and the pro-Western Russian leader Boris Yeltsin had consolidated his position of power after putting down a coup attempt by hardliners the previous year.

Both the LDP and the JSP failed to anticipate how much this new international environment would change the political environment in which they competed. For the JSP, the change meant that it could no longer scare up support from its base by appealing to fears that Japan might become involved in a Cold War conflict. But that did not keep the JSP from trying. Indeed, exactly as the path-dependent model predicts, the JSP – responding to party activists who shared its long-time commitment to pacifism – attempted to keep the old cleavage alive by arguing that the LDP's efforts to cooperate with the United States during the first Gulf War in 1991 were dangerously militaristic. Voters, however, could see that the material conditions had changed – the Soviet Union had broken up and Saddam Hussein was in no position to attack Japan – and the JSP's efforts not only failed but backfired by revealing how out of touch the party was.

During the 1991 Gulf War, the JSP had helped to block LDP-supported legislation that would have allowed Japan to send a 'peacekeeping' force abroad to assist the United States in the region. As a result, Japan was not able to make a commitment of forces until the fighting was over (it sent minesweepers), but sent a large sum of money instead. Although world opinion rebuked Japan for its inability to move beyond 'chequebook diplomacy,' the JSP used all of the parliamentary manoeuvres at its disposal – including 'cow walking' to slow down the voting process[5] – in an effort to stop the LDP from pushing through a Peace Keeping Operations Law in spring 1992. The televised coverage of octogenarian JSP Diet members being taken to the hospital after their attempt to cow-walk overtaxed their physical capabilities provided an apt image of the JSP's outdated and futile politics.

The LDP seemed to be in a much better situation in the aftermath of the end of the Cold War – after all, it had backed the winner. But it, too, failed to anticipate how the declining salience of the Cold War cleavage in domestic politics would affect the party's fortunes (Curtis 1999, 78–9). The party had come to rely on support from voters who backed it because it was the only one with a commonsense security policy, even if they had to hold their noses while doing so because they felt the party was overly solicitous of vested interests, if not outright corrupt. By the time of the 1993 lower house election, however, the LDP could no longer mobilize these voters merely by recycling slogans about the party's support for the United States-Japan alliance. Neither could the party contain internal factional conflict by relying on the fears of disgruntled party members in the Diet that they would be forced to cooperate with the Socialists if they left the party. With the security stakes lowered, renegade LDP members now could imagine a centrist coalition that might even include breakaway moderate Socialists.

If the end of the Cold War had been the only shock to the Japanese party system, the LDP and the JSP might have adapted by finding *other* reasons for the voters to support them. At the start of the 1990s, however, the only other reasons on voters' minds had to do with corruption and money politics – in the latest round of scandals, Sagawa Kyuubin, an express delivery company, had delivered a shopping cart full of cash to the boss of an LDP faction (Schlesinger 1997, 246). The problem for both the LDP and the JSP was that the media and the public had latched onto *electoral reform* as the only way to clean up Japanese politics. Japan's multi-member electoral districts were blamed for fostering factionalism and corruption. To raise the necessary funds, LDP members forced to compete against each other in these districts had to turn to faction bosses to get extra cash and make deals with vested interests in their districts and at the national level. Only a shift to a more party-oriented electoral system – single-member districts, proportional representation (PR) party list, or a mixture of the two – the argument went, would give voters the power to kick out poorly performing parties.

While the electoral reform issue was esoteric and difficult for voters to understand fully, it resonated with concerns of urban and suburban salaried workers that had been building since the 1970s. For them, the LDP was too close to farmers and to the construction industry, and directed too much of the nation's tax revenues to rural areas. It wasted taxpayers' money by building white elephant projects, such as the three bridges that connect the main island of Honshu to Shikoku. It over-regulated the economy to protect its clients, making it difficult for businesses – and even local governments – to make their own decisions. When the governor of Kumamoto Prefecture, Hosokawa Morihiro told the story of how he had been unable to move so much as a bus stop without permission from bureaucrats in Tokyo, it resonated with fed-up citizens throughout Japan.

The problem for the LDP and the JSP was that, on this set of issues, their constituencies were split down the middle. The catch-all LDP coalition certainly included business interests that supported deregulation, fiscal restraint, and other such neoliberal policies, and Prime Minister Nakasone had sought to move the party in this direction in the 1980s by privatizing the national railways and pushing through administrative reforms. But the party also catered to farmers, construction firms, and other segments of the economy that depended on protection, regulation, and government contracts to stay in business. Not only was the party base fundamentally split (Pempel 1998; Vogel 1999), on the issue of electoral reform the party itself was torn between a reformist wing that believed reform could help remake the party system and enable the party to exercise more leadership (Ozawa 1994) and a large group of Diet members who worried that reform threatened their ability to win re-election. These divisions immobilized the party.

The JSP was in no better position to take advantage of the new cleavage over electoral reform, fiscal restraint, decentralization, and deregulation. The party had opposed Nakasone's reform agenda of the 1980s, and in 1994, when Hosokawa, now prime minister, announced a deal to open Japan's rice market, the JSP, then part of the ruling coalition, was unenthusiastic at best. Many in the party saw deregulation as part of a right-wing neoliberal conspiracy to give free rein to market forces, allowing companies to cut corners on safety and their commitments to their workers. Finally, the party was even less supportive of electoral reform than the LDP – worried in particular that its members would find it difficult to win seats in single-member districts.

The confluence of this set of developments – corruption scandals, the rise of the issue of electoral reform, growing support for more market-oriented economic policies, and the end of the Cold War – created in

Japan exactly the kind of cleavage structure that makes party systems vulnerable to change. With neither the LDP nor the JSP representing voters who favoured political and economic reform, the system was ripe to be challenged by new parties with new positions.

All the parties that arose during the tumultuous years of the 1990s sought to confront both the LDP and the JSP from more reformist positions. In 1992, Hosokawa, the fed-up governor of Kumamoto, formed the Japan New Party (JNP), explicitly committed to an agenda of decentralization, deregulation, and political reform. In the 1993 election, the party won seats almost exclusively in urban areas where its reform agenda appealed to unaffiliated voters of the 'new middle mass.' Similarly, in 1993, two groups of largely reformist politicians broke away from the LDP to form Shintou Sakigake (New Party Harbinger) and Shinseitou; these parties, too, received substantial support from unaffiliated, mostly urban and suburban voters (Reed and Scheiner 2003).

After the LDP failed to win a majority in the 1993 lower house election, these new parties became the core of a ruling coalition that also included the Socialist Party, Koumeitou, and the Democratic Socialist Party (DSP). They did not agree on much, but they were able to push through electoral reforms that replaced the old multi-member system for the lower house with a new, mixed-member system that would elect 300 members in single-member districts and another 200 by PR. Electoral reform therefore came *after* the earthquake that collapsed the seat totals of the two dominant parties of the 1955 System. Once adopted, however, these reforms became a force in the background shaping how the party system would continue to evolve.

Between 1993 and 1996, largely in response to the way the new electoral system punished smaller parties – to win a single-member seat, a party needed to win 40–50 per cent of the vote – the party system went through another round of realignment. The result was the formation of two, relatively large, new parties, each containing reformist politicians who had created the JNP, Sakigake, and Shinseitou in 1992 and 1993, as well as politicians from the old party system. The New Frontier Party (NFP), organized by Ozawa Ichirou of Shinseitou, included politicians from the DSP and Koumeitou. The Democratic Party of Japan, formed by Hatoyama Yukio and Kan Naoto of Sakigake, included a contingent of Diet members who had decided to leave the Socialist Party.

Both new parties challenged the LDP and the Socialists – by this time joined in a ruling coalition – from policy positions that were distinctly reformist. Figure 2.3 shows the positions of the DPJ and the NFP in 1996

Figure 2.3: Japanese Parties in Policy Space, 1996

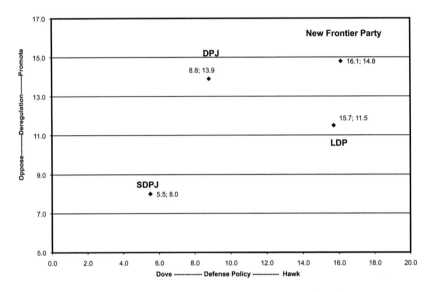

Note: Scores on the x- and y-axes were assigned by experts on Japanese politics to each party's policy platform on a 20-point scale where 0 and 20 represent the extremes; for details, see Katou and Laver (1998, 256–257).

relative to the dominant parties of the 1955 System (Kato and Laver 1998, 256–7). The plot shows how the DPJ and the NFP differed on the dominant issue of the old party system, defence; on deregulation, however, which cut across the old cleavage, both were pro-reform. During the 1996 election, the two parties challenged the ruling coalition by advocating reduced public works spending, fiscal restraint, decentralization, and economic reform.

Just as the model of party system change suggests, the system that took shape after 1996 was an awkward amalgam of the old and the new, reflecting the strategic incentives of the new parties to locate themselves relative to the remnants of the old. The cleavage over security policy had declined in salience, but it was still critical to the way party activists and many voters thought about party politics. The DPJ, which had located itself in the middle of the debate over defence policy, was therefore in a better position to challenge the old parties than was the NFP, which essentially supported the LDP's more hawkish policies; indeed, the NFP could distinguish itself from the LDP *only* on the new issue dimension. The DPJ, on the other hand, could draw voters who continued to be uncomfortable with the conservative parties' hawkish security policies while tapping into voter disgust with the LDP's profligate spending on public works, its mismanagement of the banking system, and other issues connected to the broad agenda of 'economic reform.'

Once the DPJ had established itself in this strategically advantageous location, it began to attract new candidates (and, after the 1997 break-up of the NFP, groups of politicians) that shared and reinforced its reformist views. Unlike the JSP, which had never attracted many ex-bureaucrats, the DPJ was able to attract and run candidates with backgrounds in prestigious ministries such as Finance and International Trade and Industry (Schoppa 2006a, 133–5). Several new candidates came from the financial sector, others had received training in the pro-market Matsushita Seikei Juku, founded by the man who built the Matsushita Electric Corporation. These were the individuals who, in 1998, took the lead in championing banking reform when the DPJ faced off against LDP leaders who were trying to bail out the bankrupt Long-Term Credit Bank. By 2000, these reformists were able to cement the DPJ's status as the neoliberal alternative to the LDP on economic policy. In the lower house election campaign held that year and in the upper house campaign of 2001, the DPJ called for deep cuts in public works spending and concerted action to balance the budget. DPJ leader Hatoyama called for *reducing* the progressivity of the income tax. The party also campaigned for the privatization of government corporations and the decentralization of government.[6]

The emergence of the DPJ as the survivor of the new party shake-out of the 1990s therefore conforms with the expectations of the path-dependent model of party system change. The DPJ positioned itself best to triangulate on the failure of the two dominant parties of the old system to respond to voters' concerns about the new issues of political and economic reform. Once it had survived, the party developed its own positive feedback loop processes that entrenched its economic reform policy line and began to 'mobilize bias,' so that the debate about economic reform became a sustained part of the political discourse. Nevertheless, as the path-dependent model anticipates, there was bound to be some awkwardness in a party system that layered a new cleavage over the old.

If the Japanese political system could have started over, *de novo*, in the 1990s, it might have developed into one that pitted a neoliberal, pro-defence party – in the northeast quadrant of the policy space depicted in Figure 2.3 – against one in favour of using social welfare programs and regulations to cushion market forces and of a more dovish security policy – in the southwest quadrant. Most 'Right' and 'Left' parties in democratic nations tend to align in this way. Instead, because the LDP occupied the southeast quadrant – supporting a relatively hawkish security policy as well as the Japanese convoy system of social protection – and the JSP occupied the southwest, the DPJ ended up locating itself in the northwest quadrant, supporting a moderately dovish security policy and neoliberal economic reform. While the DPJ's strategy made sense, given the prior locations of the LDP and the JSP, the party has run into a variety of difficulties that are directly attributable to this decision.

For one, the DPJ has suffered from schisms – it turns out that few politicians, even within the DPJ, support this combination of views. Those who ardently supported economic reform tended also to favour a relatively hawkish security policy,[7] while those on the dovish wing[8] tended to oppose rapid economic reform, especially if it risked bankrupting small firms and pushing workers out of jobs. The DPJ has been able to establish itself as more dovish than the LDP yet more neoliberal on economic policy only by forcing these disparate camps to bridge their differences. As a result, it has suffered since its inception from a reputation for divisiveness and infighting.[9]

The DPJ's strategic location decision also has left it vulnerable to being outflanked on the Right, particularly by the LDP. During the 1990s, the LDP found it difficult to appeal to voters who cared about the new issues of political and economic reform. Its support base, especially the construction industry and farmers, demanded large expenditures on public works and farm subsidies. Banks and their borrowers pressured the party to keep the 'convoy' system going so that they would not face bankruptcy. The inability of the LDP to escape from the feedback loops that reinforced this 'mobilization of bias' created the opening that enabled the DPJ and other new parties to challenge from the reformist direction. Indeed, even as late as 2000, the LDP was moving *away* from deregulation, rather than towards it (see Figure 2.4).

The ascension of Koizumi Jun'ichirou to the leadership of the LDP in 2001 marked an abrupt change in this pattern, as he moved the party boldly in a neoliberal direction in order to outflank the DPJ on the issues it had championed. A number of factors played a role in enabling Koizumi to break the feedback loops that had kept the LDP rooted in its old position. First, the party was extremely worried about

Figure 2.4: Japanese Parties in Policy Space, 1996, 2000, and 2003

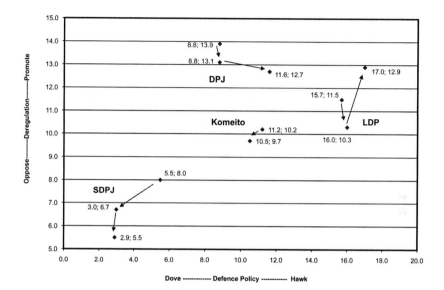

Note: Scores on the x- and y-axes were assigned by experts on Japanese politics to each party's policy platform on a 20-point scale where 0 and 20 represent the extremes; for details, see Katou and Laver (1998, 2003); and Laver and Benoit (2005).

its electoral prospects, despite the fact that it had managed to hold onto the prime ministership after lower house elections in 1996 and 2000. It had been able to do so in large part because it managed to time these two elections so that they were held at the rare moments (in a decade of economic stagnation) in which a few quarters of economic growth left voters optimistic about the future. In recent upper house elections, scheduled at set dates every three years, the party had done very poorly. In 1998, it lost the election badly, winning just 25 per cent of the party vote and losing most of its seats in urban prefectures, and it seemed headed towards a similar performance in the upper house election slated for July 2001. Outgoing prime minister Mori Yoshirou had the support of just 8.6 per cent of the public.[10] And the party was especially vulnerable in urban areas, where the DPJ had proven itself effective in appealing to 'floating' voters, who now made up about half the electorate.

Koizumi was also able to lead the party in a new direction by taking advantage of institutional changes in the Japanese political structure, especially the electoral reforms of 1994 and administrative reforms of 2000. The LDP had always included some politicians who found neoliberal economic policy attractive, and at least some of the business community saw the need for Japan to move in this direction. Until these institutional reforms, however, LDP prime ministers had been too beholden to faction bosses and bureaucrats to lead the party in a more reformist direction. Koizumi's election as party leader in 2001, therefore, marked the first real opportunity for a party reformist – Koizumi was famous for tilting at the windmill of postal reform, against the objections of party bosses – to change the party's orientation. The positive feedback loops that had kept the LDP wedded to its 'convoy capitalist' position did not go away. The faction bosses with ties to vested interests fought to block Koizumi's reforms, and, in many cases, succeeded in watering them down, but they could not stop Koizumi from boldly declaring that *his* LDP was now the party of reform. It would cut public works spending (while the DPJ only promised to do so). It would privatize public corporations, including the post office (while the DPJ was beholden to the power of the postal workers' union within the party). It would decentralize government. In short, Koizumi essentially stole the reformist thunder of the DPJ and established the LDP as equally reformist on the dimension of economic reform. Outflanked, the DPJ now could distinguish itself from the LDP only on the old issue of security.

In the 2005 election, Koizumi's manoeuvre was wildly successful, and the LDP won almost 300 out of 480 seats. The party did extremely well in urban areas with large numbers of floating voters, winning virtually all single-member districts in these areas. Yet, ironically, by moving the LDP in a neoliberal direction, Koizumi created an opportunity for the DPJ to move out of the awkward northwest quadrant, where it was being pulled apart by efforts to combine a moderate position on security issues with a neoliberal economic agenda, into the 'natural' southwest quadrant of a progressive party, where it could promote social democratic safety net programs along with a moderate security policy.

Indeed, this is exactly what Ozawa Ichirou began to do when he took over the DPJ leadership. Ahead of the 2007 upper house polls, he aggressively reached out for the votes of farmers by promising to implement a system of income supplements as an alternative to the intrusive regulatory scheme managed for the government by the farm cooperatives (*noukyou*). By the time of the 2009 election, he and new party leader Hatoyama Yukio were sounding much more like social democrats than neoliberals. They still called for a reduction in spending on public works, proposed to shrink the bureaucracy by 20 per cent, and end the practice of *amakudari* – the retirement of senior bureaucrats into sinecures in public corporations or special interest groups – so they had not abandoned their neoliberal critique of the LDP entirely. In its 2009 'Manifesto,' however, the DPJ also proposed to increase child allowances to the equivalent of US$276 a month until children turned 13, eliminate public high school fees, expand college scholarships, implement pension reforms to make the system more financially sustainable, restore social insurance cuts, and (in order to reinvigorate rural areas) abolish tolls on roads and reduce gasoline taxes.

The DPJ's move was well timed, for the deep recession that set in after the 2008 global financial crisis made Japanese – already anxious about the effects of Koizumi's reforms on their social security and disturbed by the emergence of a growing gap between poorer and richer segments of society – even more nervous. The public still wanted 'reform,' but it wanted safety net programs as well.

The shift in public sentiment was so strong that, by the time of the 2009 election, the LDP under Prime Minister Asou Tarou had moved back in this direction. Its platform also called for an expansion in child allowances and scholarships, along with more aid to struggling firms and regions. While voters over the 2001–05 period were presented with two parties favouring neoliberal reform, in 2009 they were forced to choose between two parties proposing extravagant levels of spending to cushion society from market forces. Japanese voters have yet to be given a clear choice between parties with distinct, coherent, and durable positions on economic policy.

Conclusion

The latest repositioning of the DPJ and LDP suggest the path-dependent evolution of the Japanese party system, set in motion by events in the early 1990s, has not yet run its course. The old party system became entrenched when the leading parties – the LDP and JSP – adopted policies that gave voters a clear choice over a cleavage that mattered. Once that happened, the mobilization of bias along this cleavage line by the two parties and the development of organizational support structures that reinforced the old cleavage line helped sustain the 1955 System even as Cold War fears dissipated.

The sudden end of the Cold War and the emergence of a new cleavage upset this equilibrium, allowing new parties to challenge the incumbent cartel from a direction that made it difficult for the old parties to adapt. This challenge ultimately allowed the DPJ to displace the JSP as one pole of the party system. But the story does not end there. The logic of path-dependent evolution led the DPJ to promote neoliberal economic reform (to attack the LDP) while positioning itself in the middle of the spectrum of the old Cold War divide over security policy (to attract moderate elements from both of the old camps that shared its economic reform agenda). While this made sense in the short term, it left the DPJ divided and open to being outflanked by the LDP. Indeed, Koizumi seized this opportunity by moving the LDP in a neoliberal direction and combining this position with a relatively hawkish security policy, giving voters a choice on security policy but not on the new economic issue dimension.

The decision of the DPJ to move in a social democratic direction between 2005 and 2009 *almost* gave the voters a real choice on economic issues. But by the time of the election, the LDP, too, had moved in this direction, cheered by vested interests who felt the party under Koizumi had abandoned them. So, whereas the 1955 System was anchored by parties that gave voters a clear choice between policies, as well as organizations that reinforced that divide, the 2000 System has yet to see either of these conditions emerge.

One possibility is that there is no clear divide on new economic issues in the way there was on security policy during the Cold War or on economic issues in the early days of industrialization. A mass of voters in the middle of the economic policy spectrum wants policy to be more efficient and less corrupt, and so is easily seduced by economic reform rhetoric, but these voters also want protection from the vagaries of market forces, so parties offer that as well. If so, the awkward dance that is the 2000 System so far, in which both leading parties flit between neoliberal reformism and support for social welfare programs, might be the closest thing to a new equilibrium we will see.

Japan, however, faces tough economic choices because of persistent economic stagnation, high levels of debt, and an aging society. As the DPJ confronts the difficult work of actually governing, it has already been forced to abandon some of the promises it made during its first year in power. Even more difficult choices lie ahead. Will it raise the consumption tax, to put social welfare programs on a stable footing, and so aggravate elements of society that hate paying taxes? Will it open up labour markets and aggressively pursue the remaining neoliberal parts of its agenda in order to generate economic growth, and so aggravate labour unions and other vested interests? With similar choices confronting the DPJ on the security policy front, it is possible that at least one more round of realignment will be needed before the parties settle.

NOTES

1 Neto and Cox (1997) make the strong version of this institutional argument, presenting data showing that most of the variation in the number of parties in competitive democracies correlates most significantly with their measure of electoral systems. They find that social cleavages that *interact with* electoral systems add a little to the correlation, but in the end they give most of the credit to electoral rules. See also Sartori (1968); and Ordeshook and Shvetsova (1994).
2 Virtually all of the analysis in his book, in fact, is devoted to explaining why positive feedback loops are likely to entrench established institutional structures and centres of power and place clear limits on how much politics will change.
3 Scarrow (2004, 94) discusses conscious efforts by the Social Democrats in Germany to appeal both to their base in the unions and to voters who value 'individualism, technological progress, and environmental protection.'
4 Both correlations were significant at the 0.01 (2-tailed) level.
5 'Cow walking' refers to the tactic, similar to the filibuster in the United States, where a minority party attempts to delay or block a controversial proposal by insisting on formal votes on a large number of amendments. Under Japanese parliamentary rules, a formal vote requires legislators to walk to the front of the Diet hall and place their vote in either the 'yes' or 'no' box. The minority party can slow down this process to a snail's pace by having legislators walk extremely slowly, consuming over an hour to carry out each vote.
6 See Schoppa (2006b, 122–8) for details; see also Miura, Lee, and Weiner (2005) for an analysis of the DPJ's 2003 manifesto in comparison to that of the LDP.
7 For example, Hatoyama, Ozawa, Okada Katsuya, and Maehara Seiji.
8 Especially those like Yokomichi Takahiro, who moved from the Socialists to the DPJ.
9 Reporting on the DPJ tends to blame its divisions on the fact that the party is made up of politicians who came from many different parties, with divided personal loyalties. My analysis suggests, however, that this

divisiveness is aggravated by the strategic incentives that led the party to locate itself in a policy space where few politicians are located. For further discussion of the DPJ's struggle with a reputation for divisiveness, see Weiner, in this volume.

10 *Yomiuri Shimbun,* 27 February 2001.

3 The Evolution of the LDP's Electoral Strategy: Towards a More Coherent Political Party

STEVEN R. REED

Japan's Liberal Democratic Party (LDP) is one of the world's most successful political parties, having ruled Japan from 1955 through 1993, almost always in single-party majority governments. The only exception was a short-lived coalition in 1983 with the New Liberal Club, a small party with only six seats, whose members had defected from and would soon return to the LDP. By the 1990s, the LDP had evolved what one can readily assume to be a nearly optimal set of strategies for maintaining its dominance in the political context of the times. But political context is never static, and two major changes in the LDP's environment reduced the effectiveness of those previously optimal strategies. The LDP now faces the challenge of reforming itself to fit the new environment.

The first change in the LDP's environment has been widely studied: the enactment of the new mixed-member electoral system first used in the 1996 election (see for example, Christensen 1994, 1998; McKean and Scheiner 2000; Reed and Thies 2001; Krauss and Pekkanen 2004). The mixed system's tier of single-member districts rendered many of the LDP's standard operating procedures counterproductive. Most notably, under the previous system of multi-member districts, the LDP almost always ran more than one candidate per district, while in single-member districts splitting the vote by running two candidates is virtually suicidal. The primary effect of the introduction of single-member districts thus has been to force voters and candidates to choose just one party or another and to force parties to choose only one candidate and only one side of any politically salient issue.

In the multi-member district environment, the LDP had evolved into an all-inclusive party, excluding only those, notably the communists, who were unwilling to engage in the politics of compromise. An analysis of the Italian Christian Democrats applies with equal force to the LDP: 'On economic matters, the [Christian Democrats] started out as [defenders] of the interests of industry and of independent farmers. But very quickly, as its links with civil society expanded and its electoral targets multiplied, the party became an avenue for the advancement of the economic interests of every relevant societal and economic group' (Bardi 2004, 129). The Christian Democrats did not need, and therefore did not develop, the capacity to choose sides. Similarly, Japan's LDP presented itself to the public as all things to all people, and one could find LDP candidates on every side of almost every issue. Groups increasingly chose to support LDP candidates who would represent them in the internal LDP policy-making process instead of an opposition party that might better represent their interests but would never control the government. In the nomination process, the LDP often allowed several candidates to run, declaring whoever won to be LDP (*kateba Jimintou* ['if you win, you are LDP']; see Reed 2009). The party thus made no decision at all but left the effective choice to voters. The introduction of single-member districts has now forced the party to develop ways of choosing a single candidate, including the even more difficult task of denying the nomination to any other candidate who might have some support in the district. The same dynamic is forcing the party to choose only one side on any issue salient to the public during an election, thus pleasing some of their support groups while alienating others.

The second major change in the political environment has not been the focus of much research (for an exception, see Kollner 2002) but probably has been more fundamental: the decline in the capacity of organized groups to deliver the vote, a phenomenon common in advanced industrial democracies. The most theoretically useful way of approaching the phenomenon is as a shift from clientelistic to policy linkages between parties and voters (Kitschelt 2000). In western Europe, it is often described as 'dealignment': the decline of voter loyalty to particular parties and the rise in the number of voters available during the election campaign. In the Netherlands and other consociational democracies, it is known as 'depillarization' (Luther and Deschouwer 1999). In a religious context, the same phenomenon is referred to as 'secularization.' In Japan, it is expressed as the decline of the 'organizational vote' (*soshiki-hyou*), the rise of the 'floating vote' (*fudou-hyou*), and the rise in the number of voters unaffiliated with any party (*mutouhasou*) (see Tanaka 1997), and it is these terms that I use in this chapter.

Traditionally, the LDP did not win elections by appealing directly to voters; in fact, it was never a particularly popular party and was seldom led by popular leaders. According to monthly polls conducted by *Jiji Tsushin*, the average support for the party between 1960 and 1990 was a bit over 32 per cent, and support for the cabinet was not quite 35 per cent. The LDP relied instead on its candidates' personal campaign organizations (*kouenkai*) and interest groups linked to the party by clientelistic ties to deliver the vote (Scheiner 2006, chap. 3). The party had little or no organization at the local level; rather, each candidate created his own personal campaign organization in direct competition with those of the other LDP candidates in the district. Indeed, intra-party competition among LDP candidates and their respective *kouenkai* was fiercer than inter-party competition between the LDP and the opposition – hardly a recipe for coherence. The decline of the organizational vote and the advent of single-member districts now have forced the LDP to find ways to avoid intra-party competition and to focus on the inter-party competition with its current biggest rival, the Democratic Party of Japan (DPJ).

In the new electoral environment, organizational support is secondary and might even be detrimental if it hampers the LDP's ability to enact reforms the public demands. The party must loosen its ties to traditional support groups, a delicate task that tends to lose some votes in the short run. Moreover, to attract the floating vote, the party must send a clear and consistent message, with backbenchers forced to parrot the party line and avoid statements or actions that could be interpreted as 'off message.' This requires the party to select a popular leader and allow that person to lead, a difficult task for a faction-ridden party devoted to the tedious process of consensus decision-making.

By the 1980s, at the latest, the LDP had evolved into a candidate-centred, clientelistic group that Curtis calls a 'franchise party': 'The party offered a known name, financial support, and other assistance to its endorsed candidates, but each candidate was in effect an independent political entrepreneur with his own local organization' (1999, 143).[1] Another label that fits is one originally developed to describe the Italian Christian Democratic Party: a 'mass clientelism party' (Belloni, Caciagli, and Mattina 1979). The LDP used such groups as farm cooperatives, construction companies, doctors, dentists, and nurses to deliver the vote. When these proved insufficient, it provided public subsidies to stimulate the organization of new groups that, quite naturally, would support the LDP.

In both policy platform and party image, the LDP was a chameleon or an amoeba, changing into whatever colour or shape seemed necessary to win the next election (Reed forthcoming). Whenever it found itself in trouble, the party changed leaders, who promptly adjusted both the party platform and the party image. Writing soon after the founding of the LDP, Quigley and Turner thought that the party would not last long because 'the merger was an entente of expediency, concealing rather than resolving factional rivalries' (1956, 302). Their analysis was correct, even though the prediction proved far wide of the mark. It was precisely the lack of organizational and policy coherence that allowed the LDP to prosper in the political environment of the time.

Now, however, the LDP needs to become a more coherent party, one that can appeal directly to unattached voters on the basis of leadership, policy manifestos, and performance in office. Support for the LDP increasingly is linked to support for the prime minister (Krauss and Nyblade 2005), so the party can no longer afford to be complacent when cabinet support drops. The LDP also needs to become more disciplined, capable of keeping its candidates 'on message' throughout an election campaign and punishing those who violate party discipline. In the 2001 upper house and 2005 general elections, Prime Minister Koizumi Jun'ichirou showed the LDP how to win elections in this new environment, but the LDP so far refused to learn the lesson. Even the shock of the devastating defeat in the 2009 election has yet to force the party to reconsider its electoral strategies.

In this chapter, I analyse the successes and failures of the LDP's attempts to become a coherent political party capable of competing in a two-party format. The evidence presented below indicates, first, that the LDP has yet to make much progress, and is unlikely to reform until it has served a second stint in opposition; and, second, that the party is not disintegrating but sooner or later should return to power.

The necessary reforms are no mystery: party reform in western Europe points in the same direction as the proposals of LDP reformers. Indeed, most of the proposed changes have been on the agenda since the 1960s, but the party has repeatedly failed to act. Can the LDP reform?

The comparative evidence from western Europe suggests that an entrenched governing party does not reform while in power. Losing, however, not only focuses a party's attention on fixing the problems that led to its defeat, but also allows it more time to spend on internal party issues. A single loss, however, is seldom sufficient. An entrenched party tends to assume that being in power is the norm, and that the first loss is an anomaly that will soon be corrected with little or no effort on its part. A second loss is normally required to shock the party into serious reform.

The most analysed party reform in Europe is that enacted in Germany by the Social Democratic Party (SPD) in 1959, which transformed itself from a mass party based on the support of labour unions into a catch-all party capable of winning power. Scarrow summarizes the process and context succinctly: 'SPD reformers finally gained the upper hand in organizational battles after the [Christian Democratic Union, CDU] won an absolute majority in the 1957 Bundestag election' (1996, 58). The Christian Democrats, themselves facing a similar problem, responded with similar party reforms: 'After the decisive SPD-[Free Democratic Party] victory at the 1972 election, however, the CDU . . . could no longer deny the necessity of accepting its role as the opposition party' (Conradt 1978, 82). By the 1976 election, the CDU had doubled its membership and reformed itself.

A similar pattern occurred in the United Kingdom, most notably in the case of Tony Blair's 'New Labour.' The process began after Labour's second consecutive defeat, when it 'came to terms with markets, back-pedalled on public ownership, and accepted lower income-tax rates, as well as the sale of council houses to tenants; it also endorsed Britain's continued membership of the European Community and some of the new trade union legislation' (Butler and Kavanaugh 1999, 4). Another relevant comparison is that with Ireland's Fianna Fail: 'In facing for the first time the prospect of two defeats in a row, the party therefore invested considerably in building up its organizational resources. . . . Rapidly, and quite abruptly, Fianna Fail had therefore moved from being close to the other extreme, where the key motor was provided by party central office, the national leadership and the national election programme' (Mair and Marsh 2004, 246). Fianna Fail thus reformed after only one loss and the looming prospect of another.

The LDP, for its part, so far has shown no signs of learning from its single defeat, devastating though it was, perhaps because the current DPJ government has not seemed a particularly formidable opponent. Before proceeding to the evidence on this point, however, one should review the basics of Japan's electoral system.

The New Electoral System

Japan's new electoral system is based on single-member districts but it also has a proportional representation (PR) tier; it is thus a mixed-member system (see Shugart and Wattenberg 2001). The allocation of seats in each tier is independent of the other tier – that is, the number of seats allocated to a party in the single-member-districts tier does not affect the number of seats allocated in the PR tier and vice versa. In this sense, the Japanese system is quite different from that of, say, Germany or New Zealand, where the allocation of seats is dominated by the PR tier, but similar to the system used in Italy between 1994 and 2001.

In mixed-member systems, the devil is often in the details (see McKean and Scheiner 2000). The key details of the Japanese system are the double candidacy (*choufuku rikkouho*) and 'best loser' provisions. Under double candidacy – a common provision in mixed-member systems – candidates on the PR list may also be nominated in a single-member district. Under the best loser provision, candidates who win their single-member districts are deleted from the PR list. Candidates ranked together are then re-ranked according to how close they came to winning their single-member districts. Specifically, they are ranked by 'seat-loss ratio' (*sekihairitsu*), the number of votes won by the candidate divided by the number of votes won by the candidate who won the single-member district. The final ranking is thus delegated to the voters.

The PR component of the new electoral system has given a few seats to small parties, but the major parties have used it to solve nomination problems in the single-member districts that are at the heart of the system (Di Virgilio and Reed 2010). Single-member districts thus are forcing the LDP to choose only one candidate per district. The PR tier has given the party some flexibility in how it reaches this goal, but it has not formed a separate arena of electoral competition between the two major parties.

In a purely technical or legal sense, the LDP has never nominated two candidates in a single-member district. It nevertheless would be inaccurate to conclude that single-member districts have ended intra-party electoral competition.

Deterring and Disciplining Independents

Under the old system of multi-member districts, the LDP not only nominated more than one candidate per district, it also found it nearly impossible to deny the nomination to any candidate who won. The party could not prevent candidates who had been denied a nomination from running as independents and could not deny any candidate who won a nomination in the subsequent election in the classic 'if you win, you are LDP' pattern. Under the new system, the LDP continues to be plagued by independent candidates. In fact, instead of declining towards the expected equilibrium of zero, the total number of LDP-affiliated independents (LDP candidates running despite not being nominated) increased from twenty-one in 1996 to forty-six in 2005, dropping only slightly to forty-two in 2009. In fact, under the new system, almost 30 per cent of independents have been elected, compared with about 20 per cent under the old system (Browne and Kim 2003, 118).

The LDP has also continued to accept winners back into the party. Right after the 2000 election, in a replay of scenes seen many times under the old system, the secretary general of the party warned that those candidates who had run as independents against party policy would find it difficult to be accepted back into the LDP.[2] Despite that warning, the party has yet to refuse to accept back into the fold by the subsequent election a winning candidate who had run for another party, violated party discipline, or taken a public stand in opposition to party policy. The traditional non-policy of 'if you win, you are LDP' clearly continues to operate under the new system.

Some independents simply compete for the single-member district nomination, precisely as they would have under the old multi-member system. In cases where two or more candidates seek the nomination, one or more of those who are not selected may choose to run as independents in the expectation that they will be nominated if they win, which looks remarkably similar to traditional practice under multi-member districts. The number of such independents rose from sixteen in 1996 to twenty-five in 2003 but fell to seven in 2005. These independents are often supported by LDP factions and/or by *kouenkai* within the district. Many are LDP members of the prefectural assembly, and many are related to retiring LDP politicians and represent an attempt to claim the nomination for their *kouenkai* against the *kouenkai* of their traditional rival from multi-member-district days. In addition, a bit less than 20 per cent of such independents win their single-member districts, a rate similar to that found under the multi-member-district system.

A typical, if somewhat prominent, case was Chiba 10th in 2003. There, an ambitious member of the prefectural assembly, Tanidagawa Hajime, secretary of the retiring member, decided he was ready to move up to the Diet and began to prepare his campaign. He gathered the support of several mayors, other members of the assembly, and one former Diet member. It did not seem to bother Tanidagawa that the LDP already had an incumbent in the district, presumably because that individual was the son of the retiring member's traditional rival. The race, therefore, became a continuation of the traditional competition between two rival *kouenkai*. Tanidagawa understood that he would have to run without the nomination because of the LDP's policy of giving preference to incumbents, but he assumed that whoever won would join the LDP and be nominated in the next election. The LDP made an effort to dissuade Tanidagawa from running, offering him a PR seat and the promise of the single-member-district nomination in the future, but Tanidagawa refused. In the event, the incumbent was re-elected and Tanidagawa finished second. Tanidagawa had acted as though he was seeking the nomination in a multi-member district, but, after his first experience under the mixed-member system, he noticed the difference: an independent cannot win a seat in the PR tier. In 2005, he ran for the DPJ. Under the old system, he would have continued to run as an independent, but single-member districts force candidates, as well as parties, to choose one side or the other.

The classic multi-member-district strategy of avoiding any nomination decision at all and allowing the voters to decide actually has been followed twice under the new system, in Miyazaki 2nd and 3rd districts in 2003. The story of the two Miyazaki districts shares much with that of Chiba 10th, except that, in these cases, the sons of the retiring incumbents expected to inherit their fathers' seats in the Diet, another LDP tradition (Ishibashi and Reed 1992). In the 2nd district, however, a member of the prefectural assembly challenged the succession, as did a former Diet member in the 3rd who had run for the New Frontier Party in 1996. The LDP had enough votes in both districts to win even with the vote divided between two candidates, so the party decided to nominate neither and let the voters decide. As expected, the voters chose one of the two independents instead of opting for an opposition candidate, but the LDP continued to have two prospective candidates for one single-member district. Neatly illustrating the link between intra-party competition and policy incoherence, both winners chose to oppose the Koizumi postal reform bill in 2005. Traditionally, winners were nominated even if they voted against their leader, but Koizumi refused to nominate the rebels. The 2003 winners thus were forced to run as independents in 2005. They both won, and Koizumi's successor soon reinstated the traditional 'if you win, you are LDP' policy and allowed them back into the party. Both were re-elected in the 2009 election. Of the 2005 nominees, one ran unsuccessfully for the DPJ in 2005 and the other ran unsuccessfully for governor with LDP support.

The official recognition of two independent candidates is, however, unlikely to be repeated. The LDP can leave the decision to the voters only if it is certain that one of the two LDP independents will win the single-member district. If the DPJ has any chance of winning the district, the LDP faces the familiar Duvergerian incentives to reduce its candidates to one, since having two candidates in a single district risks dividing the vote and giving the seat to the opposition. In fact, in 20 per cent of the districts in which LDP independents have challenged LDP nominees, both candidates lost. Furthermore, based on the PR returns broken down by single-member district, the DPJ is already the first or second choice of voters in every district, and all it needs is suitable candidates – among them disgruntled LDP candidates who have been denied that party's nomination – to make all districts competitive.

In two cases, Kumamoto 3rd in 2003 and Kanagawa 8th in 2005, the LDP managed to win two seats in a single-member district, with the independent challenger winning the district and the incumbent nominee winning a PR seat. These two cases appear to be a perfect replication of competition under the multi-member-district system, where two LDP candidates would run against each other and both would win. Appearances, however, are deceiving. The LDP did not gain a seat by having two winners in a single-member district, since it would have won the same number of PR seats whether the independent ran or not. It just happened that one PR seat was allocated to a losing LDP candidate in a district where an LDP independent won the single-member district and was nominated *ex post*. As well, for the next election, the party will have two candidates in one single-member district and must decide which to nominate. This intra-party competition, indeed, is the problem the party faced under multi-member districts and is one reason the LDP supported changing the electoral system.

With respect to independent candidates, therefore, traditional practices persist even when they appear counterproductive under the new electoral system. The LDP has yet to develop the capacity to prevent independents from running or to deny winners re-entry into the party. Indeed, after the 2009 defeat, the party made overtures to winning independents who had not yet sought or been asked to return to the LDP. For example, Hiranuma Takeo, a prominent opponent of the Koizumi reforms who won his single-member district in 2005, refused to sign a promise to support postal privatization and therefore was not allowed back into the party; after the 2009 defeat, however, the LDP sought to bring his personal support group into the LDP fold. Similarly, overtures were made to Nakamura Kishiro, a convicted felon who managed to win his single-member district in 2005 and again in 2009 against both LDP and DPJ opponents. These overtures failed, however, presumably because both candidates were exploring other options – the LDP is less attractive in opposition than it is in power.

Deselecting Scandal-tainted Liabilities

The LDP has experienced major corruption problems since it was founded in 1955. The party declared a policy of not nominating any candidate under criminal investigation, but in its very first election in 1958 it wound up nominating seven such candidates (Reed 2009). Under the old multi-member-district system, the tradition developed that an LDP incumbent involved in a corruption scandal would resign from the party and run as an independent while maintaining his ties to and power within the party, which would still be represented in the district by other, officially nominated candidates. The party needed to take no formal action of its own other than to deselect the scandal-tainted candidate and to leave the decision to the voters. At the same time, scandals tended to drag on for weeks or even months while the tainted candidate made up his mind to resign (under pressure from the party behind the scenes). A tainted candidate who was re-elected as an independent, however, would be allowed back into the party to be nominated in the next election.

Under the new electoral system, the stakes have risen. With only one nominee per district, deselection is insufficient to dissociate the party from a scandal-tainted candidate. Instead, the party must also nominate another candidate, since a deselected candidate who runs unopposed clearly would be viewed as the LDP candidate. The DPJ for its part has proven quite effective in dropping any candidate tainted by scandal, which has forced the LDP to change its method of dealing with candidates who are an electoral liability. Since the introduction of the new system, the LDP has tacitly supported scandal-tainted incumbents running as independents only three times. The most prominent example is that of Fujinami Takao in Mie 5th district.

Fujinami, who had been convicted in a corruption scandal, ran as an independent in the 1990 and 1993 elections, losing in the latter. Before the 1996 election, however, he was found not guilty on appeal and could therefore receive the LDP nomination. He then won by an overwhelming margin in the new Mie 5th district, but on further appeal his conviction was reconfirmed before the 2000 election. Fujinami decided to run as an independent, and the LDP chose not to nominate another candidate in the single-member district. It thus was obvious to any observer that Fujinami was the LDP candidate in Mie 5th district, which he won in 2000, but only by an extremely narrow margin. He then retired before the 2003 election. In Fujinami's case, the LDP followed its traditional practice of taking no responsibility for its candidate's misdeeds and leaving the decision up to the voters. The voters indicated that, if Fujinami were the LDP candidate in 2003, the DPJ would probably win, and Fujinami therefore retired. In the event, the DPJ had trouble finding a candidate to run against Fujinami's successor, and the LDP won the district in the next three elections, albeit against increasingly strong challenges from the DPJ.

The tradition of 'if you win, you are LDP even if you have been convicted on corruption charges' did not disappear immediately but has not been repeated since the 2003 election. In fact, the LDP has become increasingly efficient at denying the nomination to scandal-tainted incumbents and then getting them to retire before the subsequent election. In 2003, for example, the LDP found an attractive young new candidate, Nakanishi, to run in the complex Tokyo 4th district. Nakanishi, however, was arrested for making unwanted advances towards a young woman during a late-night foray into the entertainment district. With unprecedented haste, he resigned his Diet seat five days later. He then ran as an independent in the 2005 election against an LDP nominee, who won, while Nakanishi's vote total dropped from more than 90,000 to less than 20,000. Both the LDP and the voters had agreed that this politician's career should end. In another case, in Shiga 4th district in 2009, the LDP took the unprecedented step of refusing to nominate the *son* of a scandal-tainted incumbent. The son took the almost equally surprising step of accepting the party's decision to nominate someone else and did not run as an independent against the party nominee.

Single-Member-District/PR Tag Teams

Choosing one candidate usually means denying another, and incurs the risk that the denied candidate will run as an independent or even defect to the DPJ. The LDP has used the PR tier to prevent such candidates from doing either. When the LDP has two potential candidates in a district, the party solves the problem by nominating both, one in the single-member-district tier and the other in the PR tier. This is a continuation of the traditional practice of using nominations in some other election to dissuade a candidate from running as an independent against the strategic interests of the party. Now, however, there is a new twist: since candidates generally prefer single-member-district to PR nominations, those relegated to the PR tier often demand another chance to run again in the single-member district. The result of such negotiations is what the Japanese call 'Costa Rica agreements,' whereby the two candidates promise to switch back and forth between single-member and PR districts (Carlson 2006). The result is a 'tag team,' with two candidates dedicated to winning the single-member district but one running with a guaranteed PR seat.

Tag teams involve some intra-party competition, but that is balanced by an incentive to cooperate – as a team, after all, both candidates have an interest in winning the single-member district and increasing the party's PR vote. The competitive aspect of tag teams tended to dominate in the first election under the new system because two candidates were competing for one single-member-district nomination, but cooperative aspects have come to the fore as teams campaign together to win both single-member districts and PR votes.

By the third election under the new system, both the LDP and the DPJ had arrived at the same stated nomination policy, indicating that this is likely to prove to be the 'optimal' nomination strategy for several reasons. First, and most obviously, there should be but one nominee per party per single-member district. The party obviously should not nominate two candidates, but neither should it allow independent candidates to split the vote. Second, all PR candidates should run in a single-member district[3] – indeed, the ideal number of pure PR candidates, those running in the PR tier but not in a single-member district, is zero. Third, all single-member-district candidates should be ranked the same on the PR list, and only those who have campaigned hard and done well in a single-member district should be given PR seats. The LDP, however, has been forced to admit many exceptions to these principles because a candidate denied the single-member-district nomination without some compensation might run as an independent or, worse, run with a nomination from another party – tag-team members allocated to PR, for example – and to give some PR candidates guaranteed PR list positions.

Tag-team PR incumbents win their single-member districts somewhat more often than do other incumbents – 83 per cent to 77 per cent for all single-member-district incumbents (in contrast, the re-election rate for

PR members of tag teams approaches 100 per cent). Most candidates, however, continue to express a strong preference for a single-member-district nomination, and typically it is only elderly candidates who seek safe PR nominations – which is why the LDP has enacted an age limit of seventy for such nominations. The key to understanding this puzzle of preferring a single-member-district nomination to a safe PR nomination is that any single election does not a career make. A candidate who wins a single-member-district seat is an asset to the party while a PR candidate who uses up a safe list seat is a liability. A pure PR candidate must continually reassure the party that he or she is performing some service to the party that is worth the cost of a safe PR nomination.[4] Most candidates also prefer to represent a single-member district of their own to use as a base to acquire status and influence within the party, especially the influence to guarantee reselection, and to obtain some measure of independence from the party leadership.

The importance of this independence was clearly demonstrated in the 2005 election, when Prime Minister Koizumi denied the LDP nomination to thirty-seven 'rebels' opposed to his postal reforms. Of the twenty-four rebels who had won their single-member districts in 2003, fifteen were re-elected in 2005, eight were defeated, and one decided not to run.[5] Of the thirteen rebels who had been elected by PR in 2003, two were elected by PR running for a new party – indeed, it seems likely that they ran for the new party because they knew they could not win their single-member districts – three decided not to run, and eight were defeated. Three of these PR rebels were involved in tag-team arrangements and, therefore, were defeated by their erstwhile team member. Most winners of single-member districts thus survived deselection, while most PR winners did not.

From the LDP's point of view, each tag-team agreement uses up a PR seat that the party could use to reward candidates who come close to winning their single-member districts, thus reducing the incentives for candidates in single-member districts to campaign hard even when they seem likely to lose the district race. The LDP thus has said it will form no new tag teams and will phase out those that exist, declaring, for example, that any candidate who fails to win his or her single-member district will not be given a PR nomination in the subsequent election[6] – although, in practice, the party has not followed that course of action. In 2005, several tag teams were dissolved because one member chose to vote against the postal reform bill and, therefore, was not nominated. Most often, tag teams are dissolved due to the death or retirement of a member, though not necessarily even then – the son of a deceased team member often claims the right to take his father's place in the tag team. Moreover, new tag teams have been formed primarily to accommodate defectors returning to the party, a phenomenon to be discussed below. As a result, the number of LDP tag teams increased from eleven in 1996 to eighteen in 2003 before falling to ten in 2005 as postal rebels were deselected and to four in 2009. The number of new tag-team relationships dropped from eleven in 1996 to two in 2005, and to zero in 2009 (three tag teams were actually dissolved in the 2009 election). Retirements, not necessarily voluntary, solved most of the problems, but one incumbent was convinced to move to a neighbouring district with a safe PR nomination. Most surprisingly, one tag-team incumbent was given a token PR nomination, but one with no chance of winning a seat. The party clearly has increased its capacity to deny incumbents renomination and to prevent them from running as independents.

Choosing between Loyal Losers and Disloyal Winners

The new parties that defeated the LDP in 1993 and competed with it thereafter were largely formed by defectors from the LDP. When these parties failed, some defectors sought ways of returning to the LDP, thus giving the LDP the choice of nominating a turncoat winner or a loyal loser. More often than not, the party has chosen the turncoat winner, but even here one can see some evolution towards a more coherent party organization.

The biggest problem occurred when the New Frontier Party (NFP), the major opposition party in 1996, broke up in 1997 and many newly homeless candidates wished to return to the LDP. For the LDP, simply having run for another party was not enough to disbar a candidate from returning to the fold, and twenty-one incumbents of single-member districts (including one independent supported by the NFP) and seven losers were allowed to rejoin the party. Fourteen of the winners went on to receive the LDP nomination in their single-member districts and seven were nominated in the PR tier. Only one loser in a single-member district, Miyagi 5th, received a nomination in 2000, but that was primarily because the nomination was not worth much – the LDP nominee had lost badly in 1996 and the newly nominated returnee also lost in 2000. In Okayama 4th, the son of the single-member district's loser received a PR nomination, but he, too, lost. In addition, two NFP losers in 1996 ran as independents in 2000 and defeated LDP nominees.

Having won their seats, they were allowed back into the party in 2003. Winning returnees were treated quite well, but losing returnees got little or nothing from the LDP.

Some NFP winners, however, were not welcomed back. The problem was usually opposition from the district party branch, which had just fought an election against the turncoat. Two NFP winners who were not allowed to return ran as independents in their respective single-member districts. One, in Fukui 1st district, ran two losing races before deciding to run for the DPJ in 2005, winning a PR seat unavailable to him when running as an independent. The other, Yamamoto Kouzou in Fukuoka 11th, ran as an independent in the 2000 election and defeated the LDP nominee, thereby securing the LDP nomination himself in 2003. In that election, however, Yamamoto lost to the previous nominee, who ran as an independent. Then, in 2005, instead of losing the LDP nomination because he had lost in 2003, Yamamoto was renominated by the LDP because his rival had voted against postal reform. The rebel, now running as an independent, duly defeated the LDP nominee once again. In this district, therefore, an independent defeated the nominee in three consecutive elections. In 2000 and 2003, the winner was nominated for the next election, but in 2005 the winner was not nominated due to a policy dispute.

All of these examples sound as though they could have occurred under the multi-member-district system, but it would be a mistake to conclude that nothing has changed under the new electoral system. In addition to Fukuoka 11th in 2005, the two cases in which NFP single-member-district winners were not nominated, the seven cases in which NFP winners were forced to run in PR, and the LDP nominees who lost their single-member districts in 1996 but were renominated in 2000 must be counted as exceptions to the traditional 'if you win, you are LDP' rule. These exceptions are few, however, and the rule continues to pay off for the party, which has won twelve of fourteen races since 1996, when the new system was enacted, in districts where it nominated disloyal NFP winners, but only four of seven races in districts where it nominated loyal LDP losers.

In 2003 and 2005, ten more candidates returned to the LDP fold from a variety of failed new parties, but only three of seven winning returnees were given the LDP nomination in their single-member districts, perhaps indicating a lessening of importance of the 'if you win, you are LDP' rule. Although most of these cases are complex and convoluted stories of negotiations among the returnee, the local party branch, and the central headquarters, re-entry negotiations appear to have become more difficult and more dependent upon the situation in single-member districts since the 2000 election.

Enforcing Policy Discipline: The Koizumi Party Reforms

Koizumi Jun'ichirou became prime minister by winning the LDP's presidential primary in 2001 (see Lin 2009) on the promise to 'change Japan by changing the LDP,' warning that, if the party did not change, he would 'break it apart.' Both the promise and the warning were extremely popular with the public and with primary voters, but, unsurprisingly, were much less popular inside the party, where Koizumi faced heavy resistance to his policies, his effort to exercise leadership, and his plans to reform the party. Koizumi's reforms were designed to change the LDP into a coherent party capable of winning elections on the basis of policies and leadership, rather than personal support for individual candidates and pork-barrel politics. Towards that end, he manoeuvred to reduce the role of factions and to increase the role of the leadership in both the party and the cabinet. One important aspect of his reforms involved the centralization of nomination policy – in particular, the use of the power of the party leader over nominations to enforce party discipline on a policy issue.

Passing the prime minister's pet project took years to accomplish and required breaking the LDP tradition of consensus decision-making by taking a majority vote even to get the bill to the floor of the Diet. Once on the floor, however, resistance turned into rebellion. Thirty-seven LDP members of the lower house voted against postal privatization, but the bill passed, only to be defeated in the upper house. Koizumi then dissolved the Diet, just as he had promised. He then not only refused to nominate any of the rebels, but also ran LDP nominees against each and every one of them. The election was to be a clear choice between those who supported postal reform and those who opposed it. Every single LDP candidate would have to support postal reform, at least during the election campaign. The party unity thus achieved was neither spontaneous nor necessarily sincere, but it was complete.

Thirty-three of the rebels ran in the subsequent 2005 election, seven for new parties formed from among them and the rest as independents, most of whom hoped to rejoin the LDP if they won.[7] Fifteen rebels won their single-member districts and two more won PR seats, while fourteen were defeated. The LDP nominees who ran against the rebels were promptly dubbed 'assassins' and eleven of them were given safe PR nominations, although four had won their single-member districts. Without the PR tier, the party leadership could never have found candidates willing to run hopeless races against established incumbents. This was then an innovative use of the new electoral system for purposes that had not been imagined, let alone intended, by the reformers who designed the system. It was also a clear violation of the principle of 'if you win you are LDP.' Indeed, it was meant to eliminate that principle altogether and replace it with a policy-based nomination policy.

Although the nominees were unable to defeat all the rebels, they performed well enough to give LDP party discipline an electoral bite it had never had before, which subsequently produced a landslide victory for the LDP in the 2005 election, with eighty-three new members who were promptly dubbed the 'Koizumi children.' Koizumi thus had kept his promise to change the LDP, and the 'new LDP' proved as popular as 'New Labour' had in the United Kingdom in 1997. The party had won based on leadership and the sending of a clear message of reform, symbolized by the single policy of postal privatization. Koizumi weakened the factions, centralized the party, and loosened ties with many of the party's major clientele groups – most notably, postmasters affected by privatization, but also medical doctors and construction companies. When Koizumi retired, the LDP was on the verge of becoming a coherent political party. All that remained was to institutionalize the gains that had been made, but that is precisely what his successors failed to do.

Failing to Learn the Koizumi Lesson

When Koizumi's hand-picked successor, Abe Shinzou, took over the reins of government, he had a large majority. Nevertheless, he quickly readmitted all the postal rebels who had won their single-member districts. With a few complex exceptions, the 2009 nominations for single-member districts went to winning rebels instead of loyal losers. This time, however, those who wished to return had to sign a statement promising to support postal reform, which maintained a semblance of policy coherence but also returned to the traditional 'if you win, you are LDP' decision rule, making the new LDP look more like the old version. That old image was reinforced when several of Abe's cabinet appointments were found to have serious corruption problems. Further, Abe was unable to build an image of strong leadership, as movement towards reform stalled yet again. Unable to govern effectively, Abe soon resigned, having squandered most of the Koizumi legacy in the court of public opinion.

It did not take long before policy coherence also disappeared. Abe's replacement, Fukuda Yasuo, pursued a policy of dialogue with the DPJ, which demanded that the government release tax revenues that had been dedicated exclusively to road construction for use in the general account, a reform proposal that Koizumi had dropped in order to concentrate on postal privatization. Both Abe and Fukuda had promised to end dedicated road taxes, but were stymied by backbench resistance. Unable to move his own party, Fukuda attempted to obtain the cooperation of the DPJ in the present by promising to end the system of dedicated road taxes in the future. The DPJ, however, doubted his ability to keep that promise – doubt that proved well founded. Although Fukuda obtained a cabinet promise to end the policy in 2009, the promise disappeared when Fukuda resigned.[8] Fukuda's replacement, Asou Tarou, seemed to have something of Koizumi's media presence and the potential to exercise strong leadership, but he, too, failed to deliver.

It is wise to remember that Koizumi's leadership was also sporadic. He promised reform in 2001 but was only able to enact it in 2005. Between the promise and its fulfilment, Koizumi's poll ratings dropped, similar to the experiences of Abe, Fukuda, and Asou. In fact, no LDP prime minister, including Koizumi, has been able to prod the party to reform at a reasonable pace. Even though every candidate in the 2005 election and every rebel who was allowed to return to the party in 2006 promised to support postal privatization, the LDP soon saw the emergence of a serious internal movement to reverse Koizumi's major policy achievement.[9] Others in the party were determined to defend the reform, and by the time of the 2009 election the LDP once again was both for and against postal privatization and unable to commit either its members or its future leaders to a coherent party platform.

After the 2009 loss, the party chose Tanigaki Sadakazu to lead the party. He immediately reinforced the message of unity at the cost of policy coherence, and attacked the 'dictatorial' tactics of DPJ secretary-general Ozawa Ichirou, who was preventing members of his party in the Diet from criticizing the DPJ government or its policies. In contrast, Tanigaki pointed out, LDP members of the Diet were free to criticize their party's leadership and its policies. He did not mention, however, that the other recent leader who was criticized for his dictatorial tactics was Koizumi, the only leader since the 1990s to lead the LDP to electoral victory. In fact, Koizumi won elections in 2001 and 2005 when he acted dictatorial and lost elections in 2003 and 2004 when he did not. The party, however, chose to ignore the lessons of the recent past and to return instead to the traditions of its golden age.

Prospects for the Future

The LDP is unlikely to prove an exception to the rule that the party will not implement serious reforms until it has lost two or more consecutive elections. That said, the LDP is not disintegrating, appearances to the contrary notwithstanding.

The main attraction of the LDP has always been its hold on power. In opposition, it suffers defections. Between the 2009 loss and April 2010, fourteen LDP members of the Diet resigned from the party, several forming new parties (the LDP similarly lost members when it was in opposition following the 1993 elections; see Reed 2003, 42). All these defectors, however, either were denied the LDP nomination – and therefore had no future in the party unless they could find some other way to win – or were not planning to run in the 2010 upper house election. As always, the best way for these defectors to return to the LDP is to win, even if it means running against the LDP under a new party label. Most of the defectors were members of the lower house and thus will have two or three years to decide which party to run for in the next election, while defectors who were elected to the upper house in 2007 will have until 2013 to consider their options.

The attractiveness of the defectors' various options will depend upon the election outcome, but one option for any defector who wins will be to return to the LDP. A 'new party boom' such as occurred in 1993 would make returning to the LDP somewhat less attractive, but it is hard to imagine a result in which the LDP was not one of the two largest parties in the upper house. The mass media continue to speculate about a wholesale realignment in which politicians forget about which party nomination is most likely to lead to their re-election and instead join parties with people who share their policy preferences. The evidence, both comparative and historical, indicates that this is highly unlikely. I know of no cases of such a wholesale realignment either in other industrial democracies or in Japanese history. Rapid large-scale changes in parties and party systems are caused by changes in the personnel represented in the legislature, not by rearranging the current personnel into new parties. In fact, since 1996, neither the LDP nor the DPJ has lost many incumbents to the other party even when in opposition; instead, both have served as magnets for candidates from minor parties and independents. I would be willing to wager that, twenty years from now, barring any major change in the electoral system, the LDP will have reformed, become a more coherent political party, and be competing with the DPJ in an institutionalized two-party system.

NOTES

1 See also Carty (2002) on the Canadian version of a franchise party.
2 *Yomiuri Shimbun*, 30 June 2000. All newspaper articles cited in this chapter are available in Japanese in Word format from the author upon request.
3 *Yomiuri Shimbun*, 8 July 2002; idem, 13 July 2003; and idem, 28 October 2003.
4 In Germany, for example, PR candidates who do not also run in a single-member district face a similar task and a similarly uncertain career (Patzelt 2000, 39).
5 The candidate who chose not to run ran instead for mayor of the major city in the district. He won, and was replaced in the single-member district by the previous mayor of the same city.
6 *Yomiuri Shimbun*, 2 March 2003.
7 *Yomiuri Shimbun*, 14 August 2005.
8 *Yomiuri Shimbun*, 29 April 2008.
9 *Yomiuri Shimbun*, 26 December 2008.

4 The Evolution of the DPJ: Two Steps Forward, One Step Back

ROBERT J. WEINER

The Democratic Party of Japan (DPJ), which assumed power in 2009 after winning a historic victory in the lower house election, came into existence only in 1996. At the time of its birth as an amalgam of former Socialists and a small group of defectors from the long-governing Liberal Democratic Party (LDP), it was the smaller of two main anti-LDP opposition parties. But the party gradually established itself as the chief vehicle of anti-LDP opposition within the new '2000 System' (see Schoppa, Chapter 1 in this volume), absorbing other anti-LDP parties as they fragmented or disappeared. In 2009, the DPJ finally shed its 'opposition' status and took charge of governing Japan for the first time. Immediately, it was hailed as a genuine counterpart to the LDP in a true two-party system.

But the DPJ is not that counterpart just yet, and even its resounding win in 2009 was not enough to make it so. The DPJ's 2009 victory was propelled less by its own strength than by the staggering unpopularity of the post-Koizumi LDP – thanks to LDP policy missteps, ministerial gaffes and scandals, and prime ministers' inability to last more than a year in office. Whether the DPJ can win future majorities on its own merits remains an open question. Analysts have long pointed to three fundamental organizational flaws in the party. First, geography: the DPJ might be overly concentrated in volatile urban areas. Second, 'quality': the DPJ has failed to cultivate high-quality candidates with political experience, prestige, or name recognition. Third, ideology: the DPJ is dangerously split between progressives and conservatives, many of whom built their identities in smaller, more homogenous parties before coalescing into the DPJ (see Figure 4.1). In the immediate aftermath of the DPJ's landslide win, criticisms of these purported organizational flaws were muted, but

Figure 4.1: Main Lineages of Party Formation in Japan, 1993–2009

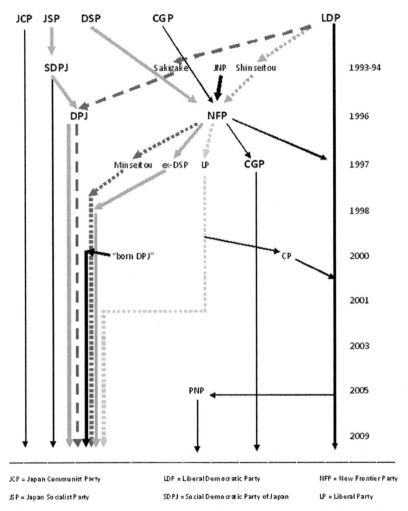

JCP = Japan Communist Party

JSP = Japan Socialist Party

DSP = Democratic Socialist Party

CGP = Clean Government Party

LDP = Liberal Democratic Party

SDPJ = Social Democratic Party of Japan

JNP = Japan New Party

DPJ = Democratic Party of Japan

NFP = New Frontier Party

LP = Liberal Party

CP = Conservative Party

PNP = People's New Party

Source: Originally constructed by Leonard J. Schoppa and modified by the author.

they are likely to return. Indeed, to the extent these problems exist, the DPJ's big win in 2009 might obscure them and lull the party into thinking them solved, which could prove damaging once the party inevitably is forced to campaign in a more normal, non-landslide election.

How severe are the DPJ's problems of geography, quality, and ideology? Has the party been able to address them as it has evolved? Are they likely to threaten the party's ability to maintain its 2009 strength? This chapter concludes that, while the DPJ needs to improve its candidate recruitment, the party is not an overly urban one, nor is its ex-Socialist contingent particularly strong – findings that suggest that, in addition to its major short-term gains in 2009, the party also has improved its long-term prospects.

The DPJ Is Not an Urban Party

The first charge is that the DPJ, despite its success in the 2009 election, still suffers from overdependence on urban areas, where voters are fickle and liable to swing completely against a party just a few years after embracing it. The election results I analyse in this section disprove this assertion.

Measuring Party Strength in Specific Districts

To gauge where the DPJ is strongest, one might use either of two benchmarks: (1) where the DPJ wins seats, and (2) where the DPJ runs strong campaigns.[1] These two measures are closely related, of course, but not exactly the same. Japan's lower house is made up of 300 members elected by plurality vote in single-member districts (SMDs) and 180 members elected through party-list voting in regional proportional representation (PR) districts. As Reed describes (in this volume), parties have the option of running lower house candidates simultaneously in an SMD and on a PR list.

In measuring the DPJ's strength, I treat as equivalent two types of SMDs: ones where the DPJ candidate wins outright, and ones where the DPJ candidate loses the district but wins a lower house seat through PR.[2] In both types, the DPJ candidate wins the seat through a strong performance in the SMD, thanks to the DPJ's aggressive use of 'shared PR ranks.' This provision of Japan's electoral system allows parties to rank multiple dual SMD/PR candidates at the same position on a PR list. Any who win their SMD race simply take that SMD seat; any who lose, if ranked high enough, take one of the party's PR seats, with ties among shared-rank candidates broken as necessary by 'seat loss ratio' (*sekihairitsu*) – the ratio of one's losing SMD vote to the winning vote in that district. When a party lists several candidates at a shared rank that is likely high enough to win a seat, it effectively tells these candidates that their PR fate depends on their SMD performance.

The DPJ had adopted this practice widely by 2003, and by 2009 had taken it nearly to its logical limit: nearly all its officially endorsed SMD candidates were dual SMD/PR candidates, and all these dual candidates were ranked together at the top position on their respective regional PR lists, above any pure PR candidates. This means that nearly all the DPJ's PR winners earned their seats not simply by virtue of high positions on the PR list, but also through strong SMD races (albeit not strong enough to win their districts outright). As a signal of DPJ strength, then, PR 'back-door' wins differ from straightforward SMD wins only in degree. Both types of winners did well enough in their respective SMDs to earn seats in the lower house, and both types will be incumbents when they run in the next election. The more important distinction is the one between all these winners, on the one hand, and candidates who win no seat at all, on the other.

Still, one might argue that even the distinction between winners and losers is only one of degree, at least as far as electoral performance goes. One also might want to distinguish *among* the winners: some scraped by and might be more likely to lose in the future, while others trounced their competition. To this end, one can use a general 'vote ratio' as a richer measure of DPJ candidate strength. An SMD loser's 'vote ratio' is simply the candidate's *sekihairitsu* – the ratio of the loser's vote to that of the winner. The loser's vote ratio is necessarily less than 1. Similarly, an SMD winner's 'vote ratio' is the ratio of the winner's vote to the SMD runner-up's vote, and is necessarily greater than 1. Of course, while vote ratios provide a more sensitive gauge of a DPJ candidate's strength than simple wins and losses, the two measures are highly correlated. All the DPJ's SMD winners necessarily have vote ratios greater than 1 and greater than those of the PR winners, and in any given year nearly all the DPJ's PR winners have higher SMD vote ratios than do nearly all its losers.[3]

Classifying Districts by DPJ Strength

I classify the strength of the DPJ in a given SMD based on the party's performance in the three most recent lower house elections: those of

2003, 2005, and 2009. It was in 2003, upon the DPJ's merger with Ozawa Ichirou's Liberal Party (LP), that the DPJ took its current form; this is also true, by extension, of the party system as a whole. The only notable party merger or split between the elections of 2003 and 2009 was the defection of 'postal rebels' from the LDP in 2005. Given this stability, any of these three most recent elections alone could provide a good map of the DPJ's district-by-district strength. Though the party's win totals varied widely across the three election years, the districts where the DPJ performed best and worst *within* each election year, as measured by vote ratios, remained fairly consistent, and so the DPJ's vote ratios in SMDs in 2003, 2005, and 2009 are reasonably well correlated.[4] Still, it makes sense to incorporate all three years' results.

I divide Japan's 300 SMDs into four categories of DPJ strength: strong, mid-strong, mid-weak, and weak. These categories are based mainly on straightforward wins (either in the SMD itself or via PR) and losses. But they also take into account vote ratios, in part because simple wins and losses do little to distinguish among DPJ candidates in 2005, when nearly two-thirds of the DPJ's candidates lost, and in 2009, when nearly all its candidates won. I discount as 'unconvincing' DPJ victories that came despite vote ratios below the party's top 200 that year, and note as 'promising' losses that came despite a ratio in the party's top 200. Finally, the categories account for exceptions caused by the failure – usually temporary – of either the LDP or the DPJ camp to prevent more than one of its candidates from running in a district.

More specifically, there are ninety-five 'strong' DPJ districts, including ninety where the DPJ candidate won convincingly in each of the three election years. Three more fit this pattern save for a loss in one year due to coordination problems in the DPJ camp. In two more, the DPJ ran no candidate in 2003 out of deference to a strong candidate from a different non-LDP party, which candidate later switched to the DPJ and won convincingly in 2005 and 2009.

Seventy-seven DPJ districts are classified as 'mid-strong,' chiefly those in which the DPJ fell short of a convincing win in only one of the three election years. Sixty are SMDs where the DPJ candidate lost in the weak DPJ year of 2005 but won convincingly in 2003 and 2009. In four more, the DPJ candidate lost in 2003 but won convincingly in 2005 and 2009. In three more, the DPJ candidate won convincingly in 2003 and 2005 but only unconvincingly in 2009. Ten more mid-strong districts would fit one of these patterns save for exceptions due to coordination problems or early years when the DPJ ran no candidate.[5]

Fifty-seven DPJ districts are 'mid-weak,' and constitute a residual set where DPJ performances were weaker than in the 'strong' and 'mid-strong' categories and stronger than in the 'weak' category. They include twenty-nine districts where the DPJ candidate lost in both 2003 and 2005 but won convincingly in the boom year of 2009, fourteen where the DPJ candidate won convincingly in 2003 but lost in 2005 and won only unconvincingly even in 2009, and four where the DPJ won convincingly in 2003, lost in 2005, and ran no candidate in 2009, among others.

Finally, there are seventy-one 'weak' DPJ districts, including sixty-nine with no DPJ winner in 2003 and 2005 and either no winner or an unconvincing winner in the boom year of 2009. In two more districts, the DPJ won once in the three election years, but only thanks to a coordination problem within the LDP camp.

The DPJ Is Not Intrinsically Urban

The conventional wisdom holds that the DPJ is an urban party, but this is misleading. The DPJ is only an urban party in that it runs poorly in the *most rural* districts. Outside of this deepest countryside, the DPJ performs similarly well across the upper three-quarters of the urban-rural spectrum, in districts ranging from hyper-metropolitan to small-city/ rural hybrids. And in the most heavily urban areas, the DPJ enjoys no more intrinsic strength than do its rivals.

For those familiar with the map of Japan, a quick glance makes this plain. Figures 4.2 through 4.4 are cartograms, with each SMD depicted by a square of equal area rather than by its actual boundaries (this keeps populous but geographically tiny districts such as Tokyo's from 'disappearing' next to sprawling but emptier rural ones). Figure 4.2 helps readers less familiar with Japan see where the most urban and most rural areas are by dividing the 300 SMDs into four urbanness 'quartiles' according to the standard urbanness criterion: the percentage of the district's population living in census-defined 'Densely Inhabited Districts.'[6] The dark masses around Tokyo and Osaka show how the most urban districts are clustered in these areas. Figure 4.3 shades SMDs according to their DPJ strength categories, as defined above. Figure 4.4 pulls out and shades only the DPJ's ninety-five 'strong' SMDs according to urbanness. Strong DPJ districts are scattered across the map, both inside and outside the dense megalopolis of the Pacific coast. Indeed, the most urban quartile has *fewer* strong DPJ districts than the second-most, and not so many more than the third.

Figure 4.2: Single-Member Districts by Urbanness Quartile

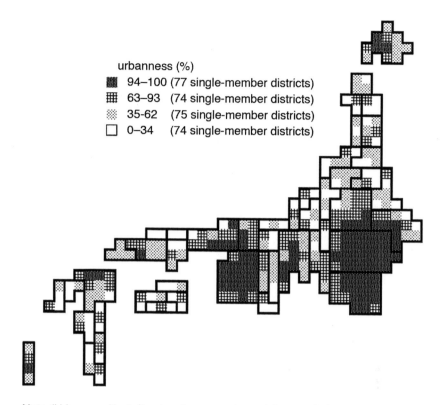

Note: 'Urbanness' is defined as the percentage of the population living in census-defined 'Densely Inhabited Districts.'
Source: Data on urbanness from Steven R. Reed.

This pattern is not simply an artefact of the 2005 election's urban LDP boom and DPJ bust or a reflection of Ozawa's subsequent efforts, during his term as DPJ leader and subsequently in the 2009 election, to bolster the party's rural support.[7] It even predates the DPJ's early mergers with more conservative parties and the LDP's coalition with the urban Clean Government Party (CGP). The DPJ's strength has been spread evenly across all but the most rural areas as long as the party has existed. Even in 1996 and 2000, the DPJ won at roughly equal rates in all quartiles but the most rural, and it proved strongest in the *second*-most urban

Figure 4.3: Single-Member Districts by DPJ Strength, 2003–09

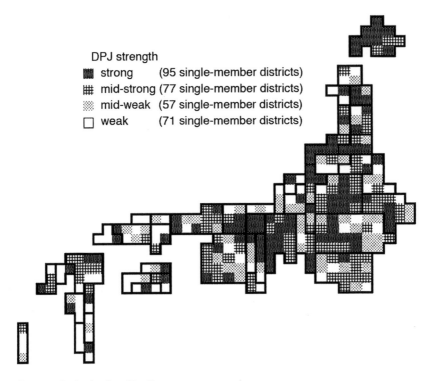

Source: Author's classification.

quartile (Table 4.1). Only in 2003 did the DPJ's candidates win more the more urban their districts.[8]

The DPJ is no more an urban party than is the LDP. The DPJ's strong and safe districts – the districts where DPJ candidates enjoyed something more than anti-LDP protest support, where they have won even in rough years and have compiled the uninterrupted strings of victories that build party seniority – are found just as often in semi-urban and semi-rural areas as in fully urban areas. In the most urban areas, the DPJ has no bedrock strength comparable to that of the LDP in the deepest countryside.

The standard 'urban-rural' dichotomy, then, is misleading. It both ignores significant pockets of non-urban DPJ strength and overestimates DPJ urban strength. But this is not to say that the best one can

Figure 4.4: 'Strong' DPJ Single-Member Districts by Urbanness Quartile, 2003–09

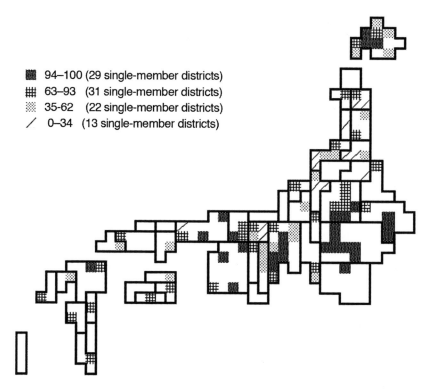

- ▓ 94–100 (29 single-member districts)
- ▦ 63–93 (31 single-member districts)
- ▨ 35-62 (22 single-member districts)
- ╱ 0–34 (13 single-member districts)

Note: 'Urbanness' is defined as the percentage of the population living in census-defined 'Densely Inhabited Districts.'
Sources: Data on urbanness from Steven R. Reed; and author's classification.

do to describe DPJ support is 'all-but-extremely-rural.' The DPJ enjoys strength in particular *types* of urban areas – and particular types of rural areas as well. One needs a more nuanced approach to DPJ geography.

One can better characterize the DPJ's geographical strengths based on four other, more tailored district features. Three of these simply reflect the prior strongholds of the three disparate '1955 System' elements now at the core of the DPJ – the former Democratic Socialist Party (DSP), the pre-1993 Social Democratic Party of Japan (SDPJ), and various conservatives – none of which was ever particularly urban. A fourth acknowledges that such urban appeal as DPJ candidates do have is concentrated

Table 4.1 DPJ Winners, 1996–2009, and Strength in Single-Member Districts, 2003–09, by Urbanness Quartile

Urbanness (%)	DPJ Winners					DPJ Strength in Single-Member Districts, 2003–09				
	1996	2000	2003	2005	2009	Strong	Mid-strong	Mid-weak	Weak	Total Number of Districts
	(number of winners)					(number of districts)				
94–100	13	32	64	30	71	29	24	16	8	77
63–93	15	41	58	33	70	31	25	12	6	74
35–62	11	26	38	31	71	22	17	20	16	75
0–34	3	11	19	18	54	13	11	9	41	74
Total	42	110	179	112	266	95	77	57	71	300

Note: 'Urbanness' is defined as the percentage of the population living in census-defined 'Densely Inhabited Districts.'

Sources: Steven R. Reed for data on urbanness; Steven R. Reed and Ethan Scheiner for data on the 1996 and 2000 elections; Matthew Carlson, Ross Schaap, and the author for data on the 2003 election; Ethan Scheiner for data on the 2005 election; and Ko Maeda for data on the 2009 election.

in the suburbs, away from the central-city strongholds of another 1955 System member, the CGP, now allied against the DPJ. Together, these four features describe a *political* geography of DPJ support.

The former SDPJ – that is, its pre-1993 incarnation, not its current rump form – was never at its strongest in Japan's biggest cities. Though the SDPJ did appeal to voters in large metropolitan areas, both as an anti-LDP protest vehicle and on ideological grounds, it was there that the SDPJ also faced the only two 1955 System parties that *were* truly urban: the CGP and the Japanese Communist Party (JCP). The SDPJ did better in 'second-tier' cities *outside* major metropolitan and industrial areas. In 'second-tier' prefectural capitals in particular, a large share of the workforce was made up of the SDPJ's public sector labour support base – especially teachers, prefectural and city employees, and other civil servants.[9] The party thus enjoyed some of its deepest pockets of strength in regions that were less urban overall: Hokkaidou, Touhoku, Shin'etsu (Nagano and Niigata Prefectures), San'in (Tottori and Shimane), Shikoku, and Kyuushuu. The capital cities of these historically strong Socialist regions remain DPJ geographical strongholds under the current electoral system. I include in this category the nineteen capital city single-member districts in these regions that fall into the middle two urbanness quartiles.[10]

The former DSP, meanwhile, relied on large- and heavy-industry private sector labour for most of its support. As a centrist party with neither the size of the LDP or SDPJ nor the notoriety of the CGP or JCP, the DSP is often overlooked in analyses of the 1955 System. But where the DSP was strong, it was often tremendously strong. It often enjoyed concentrated vote support in 'company towns' (*kigyou joukamachi*) such as Toyota City, whose Aichi 11th district the LDP did not even bother to contest in 2003, or Nobeoka City, home to Asahi Chemical and whose city council's largest bloc still calls itself the 'Fraternity Club' (*Yuuai Kurabu*, '*yuuai*' being a term long associated with the DSP). More generally, the DSP was at its strongest in certain industrial areas of the Pacific coast megalopolis between Shizuoka Prefecture and northern Kyuushuu, with a few added pockets of strength in isolated company towns and big-city industrial wards. Under the current electoral system, I categorize as former DSP strongholds those forty-eight SMDs carved out of the eighteen multi-member districts where the DSP won a seat in at least two of the last three pre-electoral-reform elections (in 1986, 1990, and 1993).[11] These forty-eight SMDs are found in all four urbanness quartiles, but the bulk are evenly spread across the top three.

Powerful conservative leaders within the DPJ have also maintained their personal spheres of influence. Individual politicians in Japan – especially, though not exclusively, conservatives – gain votes at least as much for their personal characteristics as for their policy stances or party affiliation. It follows that the home regions of senior DPJ leaders have become solid DPJ strongholds. This is especially so in these regions' rural areas, where one should expect personal characteristics and connections to shape voting behaviour most effectively. To avoid an overly expansive definition of 'leader,' I include only current and past heads (*daihyou*) of the party – Hatoyama Yukio, Kan Naoto, Maehara Seiji, Okada Katsuya, and Ozawa Ichirou – and add Hata Tsutomu, a leader of several DPJ predecessor parties and a former prime minister.[12] I narrowly define 'home region' as one's home prefecture. Though personal political influence can travel across prefectural borders, it operates most effectively within prefectural party federations (which oversee candidate selection), through networks of home-prefecture local politicians, and among prefectural media and citizens, who define 'native son' on a prefectural basis. I include only SMDs in the bottom two urbanness quartiles, where, again, personal-bailiwick effects should carry the most weight (this assumes away any personal-bailiwick influence by Kan, whose home prefecture of Tokyo has no SMDs in the bottom two urbanness quartiles). The category of 'rural areas in DPJ leaders' home prefectures' is thus made up of twenty SMDs in the more rural parts of Hokkaidou (home also to ex-Socialist DPJ heavyweight Yokomichi Takahiro), Iwate, Nagano, Mie, and Kyoto Prefectures.

Of course, the DPJ's appeal to voters is not carried over entirely from its predecessor parties. The party might not yet have a cogent statement of what it stands for, but it is at least *not* the LDP, and at the same time not the thoroughly leftist party the SDPJ once was. The party offers (or, perhaps, 'sells') the prospect of a break with traditional social values, long-entrenched patterns of governance, and disproportionate influence on the part of agriculture, small business, and other less-efficient economic sectors. This is an appeal based more on policy and party image than on organization and candidate personalities, and, as Schoppa notes (in chapter 2 of this volume), it indeed plays best in urban areas, particularly in large metropolitan areas like the Tokyo and the Osaka-Kyoto-Kobe conglomeration. Metropolitan-area residents (as opposed to those in the more 'provincial' cities described above) are more affluent and educated and more likely to identify with more efficient economic sectors, more 'modern' social values, and change for change's sake. They are also less likely to belong to the social and organizational networks the LDP has traditionally relied upon to mobilize voters.

But this description does not fit all metropolitan-area voters equally well. It applies most widely in wealthier and more purely residential suburban areas, those sometimes described as *yamanote*, or, loosely translated, 'uptown.' It fits less well in 'downtown,' or *shitamachi*, areas, which house more small business and industry and whose residents hew somewhat closer to the demographic and organizational profile of the LDP's more rural supporters. Indeed, the LDP has long enjoyed support in downtown metropolitan areas – as has its current coalition partner, the CGP.

To describe where the DPJ does well (and does not) within large metropolitan areas, one might focus on demographics and identify *yamanote* districts by their residential character. *Yamanote* SMDs could be those with a ratio of daytime to nighttime population less than, say, 0.95, indicating 'bedtowns' whose residents are more likely to lack occupational or organization ties to their home communities. But one might also jump to a more immediately political description: the DPJ does well where the CGP does not. Since CGP supporters tend not to be 'uptown' types, their presence has always been a good proxy for a district's 'downtown-ness' and relative resistance to the DPJ's type of appeal (CGP support correlates well with daytime-nighttime ratios, for example, though there is relatively greater support in the Kansai region than these ratios would predict).[13] Now that the CGP allies itself with the LDP and actively directs its supporters away from the DPJ, this particular portion of downtown resistance to the DPJ has become explicit and institutionalized. Note again, though, that the LDP, too, has always done well in *shitamachi* areas. CGP strength is a better proxy because that party *only* does well there.

I define as metropolitan SMDs those in the top two urbanness quartiles that lie within the census-defined major metropolitan areas surrounding the cities of Sapporo, Tokyo, Nagoya, Osaka-Kyoto-Kobe, Hiroshima, or Fukuoka-Kita-Kyuushuu. Among these, I define as 'uptown,' or low-CGP metropolitan SMDs, those whose voters' CGP vote in the lower house's PR portion falls below these districts' mean of about 15.5 per cent. There are seventy-nine such districts, sixty-four of which are not already identified as promising DPJ districts under one of the three previous categories.

These four features – the capital cities of historically strong Socialist regions, former DSP strongholds, rural areas in DPJ leaders' home prefectures, and low-CGP metropolitan areas – amount to a political geography of DPJ strength (they are not necessarily the *cause* of DPJ strength). The aim here is simply to establish a geographical shorthand slightly more nuanced – and more political – than 'urban' to identify SMDs where DPJ candidates win most consistently and to whom the DPJ's core legislators are thus responsible. The four 'political geography' features are slightly less parsimonious than 'urbanness,' but this lets them better describe where the DPJ does well.

Of course, in many SMDs, these two approaches overlap (if one takes 'urban' to mean the top two urbanness quartiles and 'rural' to mean the bottom two quartiles). But forty SMDs also fit the political-geography profile of DPJ strength despite being rural, and forty-nine others fall outside the political-geography profile despite being urban. (These eighty-nine districts' cells are shaded in Table 4.2.) To the extent that the DPJ indeed tends to do well in the former group of forty districts but not in the latter forty-nine, the political geography profile is an improvement over the 'urban versus rural' approach.

Table 4.2   Single-Member Districts by Urbanness Quartile and Political Geography Feature

Urbanness (%)	Political-Geography Feature			
	Former SDPJ or DSP District, or Rural Portion of Party Leader's Home Prefecture	Low-CGP Metropolitan	Others	Total
	(number of districts)			
94–100	12	42	23	77
63–93	26	22	26	74
35–62	27	0	48	75
0–34	13	0	61	74
Total	78	64	158	300

Note: 'Urbanness' is defined as the percentage of the population living in census-defined 'Densely Inhabited Districts.'

Sources: Steven R. Reed for data on urbanness; Lijphart Election Archive (http://ssdc. ucsd.edu/lij) for data on pre-1993 elections; Steven R. Reed and Ethan Scheiner for data on the 1996 and 2000 elections; Matthew Carlson, Ross Schaap, and the author for data on the 2003 election; Ethan Scheiner for data on the 2005 election; Ko Maeda for data on the 2009 election; and Sugawara Taku (http://freett.com/sugawara_taku/data/pr03_00.html) for CGP data.

Among the ninety-five 'strong' DPJ districts (as defined above), nineteen fit the political geography profile despite being rural, while only eight fall outside the profile despite being urban (Table 4.3).[14] To view this another way, 32 per cent of all districts are strong DPJ districts. As might be expected, districts that are both urban *and* fit the political geography profile beat this average: 51 per cent are strong DPJ districts. But 48 per cent of districts that are *rural* and fit the political geography profile are strong DPJ districts as well. Meanwhile, among districts that are urban but lack any of the political geography features, only 16 per cent are strong DPJ districts.

If one looks at both strong and mid-strong DPJ districts together, the political geography profile's predictive advantages are smaller but still present. There are only barely more districts that fit the political geography profile despite being rural (twenty-seven, or 16 per cent) than there are urban districts that the political geography profile misses (twenty-six, or 15 per cent) (Table 4.4). But, again, the political geography profile is more precise. Fifty-seven per cent of all SMDs are either

Table 4.3   Number of 'Strong' DPJ Single-Member Districts by Urbanness Quartile and Political-Geography Feature

| Urbanness (%) | Political-Geography Feature | | | Total |
	Former SDPJ or DSP District, or Rural Portion of Party Leader's Home Prefecture	Low-CGP Metropolitan	Others	
	(number of districts)			
94–100	7	20	2	29
63–93	18	7	6	31
35–62	12	0	10	22
0–34	7	0	6	13
Total	44	27	24	95

Note: 'Urbanness' is defined as the percentage of the population living in census-defined 'Densely Inhabited Districts.'

Sources: Steven R. Reed for data on urbanness; Lijphart Election Archive (http://ssdc. ucsd.edu/lij) for data on pre-1993 elections; Steven R. Reed and Ethan Scheiner for data on the 1996 and 2000 elections; Matthew Carlson, Ross Schaap, and the author for data on the 2003 election; Ethan Scheiner for data on the 2005 election; Ko Maeda for data on the 2009 election; and Sugawara Taku (http://freett.com/sugawara_taku/data/pr03_00.html) for CGP data.

Table 4.4   Number of 'Strong' and 'Mid-strong' DPJ Single-Member Districts by Urbanness Quartile and Political-Geography Feature

Urbanness (%)	Political-Geography Feature			Total
	Former SDPJ or DSP District, or Rural Portion of Party Leader's Home Prefecture	Low-CGP Metropolitan	Others	
	(number of districts)			
94–100	10	33	10	53
63–93	23	17	16	56
35–62	19	0	20	39
0–34	8	0	16	24
Total	60	50	62	172

Note: 'Urbanness' is defined as the percentage of the population living in census-defined 'Densely Inhabited Districts.'

Sources: Steven R. Reed for data on urbanness; Lijphart Election Archive (http://ssdc.ucsd.edu/lij) for data on pre-1993 elections; Steven R. Reed and Ethan Scheiner for data on the 1996 and 2000 elections; Matthew Carlson, Ross Schaap, and the author for data on the 2003 election; Ethan Scheiner for data on the 2005 election; Ko Maeda for data on the 2009 election; and Sugawara Taku (http://freett.com/sugawara_taku/data/pr03_00.html) for CGP data.

strong or mid-strong DPJ districts. Unsurprisingly, districts that are both urban and fit the political geography profile beat this average: 81 per cent are either strong or mid-strong DPJ districts. But of the forty districts that are rural but fit the political geography profile, 68 per cent are strong or mid-strong DPJ districts. Meanwhile, among the forty-nine urban districts not already identified by the political geography profile, only 53 per cent are strong or mid-strong for the DPJ – that is, fewer than average.

The DPJ Still Lacks Quality Candidates

All parties, regardless of the political system in which they operate, benefit from high-quality, appealing candidates. Such candidates not only are better able to win the election immediately at hand, but also provide a more stable linkage with voters than ideology, popularity, specific issues, or protest voting. They promise more staying power and more durable incumbency advantages, all else being equal.

For the DPJ, candidate quality is particularly important. Even in Japan, whose party system is often characterized as focused on candidates rather than parties, some parties do manage to build voter loyalty through well-defined ideologies, well-honed organizations, and/or long histories. The DPJ enjoys none of these advantages. It is a young party, and its most salient appeal is that it is not the LDP. This leaves more of its success dependent on the strength of its individual candidates. Of course, not being the LDP is enough to win quite handily at times, as in 2009. In both the DPJ boom election of 2009 and the LDP (or Koizumi) boom election of 2005, candidates' party affiliation proved at least as important as their personal characteristics – though personal characteristics were still significant (Reed, Scheiner, and Thies 2009). In the DPJ's early years, however, when party affiliation hardly mattered, candidate selection was the DPJ's Achilles heel: it lacked many 'quality' candidates, and thus lost elections it might have otherwise won (Scheiner 2006). In future elections, under more normal electoral conditions, the DPJ will face a similar challenge.

In 2009, the DPJ was facing its fifth lower house election. Its losses in 2005, unfortunate as they were for the party, gave it a chance for a personnel makeover, and the party's success in the 2007 upper house election was well timed to help it recruit stronger candidates in 2009. But has the DPJ indeed improved its candidates since the 2000 election, the party's first year as the leader of the opposition? Is this why the party did so well in 2009?

The conventional definition of 'quality,' as Scheiner (2006) aptly codifies for Japan, is based on candidates' (and their families') experience in government and electorally advantageous professional backgrounds. It ignores other, less objective advantages such as charisma, long-time residence in the district, or policy expertise obtained outside elected or appointed government office. 'Quality' lower house candidates are defined as those with prior experience as national bureaucrats or high elected officials (as either an upper house member, prefectural governor, prefectural legislator, or city mayor), the children or other close relatives of former lower house members, and television news reporters and presenters (who qualify by virtue of their name recognition and apparent knowledge of current affairs). Candidates common in the DPJ but whose career backgrounds are left out of this definition include bankers; officials of non-governmental organizations; doctors, lawyers, and other professionals; non-television journalists, commentators, and think tank members; celebrities, including non-entertainment celebrities such as well-known plaintiffs in medical malfeasance cases; union officials; other businesspeople (*kaishain* or *sarariiman*); graduates of Matsushita Seikei Juku and other policy and political training academies; city-level legislators; and Diet members' aides (*hisho*). The last three of these – political training academy graduates, city legislators, and Diet members' aides – come closest to fitting the existing definition of a quality political background, but can reasonably be left out if one is comfortable with a strict standard.

Note that these criteria include three of the four pools from which the LDP traditionally has recruited most of its own candidates, the excluded fourth being Diet members' aides. The standard definition of candidate quality is thus somewhat LDP-centric – which implies that, as the DPJ increases its candidate quality, it is becoming more like the LDP. It is also biased in favour of government experience. For example, among the finance-savvy candidates who pushed the DPJ towards neoliberal reforms (see Schoppa, Chapter 2 in this volume), those who toiled in economic ministries count as quality recruits while those who entered politics directly from banks or policy schools do not. 'Quality' identifies the family and career experiences most directly applicable to campaigning and/or legislating, not policy knowledge per se.

Discussions of 'quality' often focus on new candidates and ignore incumbents and former incumbents. Since quality is a proxy for electability and experience, the implicit assumption is that incumbents and former incumbents are quality candidates by definition, no matter what their backgrounds might be. This is consistent with the fact that incumbents indeed win at higher rates; it is also consistent with parties' practice of routinely re-endorsing incumbents (though the fact that even weak incumbents are also routinely re-endorsed suggests this practice might reflect simple inertia as well). I thus use a broader definition of quality and explicitly include incumbents and former incumbents. But I withhold the 'quality' label from those few former incumbents and otherwise-'quality' newcomers who clearly defy expectations of electability by losing twice or more in a row. This is typically the point at which Japanese parties rescind endorsements – if the two-time loser candidate has not already bowed out.

If the DPJ were aggressively upgrading its candidate roster, then, its candidate slates increasingly would be made up of what I call 'broad-quality' candidates: incumbents, quality newcomers, and former incumbents and quality challengers being given just one more chance after having lost in the previous election. We should see less reliance on non-quality challengers and less recycling of 'third-chance' candidates with two or more consecutive losses to their names. How well has the DPJ done this?

The record is mixed. By the most important measure, the overall number of broad-quality candidates, the party took a step backward in 2009. In 2000, the DPJ ran 141 such candidates, covering 47 per cent of the 300 SMDs (Table 4.5).[15] Though the party absorbed several dozen incumbents of other parties via mergers, it was still too young to have demonstrated enough long-term viability to attract many well-qualified challengers. In fully fifty-six districts, the DPJ failed to run any candidate at all. The party improved over the next two elections, and by 2005 was placing broad-quality candidates in 71 per cent of SMDs. In 2009, though, broad-quality candidates ran in only 197 districts, or 66 per cent of the total.

This backsliding hides a few mildly encouraging caveats and sub-trends. First, the DPJ's poor electoral performance in 2005 saddled it with a more challenging task in 2009. Incumbents are broad-quality by definition, so the more of them a party retains, the easier it is to assemble a high-quality overall slate of candidates. The relatively successful 2003 election left 171 SMDs stocked with DPJ incumbents for 2005. The party installed only forty-three additional quality candidates in the remaining 129 districts – that is, only one in three – but this was enough to yield broad-quality candidates in 71 per cent of districts overall. In 2005, though, voters removed nearly half the DPJ's incumbents, so that the party faced the 2009 election with only 103 incumbents ready to run in districts they had won in 2005. To maintain its overall quality level, the DPJ would have needed to fill 111 of the remaining 197 districts – more than half – with broad-quality candidates.

Second, the party *has* improved – moderately – the quality of its new recruits. Among challengers (as opposed to incumbents or former incumbents) newly recruited to their SMDs as DPJ candidates, 45 per cent were quality candidates in 2009, compared with about 35 per cent in the two previous elections and 26 per cent in 2000. This reflects the DPJ's weaning itself off non-quality newcomers more than any great new skill at finding quality ones. The party unearthed thirty-eight new quality challengers in 2009 – certainly an improvement over 2005 (when it had fewer open districts to fill), but only a few more than it found in 2003 or even 2000.

Third, the DPJ has returned to aggressive weeding out of the previous election's non-broad-quality losers (Table 4.6). It was quite

Table 4.5   Broad-Quality DPJ Candidates, Lower House Elections, 2000–09

Broad-Quality Candidates among:	Lower House Election							
	2000	2003	2005	2009	2000	2003	2005	2009
	(number of quality candidates)				(% of quality candidates in category)			
All single-member districts	141	171	214	197	47	57	71	66
All DPJ candidates	141	171	214	197	58	64	74	72
Candidates with variable quality								
Newly recruited DPJ challengers	33	34	23	38	26	34	35	45
Prior-election losers[a,b] (except one-loss incumbents)	4	5	9	8	31	14	21	22
Broad-quality-by-definition candidates								
Incumbents[a,b]	36	91	171	103	100	100	100	100
One-loss prior incumbents[a,b]	8	3	6	39	100	100	100	100
Incumbents (and one-loss prior incumbents)[a] in new districts	18	16	0	4	100	100	n/a	100
New-to-DPJ candidates (and one-loss prior incumbents)	42	22	5	5	100	100	100	100

Note: Candidates exclude purely proportional representation candidates.
[a] Only those who ran as DPJ candidates in prior election.
[b] Only those who ran in the same single-member district in prior election.

Sources: Steven R. Reed and Ethan Scheiner for data on the 1996 and 2000 elections; Matthew Carlson, Ross Schaap, and the author for data on the 2003 election; Ethan Scheiner for data on the 2005 election; Ko Maeda for data on the 2009 election. Data on DPJ candidates' backgrounds were compiled from newspaper reports and from parties' and individual legislators' personal web pages, among other sources; specific sources are available from the author upon request.

aggressive in 2003, in part to make room for new candidates from the newly absorbed Liberal Party. That year's was also a less discriminate house-cleaning, with quality losers even more likely to be cashiered (or to stand down proactively) than non-quality ones. In 2005, though, fewer than half of 2003's losers were removed, including fewer than half of the non-broad-quality losers among them. The DPJ particularly indulged former-incumbent losers and new candidates who had lost for only the first time. This might be because the party had little time to find new candidates: less than two years had passed since the previous election, and 2005's was a snap election at that. The DPJ might also have felt less urgency, given its relative success in 2003. In 2009, in contrast, the party again removed more than half of its losers. More important, it discriminated more sharply between broad-quality and non-broad-quality losers, removing just under half of the former but two-thirds of the latter.

Fourth, the DPJ now must assemble its candidate roster without poaching other parties' incumbents, whether individually or through party mergers. In 2000, forty-two such party switchers accounted for fully 30 per cent of the party's broad-quality candidates; in 2003, twenty-two accounted for 13 per cent; in 2005 and again in 2009, though, there were only five. Mergers with the People's New Party, SDPJ, or other minor parties might occur in the future, but these parties' incumbent rosters are small.

At the same time, and fifth, a large portion of the DPJ's backsliding on overall broad quality is attributable to its increasingly strategic reluctance to run its own candidates in losing efforts. In twenty-one SMDs in 2009, the party endorsed no candidate of its own, instead giving its official recommendation (*suisen*) to another anti-LDP candidate – in most cases one from the SDPJ or People's New Party.[16] In six more districts, the DPJ neither ran nor recommended any candidate at all. I count these twenty-seven districts against the party's overall quality performance in 2009: they constitute 9 per cent of districts in which the DPJ failed to offer voters a quality standard-bearer. Still, in thirteen of these, the DPJ had run a non-quality candidate in 2005, and thus in 2009 at least achieved a more *efficient* form of non-quality than it had before: it strategically opted to bow out rather than invest time and funds on a non-quality candidate who was likely to lose.[17] This is the approach long practised more radically by the CGP: either run a likely winner or offer no candidate at all. It also avoids splitting the non-LDP vote and builds relations with potential governing coalition partners. If one

Table 4.6 DPJ Election-to-Election Candidate Removal Rates, 2003–09

	Number in 2000	Share Removed for 2003	Number in 2003	Share Removed for 2005	Number in 2005	Share Removed for 2009
Winners	110	0.13	179	0.04	112	0.07
Losers	132*	0.70	90	0.46	179	0.58
Broad-quality losers	35	0.77	25	0.40	92	0.48
Incumbents	18	0.83	12	0.50	78	0.49
Quality newcomer two-time losers	17	0.71	13	0.31	14	0.43
Non-broad-quality losers	97	0.67	65	0.48	87	0.67
Former incumbents	14	0.64	6	0.33	9	0.78
Quality newcomer two-time losers	4	0.75	2	0.50	10	0.60
Non-quality newcomer one-time losers	66	0.68	37	0.35	34	0.56
Non-quality newcomer one-time losers	13	0.62	20	0.75	34	0.76

* Excludes two losers 'removed' by the elimination of the district via redistricting, rather than at the DPJ's discretion.

Sources: Steven R. Reed and Ethan Scheiner for data on the 1996 and 2000 elections; Matthew Carlson, Ross Schaap, and the author for data on the 2003 election; Ethan Scheiner for data on the 2005 election; Ko Maeda for data on the 2009 election. Data on DPJ candidates' backgrounds were compiled from newspaper reports and from parties' and individual legislators' personal web pages, among other sources; specific sources are available from the author upon request.

ignores the DPJ's blank districts, its quality rate among those candidates it *did* field was 72 per cent – though this still falls slightly below the 2005 rate of 74 per cent.

These caveats and bright spots notwithstanding, the DPJ needed to compensate for its 2005 losses by markedly improving its candidate recruitment efforts, and it failed. It improved new-candidate recruitment only moderately in 2009 – and new candidates accounted for only about a quarter of all candidates to begin with. The party weeded out many of 2005's non-quality losers – but not enough, given how many there were to begin with. The party's strategic concession of certain weak districts to other opposition candidates might be praised on efficiency grounds, but this is still just another form of failure to recruit candidates (or to poach the very non-DPJ candidates it recommends).

Reed (in this volume) holds that the DPJ will assemble a full roster of competitive candidates sooner rather than later. The party might well prove capable of this eventually, but 2009 apparently was too soon.[18] More troubling for the DPJ's longer-term prospects is that it posted lacklustre results under prime recruiting conditions. First, it had been apparent at least since the DPJ's upper house win of 2007 that the party was likely to do well in the next lower house election. Second, the party both enjoyed an atmosphere of urgency *and* ultimately had time on its side. The DPJ had lived under near-constant threat of lower house dissolution since at least fall 2007, when its upper house victory triggered a series of LDP prime ministerial resignations and policy impasses. But two more years elapsed between elections, time the party spent under the electoral gun, and more time than had passed between the 2003 and 2005 elections altogether. Third, the DPJ was simply older: electoral trends of the day aside, each passing year strengthens the DPJ's image as an established party and gives it more time and ability to locate and cultivate prospective candidates.

Yet the DPJ failed to convince many new quality candidates to run under its banner. It even dragged its feet in installing those candidates it did find – and the later endorsements are made, the less time a candidate has to campaign effectively (of course, informal activity might take place beforehand, but securing an official endorsement legitimizes and amplifies the campaign). Even in late 2007 – two years after the 2005 election and months after the momentum-shifting 2007 upper house victory – internal party turmoil kept candidate recruitment stalled.[19] As late as November 2007, the party had named candidates for only about two-thirds of the 300 SMDs, and for fewer than half of the districts without DPJ incumbents. Until fall 2008, it made no significant additions to its candidate roster beyond this.[20] The LDP, by comparison, found official candidates for all but fifteen SMDs by fall 2007, two years before the 2009 election.

Perhaps a larger problem, under the surface, is the DPJ's failure to increase its *supply* of potential quality candidates. While the DPJ has little power to create more bureaucrats, newscasters, or incumbents' offspring (of candidate-eligible age, at least), the party *can* play a part in creating more DPJ local politicians and upper house members. But raiding the upper house delegation to find better lower house candidates might be self-defeating. Indeed, the DPJ's resounding upper house victory in 2007 might have contributed to its poor 2009 lower house recruiting, as two dozen promising newcomers became upper house incumbents instead. This leaves local-level politicians – naturally hungry for higher political office and already more plentiful than other types of potential quality candidates.

Local-level DPJ politicians have always provided more of the party's quality new recruits than has any other single source, but the party has done little to create more of them. At the local level, the DPJ is still a minor party as of this writing. As noted above, the DPJ has just begun to abandon unpromising lower house districts, but at the local level this is a long-established norm – with bigger consequences. In the 2007 prefectural legislature election cycle, the party ran only 13 per cent of all candidates, or 1 for every 5.4 available seats.[21] On the eve of the 2011 local elections, it held roughly 15 per cent of the prefectural legislature seats, or perhaps as many as 20 per cent once affiliated independents are accounted for (Weiner 2008). Both numbers are about one-third those of the LDP. In prefectural governors' and municipal mayors' races, meanwhile, the DPJ rarely runs candidates of its own, preferring to back independent coalition candidates – even ones whom the LDP backs simultaneously. Relatively few chief executive candidates win who are not backed at least in part by the LDP. And of the few governors and big-city mayors who do take a clear DPJ partisan stance (or at least a clear anti-LDP one), many are DPJ politicians who *left* the lower house, including several who at one point vied for the DPJ party leadership. It is the DPJ's lower house delegation that supplies quality candidates for local chief executive races, not the reverse. While the DPJ has the opportunity to work at cultivating a pool of higher-quality partisan candidates at the local level, it seems unwilling to do so.

The DPJ Is Not Hostage to Its Ex-Socialists

The third and last apparent organizational obstacle to the DPJ's success is internal ideological division. The DPJ originally was created by Diet members who split from the SDPJ and Sakigake (which itself was composed of 'liberal conservatives' who had split from the LDP) at a time when the New Frontier Party (NFP) still provided a home for most non-LDP conservatives. After the NFP collapsed, though, many of its conservatives and ex-DSP members streamed into the DPJ. Finally, in summer 2003, the LP, at the time home to many remaining ex-NFP conservatives, merged into the DPJ as well. Meanwhile, the DPJ's growing size and (relative) longevity established it as an attractive launching pad for various ambitious newcomers, from aspiring politicians with non-traditional (and non-quality) backgrounds to 'standard-issue' conservatives who turned to the DPJ only for lack of an open slot in the LDP.

The resulting party is a mélange of ideologies, political styles, and organizational types. But observers who voice concern over internal DPJ division generally have in mind the presence of former Socialists (I include in this group candidates with SDPJ or public sector union ties who were never SDPJ Diet members).[22] While the party hosts a variety of other political lineages, most can be seen as variations on Japanese conservatism. Former Sakigake members straddle the boundary between conservative and progressive; the conservative bona fides of former LDP members go without saying; and even the former DSP, though allied with private sector labour, often proved at least as conservative as the LDP on a number of issues, including national security. DPJ members without discernible ties to these predecessor parties still often have similar career backgrounds – bureaucrats, small business-people, bankers. The distinction between these DPJ members and ex-Socialists, however, is clearer. Former Socialists are distinct not only in their ideological backgrounds, but also in their reliance on mass support organizations in the form of public sector labour. The internal disputes most cited as likely to pull the DPJ apart are 1955 System holdovers such as expansion of the Self-Defense Forces. Issues where Socialists traditionally displayed common ground with conservatives, such as trade protection, often link the DPJ's ex-Socialists more closely to old-line conservatives within the LDP than to the more 'modern' conservatives within their own party.

But concern over ex-Socialists' divisive influence might be overblown.[23] Ex-Socialists make up an ever-smaller share of the DPJ's lower house delegation, and are likely to grow only scarcer. This is in part because of the DPJ's successive mergers with more conservative forces, but also because the ex-Socialists themselves have been victimized by poor timing and comparatively poor electoral fitness. And to the small extent ex-Socialists do continue to survive within the DPJ, they will hardly be a cohesive force.

In 1996, ex-Socialists accounted for half the DPJ's candidates in SMDs and 60 per cent of its winners (Table 4.7).[24] By 2000, with the DPJ having absorbed much of the NFP, ex-Socialists accounted for about a fifth each of the DPJ's candidates and winners. By 2003, upon the DPJ's absorption of the LP, ex-Socialists had been reduced to roughly 15 per cent of both candidates and winners, and in 2005 their share of each again dipped, though slightly. By 2009, ex-Socialists constituted only 10 per cent of the party's SMD candidates and winners.

Why have the ex-Socialists gradually disappeared? The most obvious answer is that conservatives have overtaken the party via merger, as noted above. That DPJ leaders at the time allowed these mergers to occur could reflect a conscious attempt to move rightward, but the mergers just as likely represented pragmatic attempts to grow larger, whatever the ideology of the DPJ's newly absorbed partners might have been (the same might be said of the party's current alliance with the People's New Party). But the addition of conservative merger-partner incumbents does not fully explain the ex-Socialists' decline. Conservative and ex-DSP forces were not simply added to the DPJ's original ex-Socialist and ex-Sakigake forces. Rather, these new forces *displaced* the old ones – and ex-Socialists have been particularly hard hit. New candidates both moved into empty districts and took over districts previously occupied by ex-Socialist candidates.

Why have ex-Socialists been passed over and replaced so thoroughly? Note that replacing a candidate (as opposed to filling an empty district) involves one prior step: candidates are replaced only after having lost; incumbents who choose not to retire are rarely forced to step down. A simple explanation for the disproportionate replacement of ex-Socialist candidates, then, might be that ex-Socialists tend to lose their elections more often, leaving themselves more vulnerable to replacement. This would be consistent with the secular decline of socialist parties' strength throughout the post-war period, continuing more rapidly since 1993 via the rump SDPJ. As Table 4.7 shows, however, ex-Socialists have won about as often as, and sometimes more than, their fellow DPJ candidates.

Table 4.7 Ex-Socialists' Performance among DPJ Candidates in Single-Member Districts, 1996–2009

Among DPJ Candidates	Lower House Election					
	1996	2000	2003	2005	2009
Ex-Socialists' number (share) of candidates	72 (0.50)	49 (0.20)	39 (0.14)	37 (0.13)	26 (0.10)
Ex-Socialists' number (share) of winners	25 (0.60)	22 (0.20)	29 (0.16)	17 (0.15)	26 (0.10)
Ex-Socialists' number (share) of newly recruited challengers	n/a	10 (0.08)	6 (0.06)	4 (0.06)	1 (0.01)
Win rate among ex-Socialist candidates	0.35	0.45	0.74	0.46	1.00
Win rate among ex-Socialist incumbents	0.53	0.64	0.91	0.59	1.00
Win rate among ex-Socialist non-incumbents	0.21	0.25	0.60	0.10	1.00
Win rate among all DPJ candidates	0.29	0.45	0.64	0.38	0.97
Win rate among all DPJ incumbents	0.57	0.77	0.90	0.55	1.00
Win rate among all DPJ non-incumbents	0.15	0.29	0.43	0.14	0.96

Source: Data on DPJ candidates' backgrounds were compiled from newspaper reports and from parties' and individual legislators' personal web pages, among other sources; specific sources are available from the author upon request.

But whether ex-Socialists win as much as other DPJ candidates in any *given* election year is not the most important question for our purposes. More important is that the DPJ's winning percentages were particularly low across the board in the party's early years, when ex-Socialist (and ex-Sakigake) members dominated the party. These DPJ pioneers faced harsh electoral conditions and suffered for it.

In the 1996 election, only about one-third of all the DPJ's SMD candidates won seats; even incumbents won at only a 50 per cent rate. The party, which had been formed shortly before the election, was considerably weaker than both the LDP and NFP, and many DPJ candidates found themselves forced to run difficult races. The fate of ex-Socialists was particularly grim. As noted above, under the old electoral system, the Socialists' strongholds were largely provincial cities and rural areas, especially those where support for other non-LDP parties never took root. The Socialists' strength in these areas was enough to win them at least one seat in a multi-member district, even in districts otherwise dominated by the LDP. When the old multi-member districts turned into SMDs, however, finishing a distant second was no longer rewarded. The position of ex-Socialists within the DPJ was further undercut by the continued presence of the rump SDPJ as a separate party. In 2000, the DPJ's results improved over those of 1996, but not by much: not quite half its candidates won, though incumbents fared better.

As a result, most of the first generation of DPJ politicians – most of whom were ex-Socialists – was tainted by failed campaigns. If these ex-Socialists had simply held onto the DPJ nomination in their districts and run again in the next election, their absolute numbers within the party might not have declined, but most Japanese parties have little patience for losers, as shown for the DPJ (Table 4.6) and by Reed for the LDP (in this volume). Even in more recent years, about half of incumbents who falter are jettisoned from one election to the next; in the DPJ's infancy, when the party was struggling to survive, its patience wore thin more quickly.

Even this would not have weakened the ex-Socialist strain within the DPJ if unsuccessful ex-Socialist candidates simply had been replaced by *new* ex-Socialists. But the pool of potential candidates is finite, and a large portion was eliminated by the party's poor showing in 1996. The ex-Socialists' candidate pool is arguably even more finite than most – and not simply because the labour unions that supply many of their candidates are in decline. That their candidate recruitment draws heavily on well-institutionalized organizations like unions is a constraint in itself. While highly organized and standardized feeder pools are able to produce a steady quantity of candidates, they tend also to develop more rigid criteria of 'appropriateness.' Candidates need to have worked their way up to a reasonably high level of responsibility within the organization, for example – one rarely sees young candidates supplied by labour unions. This phenomenon is not limited to unions: parties searching for former bureaucrats as candidates often limit their potential candidate pools in similar ways (Kataoka 1994). Nor is this limited to public sector unions: the former DSP, in part for this reason, also produces very few new candidates.

Ex-Socialists' strong organizational backing also makes them *less* attractive as candidates amid partisan dealignment. This is not to say that unions are ineffective vote mobilizers relative to their size. Quite the opposite: Japan's main labour umbrella organization, Rengou, and its constituent unions often represent a DPJ candidate's largest single vote-support base, even if that candidate is conservative.[25] Ex-Socialists, though, cannot count on reciprocal support. Traditional conservative organized vote support either attaches itself to particular conservative candidates or continues to nurture its 'Socialist allergy.' The unaligned voters on whom the DPJ relies for much of its support also nurture an 'established organization allergy' of their own. As with the CGP in its alliance with the LDP, ex-Socialists' support organizations are valued for their ability to deliver votes, but are less often invited to provide candidates.

As a result, the ex-Socialist contingent within the DPJ has always been incumbent-heavy. Those who survived the party's early years continue to survive about as well as other DPJ officeholders, but there has been disproportionately little infusion of new blood: from 2000 through 2005, less than 10 per cent of the DPJ's newly recruited challengers were ex-Socialists; the new-recruit class for 2009 had exactly one ex-Socialist.

Ultimately, then, ex-Socialists (and, to a lesser extent, ex-Sakigake members) have suffered for founding their party and becoming the first to join electoral battle. The first post-reform elections effectively removed the bulk of the DPJ's early candidates from future contests. For ex-Socialists in particular, the very solidity of their organized support has led to inflexibilities in new-candidate recruiting, and the unpopularity of their ideological lineage prevents catch-all appeal. These handicaps have dampened their prospects of a quick rebound from early losses, and they now seem to guarantee that the ex-Socialist strain within the DPJ's lower house delegation will survive only as long as do its current incumbents.

Moreover, the ex-Socialists who remain – just 10 per cent of the party's lower house delegation – are not a unified bloc within the party. On the eve of the 2009 election, the DPJ housed about eight factional 'groups' roughly similar to the LDP's factions (though much less institutionalized).[26] One was a group made up exclusively of former Socialists and led by Yokomichi, but this included only seven of the seventeen ex-Socialist incumbents and former incumbents with known group affiliations.[27] Three more ex-Socialists were aligned with the group of young Sakigake-style conservatives led by Maehara and Edano Yukio, two with a 'Constitutional Protection' group, two with Kan's Sakigake/Socialist hybrid group, two with Hatoyama's Sakigake/Socialist-traditional conservative hybrid group, and one with Ozawa's conservative group.

If anything, concentrated Socialist influence on the DPJ is more likely to come from outside the lower house. Candidates with clear public sector labour affiliations currently account for about one-sixth of the DPJ's upper house delegation, partly reflecting the party's practice of nominating representatives of large, nationwide unions for the upper house's single, nationwide PR district (as the LDP does with its own affiliated organizations) and prefectural districts (which are larger than SMDs). Such candidates also might be relatively more dependent on their sponsoring organizations than on the DPJ per se. Just as important, and ironically, the SDPJ itself now has more influence than the former Socialists who left the SDPJ for the DPJ. Although the DPJ won a landslide share of seats in the 2009 lower house election, it relies on SDPJ votes in the upper house to reach the majority threshold there – giving the SDPJ the status of a junior but co-equal member of the governing coalition despite its small size. Each coalition partner, no matter how small, has a place in various coalition coordination organs; ex-Socialists within the DPJ have no such formal representation. The SDPJ can credibly threaten to bring down the government (or make it impossible to pass legislation in the upper house) by defecting; ex-Socialists within the DPJ are less credibly able to threaten to quit their own party.

Conclusion

Despite the DPJ's resounding victory in the 2009 lower house elections, one should be wary of assuming the party is as strong as the returns suggest. The DPJ benefited enormously from intense dissatisfaction with the LDP. Now that it leads the government, even its shrewdest policy-making decisions are likely to alienate some voters who supported the party as an anti-LDP blank slate. Accordingly, one should assess the DPJ's longer-term prospects independently of this single exceptional election.

In this chapter, I have examined three areas long viewed as more fundamental stumbling blocks for the DPJ, ones that could persist and prove harmful under more normal electoral circumstances: reliance on a fickle urban electorate, candidates' poor quality, and internal ideological division. At least two of these weaknesses, though, prove overstated.

First, the DPJ is not particularly urban; rather, its strongest districts are spread across all but the most rural areas of Japan. Like the LDP, the DPJ aggressively competes for Japan's most urban seats but enjoys no particularly deep roots there. Political geography offers a better shorthand than 'urban' for mapping DPJ strength. The DPJ is strongest where its predecessor parties were strong, particularly in capital cities outside large metropolitan areas, areas of concentrated private sector labour once supportive of the former DSP, and rural areas within the home prefectures of DPJ leaders; and *within* large metropolitan areas, it is strongest in uptown (*yamanote*) rather than downtown (*shitamachi*) regions.

Second, the DPJ is not particularly fractured across progressive-conservative lines, at least within its lower house delegation. Ex-Socialist-affiliated lower house members are no longer a large force within the party. This reflects not only successive absorptions of conservative anti-LDP parties, but also a weeding out of Socialist personnel during the DPJ's early years through both their own electoral losses and the party's failure to replace them with their own kind. Remaining ex-Socialists, meanwhile, are spread across multiple intra-party factions.

As for its third weakness, the DPJ has made only halting progress in recruiting strong, high-quality candidates. This did not hurt the party directly in 2009, when an amazing 97 per cent of its SMD candidates (and 92 per cent of its non-broad-quality candidates) won their seats. In more 'normal' future elections, however, the effects of poor-quality candidates might linger. Indeed, the party's great success in 2009 might have the unintended consequence of prolonging its candidate-recruitment problems. Since parties rarely remove their first-term incumbents, the DPJ's candidate slate in the next lower house election likely will be filled with weak candidates who luckily survived in 2009. An election in which 'natural selection' had operated more harshly might have offered the DPJ a better chance to cultivate candidates with greater staying power.

Overall, then, the DPJ is improving its long-term prospects, whatever the short-term results of the 2009 elections. One can also interpret these patterns in another way. They suggest the DPJ is becoming more like the LDP: more rural, more internally homogenous and conservative, and (fitfully) moving towards recruitment of the same types of candidates and sometimes the very same candidates – not to mention similar mutual poaching of policy positions (see Reed, in this volume).

That fortifying the DPJ's infrastructure implies convergence with the LDP is not coincidental. In any party system, all else being equal, parties should enjoy more success and longevity to the extent that they sink their roots in less volatile districts, rely on candidates whose appeal is based on stable and easily graspable personal characteristics (something more often associated with conservatives) than on party image or ideology, and encourage intra-party competition based on office seeking rather than on ideological differences. Such an approach helps parties establish safe districts, ride out spells of unpopularity without severe losses, and withstand the rigours of governing without fragmenting. This has been the LDP's model, and a similar version likely would benefit the DPJ as well, however much the 2009 election might suggest that old ways of Japanese politics are changing. Indeed, one might view the DPJ as a microcosm of the pre-realignment party system: the same attributes that let the LDP prosper also have let LDP-like members within the DPJ prosper. Whether the convergence of Japan's two main parties – ideologically, geographically, and in their personnel – will benefit Japan's citizens is a separate question, but this is the narrowing path its two main parties are likely to follow.

NOTES

1 Unless otherwise specified, all discussion of lower house election results is based on raw data collected and generously provided by Steven R. Reed and Ethan Scheiner for the 1996 and 2000 elections, by Scheiner for the 2005 election, and by Ko Maeda for the 2009 election; and collected by Matthew Carlson, Ross Schaap, and the author for the 2003 election.
2 I classify as DPJ candidates not only those with official endorsements from the party, but also a small number of nominal independents with close ties

to the DPJ and who joined or were likely soon to join the party upon winning their seats. Classifications are based largely on newspaper coverage; sources are available from the author upon request.

3 Exceptions occur because the ability of a loser of an SMD to win a PR seat depends not only on his or her own performance in the district, but also on how many seats his or her party wins in the PR region, which, in turn, depends on factors beyond the candidate's control that vary across PR regions. All else being equal, it takes a higher vote ratio to secure a PR seat in those PR regions where the DPJ as a whole wins smaller PR vote shares and fewer seats, where there are more strong SMD losers to compete with, where there are more PR-only candidates ranked high on the list, and where there are fewer seats at stake on the PR list.

4 Across all 300 SMDs, DPJ vote ratios' correlation coefficient is 0.60 between 2003 and 2005, 0.73 between 2005 and 2009, and 0.49 between 2003 and 2009. If one removes one outlier SMD with an extremely high vote ratio in 2003 and any SMDs in which the DPJ failed to run a candidate in either of the years in question, the correlation coefficient is 0.78 between 2003 and 2005 ratios (across 263 SMDs), 0.73 between 2005 and 2009 (across 270 SMDs), and 0.69 between 2003 and 2009 ratios (across 249 SMDs). I assign SMDs with no DPJ candidate at all a DPJ vote ratio of zero. In districts with more than one DPJ candidate (as sometimes emerge once one acknowledges DPJ-affiliated independents), I ignore all but the top DPJ finisher. These cases usually reflect party mergers that leave more than one DPJ affiliate in the same district. In almost all such cases, there is only one additional candidate so ignored, and that candidate's vote share is far below the main DPJ candidate's.

5 In one case, the DPJ ran no candidate in 2003 *or* 2005, but its convincing win in 2009 (the candidate posted the party's nineteenth-highest vote ratio) counterbalances its earlier absence.

6 True quartiles each would contain 75 of the 300 SMDs, but rounding sometimes leaves districts with the same Densely Inhabited District (DID) shares on opposite sides of a quartile cut point. To avoid this and keep all SMDs with the same DID population share in the same quartile, the 'quartiles' used here range from seventy-four to seventy-seven SMDs each. DID data were collected and generously provided by Steven R. Reed.

7 See, for example, 'Chouson-bu de no touhyou-saki, minshu ga jimin o uwamawaru . . . yomiuri keizoku chousa,' *Yomiuri Shimbun,* 14 July 2007.

8 The same trend holds for vote ratios rather than wins. And even in 2003, more DPJ incumbents lost in the most urban quartile than in the second quartile.

9 Prefectures' 1st districts always contain their capital city, hence the Japanese term '1st-district phenomenon' (*ikku genshou*) to describe the DPJ's strength there.

10 This excludes three capital city SMDs in these regions. Hokkaidou 1st, which contains part of Sapporo, is in the most urban quartile. In Tottori 1st and Shimane 1st, the prefectural capital portions of the districts are so small that these districts fall into the most rural quartile.

11 Analysis of pre-1993 lower house election results is based on raw data drawn from the Lijphart Election Archive (http://ssdc.ucsd.edu/lij) data set, downloaded in January 1996, with slight subsequent corrections by the author.

12 A more expansive accounting of SMDs where the DPJ benefits from strong personal followings could include the four dozen or so whose DPJ incumbents – some national figures, some only local powers – have been in office since before electoral reform, but this would verge on tautology.

13 Analysis of CGP support by lower house SMD is based on data compiled by Sugawara Taku, available online from http://freett.com/sugawara_taku/data/pr03_00.html; accessed 19 January 2009. Data on daytime-nighttime ratios are drawn from the 2005 'Todoufuken-betsu shikuchouson-betsu shuyou toukeihyou' census data set compiled by the Ministry of Internal Affairs and Communications, Statistics Bureau; available online at http://www.e-stat.go.jp/SG1/estat/List.do?bid=000001007609&cycode=0, accessed 30 December 2008.

14 If anything, the political geography profile *understates* rural DPJ strength. Sixteen additional strong DPJ districts are both rural and fall outside the profile's bounds. Many of these represent slightly more subtle (or, perhaps, stretched) variations on the political geography features: more than half are in the historically strong Socialist regions of Touhoku, Shin'etsu, and Kyuushuu; several are represented by former LDP lower house members or their children (including Tanaka Makiko, counted here as a DPJ independent); and several are neighbours of former DSP strongholds.

15 As noted above, when more than one DPJ-affiliated candidate runs in the same SMD, I ignore all but the top finisher, no matter which of them the party officially endorsed. This leads to a slight overstatement of the broad quality of the candidate pool in each of these two years, since none of the three candidates so ignored in 2000 was of broad quality and six of the eleven in 2003 were. Data on DPJ candidates' backgrounds were compiled from newspaper reports and from parties' and individual legislators'

personal web pages, among other sources. Specific sources are available from the author upon request.

16 In one more SMD, an unendorsed, DPJ-affiliated independent ran alongside an SDPJ candidate officially recommended by the DPJ.

17 The party also might have strategically withheld funds from the less promising of the candidates it *did* run (Toshikawa and Katz 2008).

18 Note that 'competitive' is a broader term than 'quality' – although, if the DPJ manages to field full competitive slates through heavy reliance on non-'quality' candidates over several elections beyond 2009, the definition of 'quality' itself might need revision.

19 See 'Parties Gird for Election Battle,' *Daily Yomiuri,* 26 November 2007.

20 Data on DPJ endorsement dates are derived from official announcements and candidate lists updated periodically by the DPJ on its web site (at URLs beginning with http://www.dpj.or.jp/news/ and with endings that vary by date).

21 The 2007 election cycle includes prefectural assembly elections held in forty-four prefectures on a single date in April 2007, plus off-year elections in Ibaragi, Okinawa, and Tokyo Prefectures between 2005 and 2008.

22 As Schoppa notes (in Chapter 2 in this volume), most analysts blame DPJ internal divisions on the varied ideologies of DPJ members' former parties. In this chapter, I similarly assume that varied party backgrounds encourage party schisms, though I argue that the DPJ is less varied than is often assumed. Schoppa, though, further argues that the DPJ has made matters worse by choosing a combination of policies that *none* of its sub-groups wholly agreed with in the first place.

23 Portions of the argument that follows build on Lee, Miura, and Weiner (2005).

24 I ignore the DPJ's PR-only candidates because they usually constitute little more than filler at the bottom of the DPJ's regional PR lists, ranked as they are below the dual SMD/PR candidates who usually claim all the party's PR seats. The 2009 election, though, was different: since so many dual candidates won their SMDs outright, more PR seats were available for PR-only candidates. PR-only candidates took forty-four of eighty-seven PR seats in 2009, and so accounted for nearly one-sixth of the DPJ's winners overall (PR-only candidates had also fared well in 1996, the last time many of them were ranked *above* the dual candidates). But since the proportion of ex-Socialists among PR-only winners was nearly equal to their share among SMD winners, their inclusion would not alter the 2009 figures reported here.

25 Hayashi Takayuki, 'Last Hurrah,' *Asahi Weekly,* 11 April 2007.
26 See Itagaki 2008; '"An-shou taiketsu" e tounai yuuwa enshutsu,' *Nihon Keizai Shimbun,* 13 September 2006; and '"Ozawa zokutou": minshu kanbu naze koshitsu,' *Yomiuri Shimbun,* 6 November 2007.
27 Group memberships are from Itagaki (2008).

5   Issue Evolution and Electoral Politics in Contemporary Japan[1]

SHERRY L. MARTIN

Japan's 1994 electoral reformers sought to create incentives for parties to compete for the 'median voter' (Downs 1957) and the alternation in power of two moderate, programmatic parties in order to promote issue-based voting by the electorate (Reed and Thies 2001). Their solution was the introduction of new electoral rules that created 300 seats in single-member districts and 180 in eleven regional proportional representation (PR) blocs. By eliminating competition between candidates from the same party and instead presenting voters with a simple choice between a single party slate (in PR) or one candidate from each party (in single-member districts), the two components of the new system encourage both candidates and parties to sell themselves using their positions on salient issues.

If the system is working as intended, Japan ought to have seen a significant increase in 'issue-based voting,' where parties offer alternative and opposing choices on salient issues that divide the electorate and where 'Downsian' voters select the party that is closest to their own position on the issues they prioritize. Although a competitive, two-party system has emerged, the Liberal Democratic Party (LDP) and Democratic Party of Japan (DPJ) continue to struggle to define party images that are rooted in issues that align voters on opposite sides of an ideological continuum. Thus, despite the efforts of electoral reformers, a decade after reform the general consensus among political researchers is that Japanese national politics has *not* become more issue oriented (see Steel 2008).

In this chapter, I focus on the movement of security and defence issues from the periphery back to the centre of electoral debates in the past decade, and I argue against the above conventional wisdom.

Empirical evidence from recent elections suggests that, if one narrows the focus to this particular policy arena, issues *are* assuming increased importance in parties' appeals and voters' decision-making. I argue that much of the existing research understates the importance that issues have attained because it looks for definitive trends towards issue-based voting that are evident across voters, elections, and different policy arenas. But not all issues are framed as 'position' issues that align voters on opposite sides of a debate. Different issues are salient to different voters, the issues that matter most to voters might differ from those that structure any given electoral competition, and different issues matter in different election cycles.

Security and defence issues are resuming prominence in electoral politics even though the LDP successfully diffused the emotionally and ideologically charged debates on these issues from the 1960s through the 1990s. Military matters are shaping voters' choices even though voters tend to subordinate security and defence concerns to economic and fiscal policy, social welfare reform, and the elimination of corruption. While these function as 'valence' issues, with all or most parties competing to convince voters that they are most in favour of various types of 'reform,' genuine, issue-based competition has emerged in the security and defence policy arena.

I begin by providing a brief review of how the LDP successfully diffused the intense security and defence debates that characterized the early post-war period such that, by the time the electoral reform package passed in 1994, these issues no longer functioned as significant predictors of voters' choices. I then use the concept of 'issue evolution' developed by Carmines and Stimson (1989) as a framework in which to discuss significant changes in the security and defence policy arena that have returned these issues to the centre of electoral competition in recent years. This is followed by empirical analyses of survey data that show shifts in public opinion on the United States-Japan security alliance and the strengthening of Japan's Self-Defense Forces (SDF), and the relationship between voters' positions on these issues and their choices in the 2005 lower house election. The DPJ used security and defence policy as a wedge issue in the 2007 upper house and 2009 lower house elections. The DPJ's management of the issue of the U.S. Marine Corps Air Station Futenma on Okinawa was a salient issue in the 2010 upper house election. I conclude with a discussion of the long-term potential of security and defence debates to realign Japanese electoral politics, with attention to how other salient issues influence vote choice.

The Demise of Security and Defence?

In the aftermath of World War Two, the U.S. Occupation encouraged peace activism as a symbolic rejection of a political culture antithetical to democracy. From 1960 through the mid-1970s, both U.S. and LDP elites sought to deflect public attention from security and defence issues that were so divisive that they threatened to lengthen Japan's democratic transition and economic recovery in a period when the United States needed a stable Japan to serve as a bulwark against further communist incursions into Asia. Rapid economic growth and a policy of seclusion diffused these issues, although they continued to lurk under the surface as grassroots movements took up single issues that fall under the security and defence umbrella – for example, the anti-nuclear movement, protests against U.S. bases on Okinawa, and the organization of feminists around militarization and violence against women. By 1970, public opinion on the United States-Japan Security Treaty had softened to the extent that its renewal did not stimulate the same level of contention it had inspired only a decade before.

The intensity of ideological divisiveness and activism around security and defence left an imprint on electoral politics, and these issues continued to structure voting behaviour well after they were resolved or lost salience. Public opinion under the '1955 System' was split over peace versus military defence and security values. Substantively, this meant that voters were split over whether the emperor should have more political power, the SDF should be strengthened, and the United States-Japan security arrangement should be reinforced. These divisions were reflected in the alignment of the party system. The parties of the Left (the Japanese Communist Party, JCP; the Japan Socialist Party, JSP) opposed expanding the political power of the emperor, questioned the legitimacy of the SDF, fought proposals to revise Article 9 of the Constitution – which forbids Japan to maintain standing military forces or to go to war to settle international disputes – and opposed the United States-Japan Security Treaty. In contrast, the LDP – though its politicians held their positions with varying degrees of strength – was traditionally more favourable towards revising the Constitution to empower the emperor and lifting the limits on Japan's military roles.

Over time, the multi-member-district electoral system then in place also contributed to the amelioration of security and defence issues because it created incentives for politicians and parties to downplay national issues in favour of local issues connected with regional or group interests that helped to organize constituency votes (Kohei, Miyake, and Watanuki 1991, 267). An analysis of survey data collected during the 1976 lower house election found that voters' positions on an array of issues that included security and defence were no longer strong predictors of vote choice (290–1). Not only had the relationship between national security policy and vote choice loosened, but no other issues were strong predictors of vote choice either. Japanese elections had become candidate-centred, 'issueless' competitions, and it was 'unlikely that a study of issues will contribute greatly to an explanation of voting outcomes' because 'over a quarter of voters have no positions on the issues, over half are unable to identify any party that represents their views, and over three-quarters fail to link their issue preferences to the party they voted for' (284). The contentious issues that had ignited the security and defence debates had been resolved (the status of the SDF, albeit temporarily), become obsolete (communist relations), or evolved into a valence issue (few think the emperor should have real power).

By the time electoral reform was enacted in 1993 and 1994, there was a broad-based popular consensus on security and defence. The Yoshida Doctrine – the consensus forged by post-war prime minister Yoshida Shigeru (1946–47 and 1948–54) and solidified under Ikeda Hayato, Satou Eisaku, Ouhira Masayoshi, and Miyazawa Kiichi – used Japan's alliance with the United States to minimize defence spending and capabilities so that resources could be funnelled into economic growth (see Samuels 2007). Consequently, the contentious bundle of issues that defined the security and defence policy arena in the 1950s and 1960s did not function as a predictor of vote choice and opened the way for party system change (see Schoppa, Chapter 2 in this volume).

Soon, however, shifts in international context and broad socioeconomic changes over the course of decades of relative quietude coalesced and reignited dormant debates about security and defence. According to Richard Samuels (2007), the Yoshida Doctrine began to unravel with increasing momentum in the post–Cold War period, leading Japanese opinion leaders to begin a new debate over the appropriate contours of a new security strategy. The re-emergence of a debate over what shape Japan's new 'grand strategy' for security and defence should take – at exactly the moment new electoral rules were creating an incentive for parties to make issue-based appeals for votes – helped make security and defence, one of the 1955 System's founding issues, once again a salient factor that structures vote choice in the new electoral system, possibly contributing to a long-term electoral realignment around two dominant parties.

Issue Evolution

Changes in the geopolitical environment that unfolded with the end of the Cold War and the beginning of the 1991 Gulf War gained momentum with the events of 11 September 2001, regional changes in East Asia – such as North Korea's missile testing and the rapid rise of the Chinese economy – concerns about terrorism, and the possible future closing of the U.S. security umbrella to produce new calculations of risk in Japan. Official discourse and public opinion about security and defence have changed dramatically over the past two decades in response to an uncertain and insecure future.

In their classic text on 'issue evolution,'[2] Carmines and Stimson (1989) demonstrate that, in the United States, changes in party elites' position on the contentious issue of race preceded and marked a course for corresponding changes in mass public opinion. The new debate on how to deal with the issue of race realigned the U.S. party system. Similarly, in Japan, security and defence policy debates warrant close attention at this juncture because they seem to fit the contours of issue evolution as defined by Carmines and Stimson: the new security policy debate is 'well fitted into new niches provided by an evolving political environment' that includes 'political leaders in search of electoral leverage,' 'unsatisfied constituencies,' and 'exogenous shocks to the system' (1989, 4). Political elites, however, must first contend with 'new issue species' that are rife with 'internal contradictions.' This framework of issue evolution enables one to index the interlocking policy changes and publics that constitute the security and defence arena and its potential to further unsettle the shifting electoral terrain of contemporary Japanese politics.

Political Leaders in Search of Electoral Leverage

The political climate began to change in the 1990s when, in the aftermath of the first Gulf War, leaders such as Ozawa Ichirou saw an opportunity for career advancement in mounting demands – inside and outside Japan – for the nation to assume new global citizenship responsibilities. Ozawa's *Blueprint for a New Japan*, published shortly after he led his followers in a split from the LDP to form the Japan Renewal Party (Shinseitou), argued that Japan needed to become a 'normal country,' one that assumes responsibilities commensurate with its influential standing in the global community. Responsibilities should include sending troops to participate in peacekeeping operations around the world, and there should be a clear definition of national interests that are both independent of and in keeping with the long-standing alliance with the United States. Over the course of the past fifteen years, Japan has adopted a series of creeping policy changes that stretch interpretation of the Constitution to enable it to assume new roles and responsibilities. Japan has engaged in 'non-combat' peacekeeping missions in Cambodia, Mozambique, Rwanda, the Indian Ocean, and Iraq, despite reservations that such activity is inconsistent with the spirit of Article 9 (Samuels 2007).

These policy changes, at a time when Japan is facing new security challenges, have reignited the debate over security policy in Japan. By the 1990s, the old debate over whether Japan should even have Self-Defense Forces or a Security Treaty was settled. Even the JCP and JSP had abandoned their hardline stances on these questions. But as Ozawa and hawkish members of the LDP began calling for the SDF to take on *expanded* roles, they ran head first into public opinion that valued the constraints that had been placed on SDF roles and missions under the Yoshida Doctrine. The hard-won status quo – acceptance of the SDF without further expansion – had become the public's most favoured position, and it is with this position that Ozawa and other political elites across the ideological spectrum had to contend before any dramatic shifts in foreign policy were possible.

Sabine Frühstück, in *Uneasy Warriors,* notes that, 'The beginning of the 1990s marked the most dramatic shift in the SDF's public relations policy: away from a strategy of relative nonengagement with public opinion that had been characteristic of the Cold War era to one of active attempts to create and control the [SDF's] public attitude' (2007, 118). Richard Samuels, in *Securing Japan,* carefully elaborates the range of ideological positions that inform an array of diverse, overlapping, and sometimes contradictory visions competing for control of the security and defence policy arena. The result of this struggle is that Japan has been slow to respond to domestic and international security crises, and political observers complain that 'postwar Japanese strategy is incoherent. . . . A foreign policy that is simultaneously UN-centered, Asia-oriented, autonomous, and consistent with the goals of the bilateral alliance with the United States ends up as a porridge' (2007, 8).

These struggles broke to the surface of electoral politics in a series of elections between 2005 and 2010 as elites elevated foreign policy to the top of the policy agenda even as the public complained that these issues deflected from more pressing domestic concerns that included economic stimulus and social welfare reform. Prime Minister Koizumi Jun'ichirou made visiting Yasukuni Shrine annually in the face of Chinese protests a point of nationalist pride, sent Japanese naval ships to the Indian Ocean, and deployed SDF troops to Iraq to help rebuild that country after the U.S.-led invasion toppled Saddam Hussein. His LDP successors (Abe, Fukuda, Asou) stopped visiting the shrine but otherwise carried forward Koizumi's policies in the Middle East. Abe Shinzou (2006–07) actually pushed forward a national security agenda that was even more assertive than Koizumi's. He used the LDP's strong majority in the Diet to push through legislation upgrading the status of the Defense Agency to cabinet rank – it is now the Ministry of Defense. He also pushed through legislation laying out procedures for holding a referendum on revising the Constitution, taking one step towards modifying the language of Article 9.

Ozawa, who by this time had become the chief electoral strategist for the DPJ and shed his earlier enthusiasm for Japan's becoming a 'normal country' in favour of a *moderate* position on defence policy change, chose that moment to focus public attention on the differences between the parties on this issue – even though they were not that large and even though some members of the DPJ supported much of the LDP's security policy agenda. These small policy differences between the two largest parties had a distinctive impact on vote choice in the 2005 election, albeit in a losing effort for the DPJ. Nevertheless, the DPJ strategy of keeping voters' attention focused on these differences appears to have been a fruitful electoral strategy in 2007 and 2009, though risky in 2010.

Unsatisfied Constituencies

Mari Yamamoto, author of *Grassroots Pacifism in Post-War Japan,* claims that the pacifism that took firm root in the national consciousness during the first fifteen years after the end of World War Two continued to constrain government officials' ability to gain public support for the U.S.-led coalition forces in the first Gulf War in January 1991. 'Opinions expressed from Tokyo sounded garbled, reflecting the dilemma of Japan, which was torn between diplomatic exigencies to fulfil its 'responsibility to the international community' as called for by the United States on the one hand, and the strong anti-war sentiment at the grassroots on the other' (2004, 1). Even if most Japanese voters did not want to desert the hard-won post-war consensus – the alliance with the United States enabled Japan to 'creatively combine economic and technological capabilities with a low-cost military posture' (Samuels 2007, 3) – voters were also very sensitive to U.S. criticism, echoed internationally, that Japan was not carrying its weight in providing global security.

Changes in the international and regional security environments, coupled with socio-demographic developments in Japan, have undermined the consensus around peace and created new demands for a more activist SDF. Younger Japanese, who do not recall the suffering of the World War Two period and the suppression of dissent under militarism, join an older generation (primarily male) that contests the terms of victors' justice and has never stopped pressing for constitutional revision. Though these *perspectives* constitute a minority of voters, their *position* has gained purchase within an electorate that increasingly views military strength as a pragmatic response to increasing regional insecurity – the rapid expansion of the Chinese and Indian economies and an unstable North Korea. Increasingly, Japanese on both sides of the debate are pressuring political elites to adopt more definitive policy positions on security and defence because the current inconsistency undermines the state's ability to project an international image of strength. Still, the lines separating opponents and proponents of rearmament remain fuzzy because there are substantial differences in opinion in both camps.

New Issue Species and Internal Contradictions

New issue species are old issues 'transformed by isolation and specialization in a new context to something quite different from their origins' (Carmines and Stimson 1989, 6). Okinawa, home to three-quarters of the U.S. bases in Japan, has become ground zero in the struggle to redefine the contours of the security relationship with the United States. It is where grassroots anti-base activism, over time, has produced alternative narratives that add more dimensions to nuanced ideological debates – for example, for many Okinawans, the anti-base movement is about Americans' undermining Japanese sovereignty through the ongoing occupation of land. As well, over time, feminist voices have emerged as a significant undercurrent in dominant debates about security and defence, expanding the character and range of grievances that constrain political elites' management of the security alliance.

Feminist activists in Okinawa argue that the peace movement and men in the anti-base movement fail to recognize the disproportionate amount of violence against women, both during World War Two and throughout the post-war period, in demands for the removal of U.S. military bases and personnel (Takazato 1996; Mackie 2003). According to activist and former local assembly member Suzuyo Takazato, 'patriarchal or military power-oriented societies place women in a subordinate position and legitimate their objectification as sexual machinery in order to achieve the goals of the nation' (1996, 136). This rearticulation of the problem enables Okinawan women to generalize and connect the Okinawan experience to the increased incidence of gender-based violence worldwide in communities that live in the shadow of militaries (Enloe 2004). This, in turn, has enabled Okinawa women to link their lives and activism to the fate of women throughout Asia, including former 'comfort women,' who have gained international recognition that the militarization of their lives constituted a violation of human rights. Feminist voices have established a direct link between the United States-Japan security alliance and gender equality and human rights in Japan and beyond.

Exogenous Shocks

Japanese domestic politics is highly sensitive to and responsive to changes in the international system, with changes in the latter inspiring large-scale, sweeping institutional adjustments. According to Pyle (2007), Japan is at a critical juncture as it abandons the policies and institutions of the Cold War. Japan's struggle to adapt to a new geopolitical context was immediately evident in its slow response to U.S. demands for support during the first Gulf War. 'The string of broken pledges of extra-monetary efforts was, in effect, the paroxysm of a ruling class that encompassed an impossibly vast range of contradictory views on the appropriate world role for Japan. . . . The LDP – as well as the broader, informal LDP-opposition alliance – incorporated a wide range of ideologies from rabid hawks to extreme doves. When Japan had been in seclusion, such distinctions had been unimportant' (Schlesinger 1997, 243). Now that the end of the Cold War has raised doubts about the dependability of the U.S. security umbrella, the threats of a nuclear

North Korea and an economically and militarily strong China have unleashed tensions previously held in check by the Cold War world order. The United States is increasing demands for Japan to assume more costs of supporting the alliance against an evolving regional and global backdrop that has changed how Japan assesses the risks and benefits that accrue to any choice it makes from a rapidly expanding menu of security options.

Security and Defence Return to Centre Stage

In this chapter, I do not seek to untangle whether opinion around security and defence changed among elites or within the mass public first, nor do I answer the question of whether elites reshaped public opinion or changed their positions in response to attitudinal changes they perceived in the public. Sorting out which side is driving change is difficult because there is a correlation between elite and mass attitudes: they have moved in the same direction over time, with both citizens and elites becoming more open to strengthening security and defence infrastructure over the past two decades than in the preceding three. Still, elites continue to struggle for clarity on security and defence, adapting a diplomatic stance and style that establishes Japan as a strong international actor while working within constitutional limits. The lines separating opponents and proponents of rearmament remain fuzzy, however, since there are substantial differences in opinion among groups in both camps. Public opinion, too, has become increasingly garbled since 1991.

Trends

In surveys of Japanese public opinion on the status of the SDF and the United States-Japan Security Treaty,[3] including three decades (1978–2008) of annual surveys conducted by the Prime Minister's Office (Japan 2009), between two-thirds and more than three-quarters of Japanese polled expressed closeness to the United States despite trade frictions and Japan-bashing in the 1980s, U.S. military misconduct in Japan, and U.S. criticism of Japan's 'chequebook diplomacy' during the first Gulf War. In an evaluation of the post–Cold War United States-Japan security relationship, Michael Green states, 'Support for the alliance is broader than ever. There are fewer opponents to the alliance among the political elite in Tokyo and Washington than at any point since the first bilateral security treaty went into effect in 1952. Public support for the security relationship also remains high in both countries' (2000, 214). Even though high support for the security relationship has been unwavering among Japanese, there is greater willingness to change the dynamics of the relationship, from rebalancing within existing parameters to changing the parameters altogether.

The United States-Japan security relationship shows signs of strain under mounting pressures for Japan to extend support to the United States in Iraq and Afghanistan and to assume more responsibility for its own security and defence. Japanese public opinion about the United States and the bilateral security relationship shifted dramatically after 11 September 2001. National election studies, conducted in Japan in 1976, 1983, 1993, 1996, and 2005, asked voters whether they agreed or disagreed with, assumed a neutral stance towards, or did not have enough information to form an opinion about the following separate, but interrelated, statements: 'Japan should strengthen its military defence capabilities' and 'Japan should strengthen the U.S.-Japan security set-up' (see Table 5.1). The most striking trend over time is the decline in the proportion of voters who felt they did not have enough information to express an opinion, which fell from 26 and 35 per cent, respectively, for the two questions in 1976 steadily into the single digits by 2005. The proportion who 'couldn't say' held steady, at roughly 26 per cent (+/–4) of voters, but this neutral response is distinct from the 'don't know' answer because it implies that voters have enough knowledge to offer an opinion. They simply find themselves in the middle of the spectrum of views, or at least find the muddled status quo satisfactory.

The rapid drop in the share of respondents unable to offer an opinion suggests that Japan's military defence capabilities and the United States-Japan security set-up are issues that engage the vast majority of voters. At the same time, the data clearly date the breakdown in the consensus behind the Yoshida Doctrine to the period between 1996 and 2005, when the North Korean threat, the rise of China, and the dangers of international terrorism all pushed the issue higher on the agenda. In the mid-1990s, the largest percentage of voters surveyed (44.4 per cent) still opposed strengthening Japan's defensive capabilities, a move that would require constitutional revision. The vast majority of voters either disagreed with the view that Japan should strengthen its defence capabilities and the United States-Japan security set-up or took the neutral position, suggesting they were content with the status quo. These voters, it seems, were 'not keen to depart dramatically from policies that

Table 5.1   Changing Security and Defence Attitudes in Japan, 1976–2005

	Year of Poll				
	1976	1983	1993	1996	2005
Japan should strengthen its military defence capabilities					
			(%)		
Agree	21.5	22.7	16.2	19.1	37.8
Disagree	27.6	45.9	48.7	44.4	31.0
Can't say (neutral)	24.0	24.0	28.8	30.4	26.8
Don't know	26.2	7.3	6.1	5.8	4.4
Japan should strengthen the United States-Japan security set-up					
			(%)		
Agree	26.2	25.3	19.9	21.7	30.9
Disagree	24.6	20.2	27.8	29.0	23.1
Can't say (neutral)	21.7	33.7	36.8	37.8	36.7
Don't know	35.4	20.4	15.1	11.2	9.3
Number of respondents	1,564	1,769	2,682	2,586	1,498

Sources: Flanagan et al. (1976); Watanuki et al. (1983); Kabashima et al. (1993–96); Ikeda, Kobayashi, and Hirano (2005).

have successfully kept a single Japanese soldier from dying in combat in over sixty years, and have seen Japan literally rise from the ashes to the second largest economy in the world' (Oros 2007).

By 2005, however, this consensus had eroded, and for the first time in thirty years the largest group of voters surveyed (37.8 per cent) favoured strengthening Japan's defence capabilities. This represents a reversal of public opinion in the space of a decade. Similarly, more Japanese (30.9 per cent) supported strengthening the Security Treaty in 2005 than in the preceding thirty years. I do not mean to imply here that there is a new consensus in favour of these views; on the contrary, there is still a large bloc of voters who disagree with these positions or adopt a neutral view consistent with support for the status quo.

As the costs of the wars in Afghanistan and Iraq mount, the United States has increased pressure on Japan to assume more of its own defence while economically and materially supporting the U.S. mission in these regions. Both demands have raised constitutional questions, however, because of Article 9, and have also contributed to a decline in Japanese public opinion about the utility of allying with the United States. What assessment, then, can one make about the relationship between these changes in public opinion and voting behaviour in 2005, the last election for which survey data are available at the time of writing?

Security and Defence Attitudes and Vote Choice

The 2005 lower house election was the first after the U.S.-led invasion of Iraq, making it possible to see if changing attitudes about the security alliance and strengthening the SDF influenced vote choice. Ishibashi (2007) finds that, even though the majority of the Japanese public opposed the Iraq war and the dispatch of the SDF in 2003, the LDP-Koumeitou coalition retained control of the lower house for several reasons. First, Iraq was less salient than domestic issues since the media focused on other issues; second, voters were unsure how Japan's relationship with the United States would affect relations with North Korea; third, the government postponed dispatch of the SDF until after the election; and, finally, the DPJ failed to offer an alternative to the LDP on security and defence. Most important, Prime Minster Koizumi successfully moved postal privatization to the top of the policy agenda (see Maclachlan, in this volume), effectively sidelining other issues. The 2005 election thus constitutes a hard test: if voters used security and defence issues to distinguish between the parties that best reflected their opinion during an election that produced a landslide victory for the LDP, then strategic party leaders can frame these issues to influence mass attitudes and vote choice in future elections. Further, if security and defence attitudes attain significance as predictors of vote choice, any geopolitical shifts that increase the salience of security and defence will increase demands on domestic elites to strategically frame them as wedge issues.

In analysing the results of the 2005 lower house election,[4] I expected voters who favoured strengthening the SDF and the United States-Japan Security Treaty to be more likely to support the LDP, while those holding opposing views vote would be more likely to vote for the DPJ. If security and defence attitudes were significant predictors of vote choice in 2005, it would demonstrate the potential for this latent cleavage to re-emerge as an indicator of vote choice over the long term. Indeed, the DPJ seized upon security and defence issues to differentiate itself from the LDP in the 2007 upper house and 2009 lower house elections. Unfortunately, tying its electoral fate to security and defence cost the DPJ seats in the 2010 upper house election after it failed to keep its 2009 election promise to find another site for the highly contentious Futenma Air Station in Okinawa.

I found that, in 2005, voters used positions on security and defence to distinguish between parties, as voters who disagreed with strengthening the Security Treaty and the SDF were significantly less likely to vote for the LDP (see Table 5.2), while agreement with this position was more likely to yield an LDP vote. Table 5.3 presents the predicted probability that a respondent voted for the LDP given his or her position on security and defence issues; subtracting the reported results from 1 yields the probability of voting for the DPJ. Just over two-thirds (67.5 per cent) of voters who agreed that the United States-Japan security alliance should be strengthened and just under two-thirds (64.6 per cent) who thought Japan should strengthen the SDF voted for the LDP. Just under half (46.4 per cent) of voters who disagreed with strengthening the security alliance and two-fifths (41.8 per cent) who disagreed with strengthening the SDF also voted for the LDP. Voters who were unable to take a position on either issue were nearly twice as likely to vote for the LDP than for the DPJ. This asymmetry reflects the lopsided LDP victory, but also suggests that the 'doves' who favoured the status quo were not as mobilized around these issues as the 'hawks' who were pushing for change.

In 2005, the DPJ stood to expand its base of support with a clearer articulation of its moderate position on security. Over the previous two decades, the strength of the political Left's resistance to remilitarization had weakened considerably in tandem with voters' growing acceptance of the Yoshida Doctrine status quo. But as LDP leaders began pushing for more hawkish policies in the late 1990s and early 2000s, the DPJ was slow to counter with a clear statement of how its policies differed from those of the ruling party. Starting in 2005, however, by staking out security policy positions that were clearly more moderate than those of the LDP, the DPJ aimed to peel away at least some moderate voters. In that year, with security issues overshadowed by postal reform, the DPJ's success in differentiating itself from the LDP on security issues and convincing voters to pay attention to this contrast did not pay immediate electoral dividends. Yet the DPJ had recognized an opportunity to use security and defence as a strategic means of differentiating itself from the LDP in subsequent elections.

Table 5.2   Security and Defence Attitudes and Vote Choice in the 2005
Lower House Election

Predictor Variables	Voted for the LDP	
	Beta	(Standard Error)
Gender (male = 1)	−0.016	(0.136)
College (some = 1)	−0.268	(0.144)
Age	0.014	(0.004)**
United States-Japan Security Treaty		
Somewhat agree	−0.098	(0.238)
Can't say	−0.226	(0.217)
Somewhat disagree	−0.726	(0.254)**
Disagree	−0.875	(0.284)**
Self-Defense Forces		
Somewhat agree	0.244	(0.220)
Can't say	0.020	(0.212)
Somewhat disagree	−0.641	(0.223)**
Disagree	−0.935	(0.257)**
Intercept	0.215	(0.341)

N = 1,078

Note: Reference category for the United States-Japan Security Treaty
and Self-Defense Forces is 'agree.'

**p <.005; *p<.05; pseudo R2: 0.069.

Source: Ikeda, Kobayashi, and Hirano (2005).

Table 5.3   Position on Security and Defence and the Likelihood of Voting LDP

	Agree	Agree Somewhat	Can't Say	Disagree Somewhat	Disagree
		(predicted probability, %)			
The United States-Japan security alliance should be strengthened	.675	.653	.723	.501	.464
Japan should strengthen its Self-Defense Force	.646	.700	.651	.491	.418

Note: Predicted probabilities are with other variables held at their means.

Source: Ikeda, Kobayashi, and Hirano (2005).

Regional Defence and Global Security Partnerships, 2007–10

The most significant predictor of vote choice in the 2005 election cycle was an issue marginal to that election period: respondents' positions on security and defence. All things equal, voters who were looking for substantive differences between the LDP and the DPJ used this less salient issue to inform their vote choice. This finding is interesting for a couple of reasons. First, a significant subset of voters does use policies to distinguish between parties. Second, the significance of security and defence is more surprising given that studies of voting behaviour typically find that attitudes about foreign policy are not significant predictors of vote choice because voters are ill-informed and foreign policy, unless it has a strong domestic component, is distant from their everyday lives. When candidates and media continually address foreign policy concerns, however, voters gain more information and attitudes crystallize and become accessible cues for voters (Aldrich, Sullivan, and Borgida 1989, 125–6).[5]

One reason security and defence issues attained increasing salience in 2005, and have done so in every subsequent election, is media coverage of the DPJ's sustained noisy opposition to LDP support of the U.S. mission in Iraq. During the years preceding the 2005 'postal' election, Koizumi stoked the flames domestically and regionally with his visits to Yasukuni Shrine and deployment of the SDF to Iraq. Each time that Japan answers the U.S. call to assume more responsibility for security and defence, parliamentary approval is required. Temporary laws were passed to dispatch forces for peacekeeping operations in Iraq, refuel U.S. ships en route to the Persian Gulf, and, more recently, fight Somali pirates in the Gulf of Aden.[6] Since 2003, the DPJ has attempted to block such legislation on each occasion, and the performance promotes public awareness. Indeed, legislative protest was a critical weapon in the DPJ's arsenal in mobilizing voters to oust the long-dominant LDP. During the 2007 upper house election campaign, for example, the DPJ opposed LDP-sponsored legislation that enabled the SDF to refuel coalition warships en route to and from the Persian Gulf, arguing that missions to support combat units were constitutionally questionable under Article 9, legislation mandating such missions threatened to erode civilian control over the military, coalition forces lacked a UN mandate, and supporting the U.S. military would make Japan less safe.

In 2009, the DPJ pledged to withdraw Japanese naval forces from refuelling coalition vessels assisting the U.S.-led counterterrorism operation in the Indian Ocean and to renegotiate bilateral agreements that commit Japan to assuming the costs of moving the U.S. Marines from Okinawa to Guam and building a replacement facility for the Futenma air base. Both pledges signalled the DPJ's commitment to transforming the United States-Japan alliance into a more equitable partnership. Even though security and defence have begun to structure electoral competition and vote choice, reviving these highly contentious issues is a risky strategy for a new party that must prove that it is able to govern. The 2009 *Sankei Shimbun* exit polls found that only 3 per cent of voters cited foreign and security policy as their primary concern (Green 2010, 10). Thus, the DPJ went against the tide of public opinion when its management of the Futenma Air Station unbalanced the security alliance with the United States. The Futenma issue was the immediate cause of the decision of Prime Minister Hatoyama Yukio to resign after his public support ratings fell below 20 per cent and more than 90,000 Okinawans demonstrated against the agreement.[7] Belatedly, the DPJ has realized that it will pay a price if it backs down from its campaign pledges, and its management of the security alliance has further exposed the party's inability to bridge the ideological divisions within its own ranks.

Security and defence debates, successfully held in decades-long abeyance by the LDP's ability to forge public consensus around economic growth, have attained increased salience over the course of the past decade. There was more movement in public opinion between 1996 and 2005 than in the preceding three decades. Resistance to strengthening the SDF has softened considerably, and debate has now shifted to the conditions under which deployment is permissible. While the range of policies being debated has therefore shifted to the right, it turns out that voters care more about this new debate than they did about the old, making it attractive to parties seeking to use issue positions to attract new voters.

Conclusion

In 2005, attitudes on defence and security issues were strong predictors of vote choice in Japan. Voters strongly opposed to strengthening Japan's military defence capabilities and who held reservations about the future of the alliance with the United States supported the DPJ. That most voters were undecided, however, benefited the LDP. The importance of this finding is highlighted by Steel's (2008) analysis of the effect of policy preferences on vote choice in a pre-reform election

(1986) and two post-reform elections (1996 and 2003) that showed that policy preferences were not significant predictors of vote choice in these post-reform elections. She writes: 'Despite the incentives in the electoral system that had the potential to encourage politicians to focus on policies, and the introduction of manifestos into election campaigns, only a few policy preferences had a modest, and occasionally substantial impact on vote choice, and most issue preferences did not play a role' (92). Steel finds that social welfare and the economic performance are valence issues: voters always favour more social welfare and a stronger economy. Consensus on these valence issues, Steel argues, produces shifts between the LDP and the DPJ from one election period to the next, but ultimately fails to align voters behind substantively different approaches to delivering social welfare and economic improvement. Given this finding and the DPJ's success in the period since it began positioning itself as a clear alternative to the LDP on security and defence, it appears that this has been a savvy strategy, at least in the short term. Now that the DPJ is in power and has begun to suffer in the polls as it attempts to implement this alternative policy, the risks associated with this strategy are proving to be substantial.

In concluding, I would like to turn attention to other issues that have more traction in the electorate. In the 2004, 2005, and 2007 national election cycles, between one-third and one-half of voters chose pension and social welfare as the most important determinants of their vote choice.[8] A research team led by political scientist Iida Takeshi analysed post-election survey data, collected with the aid of the *Yomiuri Shimbun* newspaper, and found that voters in 2009 had more confidence in the LDP's ability to manage security policy and more in the DPJ's ability to handle fiscal reconstruction, pension reform, and a host of other policies, including immigration, associated with demographic change. Why, then, is social welfare not a better predictor of vote choice?

The significance of foreign policy in structuring elections suggests that there is a latent potential for more issue-oriented electoral competition around issues about which voters care, since parties so far are not offering clear-cut, substantive alternatives on social welfare and other issues. During the 2009 lower house election campaign, political analysts and many voters complained that the quality of debate on issues such as counterbalancing economic recovery against a ballooning national debt and rising social welfare demands was 'disappointing.'[9] The DPJ promised to reduce wasteful spending, reduce highway tolls, provide income supports to farmers, and extend cash allowances to families with children. The LDP's policies were not dramatically different, promising to reduce wasteful government spending, extend child care allowances, support companies that did not lay off workers during the economic downturn, assist families in educating children, provide vocational training and job placement services, expand and strengthen the pension system, and support the agricultural, forestry, and fishery sectors. There is thus a great deal of overlap in the campaign promises documented in manifestos issued by both parties.

Security and defence represent only one set of issues that can be exploited to produce issue-based electoral competition in Japan. The DPJ paid for mismanaging the security alliance with the United States in the 2010 upper house election. In retrospect, it appears that the party would have been more successful had it found a way to differentiate itself from the LDP on the socio-economic issues that matter most to voters in an era when demographic shifts and economic transformations are presenting the Japanese government with some difficult policy choices.

NOTES

1 This chapter draws heavily from my previous work on the relationships among sex, vote choice, and evolving security and defence debates presented in two venues: the Program on U.S.-Japan Relations at Harvard University and the Woodrow Wilson International Center for Scholars. Both papers, which include more extensive presentation and analyses of data, are available online (see Martin 2008a and 2008b). I thank numerous colleagues and anonymous reviewers whose feedback has enabled me to expand upon and update this earlier work.
2 Carmines and Stimson 'define issue evolutions as those issues capable of altering the political environment in which they originated and evolved' (1989, 12).
3 In analysing these trends in opinion, I use surveys from 1976 until 2005, the last election for which I have data. The analysis is based on identical questions asked in the 1976 Japanese Political Consciousness and Behavior Study (JABISS) and the Japan Election Studies (JES1, JES2, and JES3) conducted in 1983, 1993–96, and 2001–05. JABISS, JES1, JES2, and JES3 surveyed a randomly selected national sample of Japanese voters ages 20 and older.
4 I constructed a binary logistic regression model using the 2005 Japan Election Study III post-election survey data to measure the relationship between my independent variables of interest – voters' positions on strengthening Japan's security forces and support for the security

alliance – and a dichotomous dependent variable that captures whether respondents voted for the LDP and coalition partner New Koumeitou (coded 1) or the DPJ (coded 0). Other independent variables include socio-economic information (age, sex, income, education, employment status, and residence), party identification (a three-category variable that captures the largest groups in the electorate – LDP supporters, DPJ supporters, and non-partisans), and voters' positions on a range of other issues that include administrative reform and social justice and welfare. Here, I report a pared-down regression model to examine the variables of interest: the relationship between security and defence attitudes and vote choice. Other issues did not attain significance due to the lack of variation across response categories – that is, social welfare and political corruption tend to be valence issues that everyone favours or opposes. Table 5.2 reports the regression estimators for each of the independent variables. To aid interpretation, I generated predicted probabilities that are reported in Table 5.3.

5 In fact, Aldrich, Sullivan, and Borgida argue that foreign policy is not unlike domestic policy: 'specific international problems, or "hot spots," tend to dominate the public's foreign policy concerns at various times with ebbs and flows not fundamentally different from that characteristic of domestic issues' (1989, 131–2).

6 Nikkei Net Interactive, 'Lower house approves antipiracy legislation over opposition,' 23 April 2009; available online at http://www.nni.nikkei.co.jp, accessed 23 April 2009.

7 Martin Fackler, '90,000 protest U.S. base on Okinawa,' *New York Times,* 4 May 2010.

8 Survey data reported by the Association for Promoting Clean Elections, available online at http://www.akaruisenkyo.or.jp/066search/index.html, accessed 17 February 2009.

9 Martin Fackler, 'Lost in Japan's election: the economy,' *New York Times,* 29 August 2009.

6 Ideas, Interests, and Institutions: Japanese Postal Privatization in Comparative Perspective

PATRICIA L. MACLACHLAN

By all accounts, the passage of former prime minister Koizumi Jun'ichirou's postal privatization bills in October 2005 marked a significant step towards a more market-oriented political-economic model in Japan.[1] On 1 October 2007, Japan Post, a public corporation launched in 2003, was divided into four separate corporations, one each for the mail delivery, postal savings, and postal insurance systems, and a fourth for Japan's nationwide network of post offices. All four entities are overseen by a semi-government holding company that must sell off its shares in the postal savings and insurance companies by 2017. Given the postal system's indispensable mail service and the financial magnitude of the postal savings system – the volume of its deposits renders it the world's largest financial institution[2] – these changes should, in principle, diminish the scope of state intervention in the communications and financial sectors and invigorate the private banks. They also threaten some of the long-standing political alliances that have buttressed the Japanese political economy for generations. For these reasons, Koizumi has been wont to proclaim that postal privatization constitutes the most momentous reform since the 1868 Meiji Restoration, not to mention a triumph of liberal capitalism after decades of state-led economic development.

My objective in this chapter is to explore the political, institutional, and ideological changes that triggered and were triggered by postal reform. I begin with an overview of two landmark reforms of the 1980s that together serve as a useful benchmark for evaluating postal privatization: the privatization of Nippon Telegraph and Telephone (NTT) and the Japan National Railways (JNR), public corporations that faced technological and fiscal challenges similar to those that confronted Japan Post. I then examine the causes, processes, and consequences of

Koizumi's postal reform plan. To conclude, I assess the long-term significance of postal privatization for Japanese interest group configurations and the political economy, as well as efforts since late 2009 to reverse some of Koizumi's handiwork.

The analysis proceeds in two sections. In the first, I examine the interplay among interest groups, institutions, and ideas in the JNR and NTT cases to identify common patterns: what kinds of reforms were approved, which ones were rejected, and why? I observe that, in each case, reformers initially sought to privatize the relevant public enterprise and then break it up along regional lines. Break-up proved particularly controversial. To varying degrees, advocates of break-up argued that a nationally unified service was too large to manage effectively and that it enabled the subsidization of loss-generating regions by more profitable ones. As proponents of the break-up of the JNR argued, it was not enough simply to grant autonomy to the regional components of a newly privatized service; only through complete independence, they maintained, would each component face the incentives to cut costs and increase competitiveness, thereby enhancing the service's overall profitability (Ishikawa and Imashiro 1998, 14). The opponents of break-up condemned such arguments, however, as pandering to the dictates of market principles. More to the point, many justifiably feared that the process would weaken or destroy labour unions and other politically influential networks that span the nation; while these networks had a fighting chance under a privatized but national service, their prospects appeared much dimmer when privatization was accompanied by break-up. Consequently, interest group opposition to the privatization of public corporations was most intense when the notion of break-up was on the table. With these observations in mind, I find in the JNR and NTT cases that radical change – defined as privatization *plus* the break-up of constituent firms – resulted when 1) opposing interest groups were divided among themselves and 2) the relevant Liberal Democratic Party (LDP) and bureaucratic actors were united behind reform. Reform fell short of this level when these conditions were absent.

In the second section, I explore the patterns of political conflict in the postal privatization process during the late 1990s and early 2000s. Using the JNR and NTT cases as a basis for comparison, I show how those patterns positioned Koizumi's radical reform proposals for failure. Put simply, Koizumi faced strong opposition from a vast alliance of influential interest groups, bureaucrats, and conservative politicians;

the ruling party was divided among itself; and the two ministries that were most closely connected to the postal system were mired in conflict. How, then, did he manage to usher his postal privatization package through the Diet? To answer this question, I show how Koizumi made creative use of new and largely untested policy-making and electoral institutions to override traditional interest group configurations and forge a temporary political consensus behind his reform package – a surprisingly effective gambit that has important implications for institutional change and innovative leadership in Japan. But, as I argue in the conclusion, since each individual postal service will *not* be broken up into regional entities and since remnants of the anti-reform postal lobby survived the passage of the privatization bills, Koizumi's gambit fell short of revolutionizing the interests, ideas, and institutions of the postal system. Fundamentally, I argue, elements of Japan's state-centred approach to capitalism remain intact – and in ways that pose a significant danger to the future of Koizumi's privatization plan.

The 1980s and Administrative Reform: The JNR and NTT

In 1981, then-prime minister Suzuki Zenkou established the Second Provisional Council on Administrative Reform or Rinchou, an ad hoc advisory council (*shingikai*) attached to the Prime Minister's Office that answered directly to the prime minister. Rinchou was by no means the first advisory council to deliberate on government reform, nor would it be the last. What was distinctive about the council was its broad deliberative mandate, the strong support of the big business community and reformist politicians in the LDP, the stature of its leader, Dokou Toshio, the highly respected chairman of Keidanren and former president of Toshiba,[3] and its role as an instrument for the leadership aspirations of Nakasone Yasuhiro, who assumed the prime ministership in 1982 (Carlile 1998, 78–81). Unlike most other advisory councils, which were attached to specific ministries, Rinchou did not serve as a mere rubber stamp for the preconceived policies of Japan's powerful mandarins (Schwartz 1993, 234). It was instead a temporary entity that stood outside normal bureaucratic channels and their affiliated vested interests and, by virtue of its enabling legislation, required the prime minister to act on its recommendations (Samuels 2003, 12). Thus, the council was mandated to recommend specific policies in the context of new global economic challenges and in accordance with neoliberal economic principles. As such, it was the anointed institutional advocate of a paradigmatic shift away from the political-economic principles of Japan's particular model of state-led capitalism.

In contrast to the United States and the United Kingdom, where concerns about business competitiveness and stagflation fuelled much of the momentum towards neoliberal economic reform from the late 1970s, the primary impetus behind the Japanese reform movement was mounting government debt (Carlile 1998, 77). The product of both slower growth rates following the two oil crises and increasing public works spending, Japan's fiscal problems were widely perceived as unsustainable. Raising taxes was, of course, one way out of the fiscal morass, but with income and corporate taxes already high and a consumption tax politically unfeasible at that time, policy-makers had to search for an alternative solution (Carlile 1998, 78). For Nakasone and Dokou, that solution was to shrink the size of government and decrease spending.

Accordingly, Rinchou recommended a zero-growth policy for subsequent rounds of national budgeting, a measure that significantly shrank annual deficits during the 1980s. More important for our purposes, the council, with Nakasone's strong endorsement, recommended the privatization and break-up of three public corporations: Japan Salt and Tobacco, NTT, and the JNR. Proponents argued that privatizing these three corporations would not only make them more efficient and profitable, but would also bring much-needed revenue to the state.

The JNR and NTT had been the targets of reform proposals well before Rinchou entered the scene. Motivating these proposals was widespread concern about the corporations' inability to keep up with technological advances in the context of mounting fiscal challenges and foreign competition. Established in 1906–07 as a government enterprise, the JNR was converted into a public corporation in 1949 at the instigation of Douglas MacArthur, who viewed the move as essential to the rapid recovery and modernization of Japan's war-torn transportation system (Kasai 2003, 3). By the mid-1960s, however, the JNR had lost its near-monopoly of the passenger transport sector as Japanese residents acquired their own automobiles and took advantage of expanding bus and airline services. The JNR's freight services, meanwhile, were losing out to the shipping and trucking industries. In 1964, after years of operating in the black, the JNR ran a deficit of ¥30 billion. After the 1973 oil shock, annual operating losses of approximately ¥1 trillion were not uncommon (Ishikawa and Imashiro 1998, 3). Despite government and corporate efforts to correct these problems, the JNR's debt continued to mushroom well into the 1980s, in part because of pressures from politicians to extend expensive train and shinkansen (bullet train) lines into their constituencies.

NTT's challenges were of a different sort. As Vogel notes, NTT felt fettered by government regulation as it struggled to keep up with developments in terminal equipment and the introduction of new transmission technologies that often transcended national borders (1996, 27–30). Unlike the JNR, NTT was not experiencing serious fiscal problems, but it suffered from low productivity levels in the face of growing international competition (Mochizuki 1993, 192). Privatizing NTT and liberalizing the telecommunications market, advocates argued, would help stimulate this increasingly important sector of the economy (Vogel 1996, 27–30).

Labour problems were also at issue. In Japan, public sector unions were far more militant than those in the private sector because they did not have the right to strike or other benefits enjoyed by their private sector counterparts. Government constraints on public sector wages were another source of labour militancy (Mochizuki 1993, 181). The JNR was particularly prone to labour problems. Following a string of layoffs in 1967 and 1968 triggered by a government-mandated rationalization plan, labour-management relations steadily deteriorated as the railway unions resorted to wildcat strikes and acts of sabotage (Kasai 2003, 42–3). NTT's labour problems were less severe but no less significant. United under a single union and fairly moderate politically, NTT employees were more accommodating of management than their JNR counterparts and less prone to disruptive activities. But their success in negotiating deals with their employer resulted in labour redundancies that, in turn, contributed to the low productivity levels that were impeding NTT's capacity to compete (Mochizuki 1993, 192).

Nakasone was determined to solve the fiscal problems of these public corporations, render them more internationally competitive, and break the political backs of the public sector unions and their supporters in the Japan Socialist Party (JSP), post-war Japan's most influential opposition party. In so doing, he hoped to strengthen support for the LDP as a dynamic conservative party while destroying the less desirable elements of the so-called 1955 System – the inefficient business practices, strong bureaucratic rule, and powerful vested interests that to date had proven resistant to reform (see Samuels 2003).

Nakasone's mission, which was reflected in and endorsed by Rinchou, represented a significant change in thinking about the relationship between business and government in post-war Japan. As a relatively late developer, Japan had long nurtured an active bureaucracy that used its regulatory powers not only to enhance market growth rates but also to fulfil certain social objectives (Carlile and Tilton 1998, 4). In time, the state forged a series of social compacts with various groups in society that exchanged individual economic sacrifices – including relatively low wages and limited formal welfare benefits – for a number of state guarantees: economic and price stability, full employment, informal social welfare benefits, and the like (see, for example, Garon and Mochizuki 1993). These arrangements resonated well with a risk-averse population that tended to distrust market competition and that looked to government authority for guidance and protection. They also facilitated a state-centred approach to advancing the public interest. In defiance of classical economic theory, which holds that the common good can be achieved when individuals are free to pursue profit, the Japanese relied on an activist state as the most viable advocate of the interests of the many. Consequently, serving the public interest in Japan meant stipulating government *responsibilities* towards different groups in society, as opposed to entrenching individual rights in law. It also meant empowering the government to fulfil certain objectives that could have been assumed by a more cost-effective market.

Nakasone advocated something much different. Like his international contemporaries, Margaret Thatcher and Ronald Reagan, Nakasone believed in small government and the virtues of the free market. By pressing for privatization and deregulation, he put his trust in the ability of businesses to govern themselves and of consumers to navigate the marketplace on their own. Although he did little to strengthen the individual rights of consumers, he advocated an approach to fulfilling the 'public interest' that was much closer to that of Anglo-American countries: what was in the interests of individuals – particularly businesspeople – was in the best interests of society. In this way, the 1980s marked the beginning of a long-term movement towards greater 'self-responsibility' (*jiko sekinin*) for consumers and producers. Nakasone, in short, sought to transform the very institutional and ideological foundations of the Japanese political economy.

As evidenced by the outcomes of government efforts to privatize the JNR and NTT, Nakasone took several steps towards achieving this goal. In 1985, NTT was turned into a joint-stock company; several years later, a portion of its shares was gradually floated on the open market (Mochizuki 1993, 194). But it was not until 1999 that the corporation was broken up into regional companies. The government, meanwhile, continues to hold approximately one-third of the conglomerate's shares

(Tilton 2004). The JNR's transformation was, comparatively speaking, more radical. On 1 April 1987, the entity was broken up into six regional companies, a freight company, and a holding company that leased out the rolling stock and maintained the infrastructure of the shinkansen network. (The holding company was dissolved in 1991 and its holdings sold to JR Central, the largest of the private firms.) Over time, two of the most profitable companies were fully privatized, and a third is close to achieving that goal. By all accounts, both the telecommunications and railway transportation sectors have become more economically efficient as a result of privatization. From an economic perspective, at least, the 1980s neoliberal reform movement was a success.

Given how contentious the JNR privatization process was, it is curious that the resulting reforms were more extensive – at least initially – than the NTT reforms. This difference can be explained by the *nature* of conflict in each case. During the early stages of the reform process, Rinchou's plans to privatize and break up the JNR faced stiff opposition from several vested interests: the corporation's militant unions fought the plans for fear they would result in layoffs; many conservative politicians protested that privatization would lead to the closure of unprofitable railway lines, thereby jeopardizing votes; and private railway companies complained that privatization would spark debilitating levels of competition (Samuels 2003, 20).

Four developments tipped the balance in favour of the reformers. First, the main opponents of privatization, the unions, were so divided among themselves that Nakasone and the various councils that were established to work out the details of reform were in a position to override them (Samuels 2003). Second, several JNR executives broke with their colleagues to cooperate with the reformers (Mochizuki 1993, 186). Third, Nakasone and his allies helped forge a consensus within the LDP in support of radical change. Finally, only one ministry – the Ministry of Transportation – was involved in the decision-making process, and it generally supported reform and cooperated with progressive railway managers to determine the details of change. The ministry's pro-reform stance was further strengthened under the leadership of Hashimoto Ryuutarou, a Nakasone supporter who served as minister of transportation from July 1986 through the passage of the JNR privatization bills the following November. For all intents and purposes, the concentration of bureaucratic decision-making power in one ministry negated the need for the kind of interministerial compromise that might have diluted the extent of reform. Although concessions were granted to vested interests during the decision-making process – including a guarantee that all JNR workers who did not opt for early retirement would be given jobs in the privatized firms – and the process was slowed by union protests, the final reform package was far-reaching in that it provided for both the privatization *and* the break-up of the public corporation.

The NTT privatization process was also marked by conflict. At first, the telecommunications union opposed radical reform in the expectation that too many jobs would be lost. Meanwhile, the 'family' of suppliers linked to NTT protested that they would lose a secure market for their goods, while senior NTT executives grumbled that privatization would jeopardize lucrative post-retirement positions in those firms (Vogel 1996, 153). Nakasone and his allies also had to contend with the conflicting interests of two powerful ministries: the Ministry of Posts and Telecommunications (MPT), which had primary jurisdiction over telecommunications, and the Ministry of International Trade and Industry (MITI), which, by virtue of its control over the computer industry, wanted a larger say over the telecommunications sector.

Over time, however, the particular structure of contending interests enabled a compromise solution that ultimately reduced the scope of reform. After dragging its feet for several months, the telecommunications union proved sufficiently united to leverage a deal from management and state reformers that exchanged union support for privatization in return for a promise that NTT would not be broken up into regional entities. The union reasoned that, while privatization would probably be good for wages, a break-up would weaken its bargaining power by forcing it to dissolve into smaller enterprise unions (Mochizuki 1993, 193). Meanwhile, the LDP lined up behind privatization after Tanaka Kakuei and his powerful faction signed off on the plan and the party reached a decision to postpone discussions of a corporate break-up (Vogel 1996, 154–5). Finally, after a lengthy impasse, Nakasone and his allies were able to broker a deal between the two feuding ministries – one that privileged the MPT (Vogel 1996). As a result of these accommodations and compromises, changes introduced to the telecommunications sector were somewhat more modest than those experienced by the JNR in that the 'privatized' firm was *not* broken up into regional entities. Consequently – and in defiance of Nakasone's and Rinchou's push for more competition – the restructured NTT retained a near-monopoly in the telecommunications sector until 1999, when the corporation was finally divided into two regional carriers, one long-distance carrier, and a holding company – all in response to growing competition from abroad. Until this reform was put in place, the privatized but still influential union, NTT, and NTT's family enterprises continued to wrest concessions from the state (Tilton 2004).[4]

The fact that the JNR and NTT were reformed at all is a telling illustration of the impact of leadership and institutional innovation on subsequent institutional change in the Japanese political economy. Progress in both cases can be attributed largely to Rinchou's ability to rise above long-standing ministerial and interest group conflicts and forge a loose consensus behind the need for reform. The council's star power and support within the business community and the general public, moreover, strengthened its legitimacy as the primary architect of reform, while giving the prime minister the political wherewithal to build coalitions in support for change. Rinchou also set a precedent for future reforms: the council not only contributed to a realignment of LDP politicians along a reform–anti-reform continuum (Samuels 2003, 27), but also served as a model for the establishment of future reform councils – none of which, however, matched Rinchou in stature.

Rinchou might have injected a certain degree of inevitability into political-economic reform during the 1980s, but it was politics that ultimately determined the divergent outcomes of the reform processes in the JNR and NTT cases. As I have argued, the scope of reform was shaped by the level of conflict among interest groups and their political patrons, on the one hand, and among LDP politicians and the relevant ministries, on the other. Briefly stated, the more fragmented were opposing interest groups and the more united were the LDP and the bureaucracy in favour of reform, the more reform approached the market-oriented ideals of Nakasone and Rinchou.

When all is said and done, however, the privatization process did not result in a radical reorganization of government-business relations, at least for the first decade following reform. Vogel (1996) argues that, in the NTT case, the privatization process actually *increased* government regulation of the telecommunications sector, thereby strengthening the hand of the state vis-à-vis the private sector. Throughout the reform process, the MPT took advantage of a privatization process involving a nearly self-sufficient public corporation to enhance its regulatory power. The MPT also became more active in formulating 'industrial policy' within the telecommunications sector, while other ministries distanced themselves from the practice (see Tilton 2004). The telecommunications sector might have been subjected to increasing levels of competition since the mid-1980s, but the role of the state in controlling that competition actually expanded (Vogel 1996).

Finally, mention should be made of the debates surrounding the 'public interest' that permeated these two reform processes. As we have seen, the Japanese have long looked to the state as the primary representative of the public interest – a tradition that was by no means overlooked during the NTT and JNR privatization processes. In both instances, although privatization undoubtedly reduced the power of the labour movement, the state prioritized full employment for workers over the goal of cutting costs. And in the JNR case, reformers struggled to strike a balance between the need for greater profitability in railway services and the need to maintain at least some level of public transportation service in remote areas of the country. One insider commented that members of the JNR Restructuring Supervisory Committee – which was established to implement Rinchou's recommendation for privatization and break-up – openly admitted that some services had to be maintained even if they were highly unprofitable (Ishikawa and Imashiro 1998, 189). These sentiments helped motivate the establishment of large 'management stabilization funds' for the three smallest regional corporations that were designed to help them compensate for the low profitability of lines in sparsely populated regions and to maintain universal service in those areas (Kasai 2003, 163–4). In a similar vein, a former JNR executive who helped guide the privatization process noted that 'unfettered competition is not always appropriate and in such sectors as transportation the public interest is best served with some limitations on the market mechanism' (171). Meanwhile, the government continues to shape the parameters of competition in the telecommunications sector through its regulatory activities, even after orchestrating the break-up of NTT in 1999 and divesting itself of a significant portion of its shares in NTT firms. The reason for this continuing government interference is fear of the negative social and economic side effects of price wars and other examples of 'excessive competition' (see Tilton 2004, 4). Japan might have been willing to take a few steps towards a more liberalized market economy in the transportation and telecommunications sectors, but not at the expense of economic security, stability, and other cherished principles of state-led capitalism.

The Privatization of the Postal Services

Like the JNR, the history of the postal services extends back to the early Meiji period. In 1871, the freshly minted Meiji state introduced Japan's first modern post offices, using the British postal system as a model.

The postal network, which expanded rapidly in subsequent years, consisted of two broad types of post offices: a small number of large entities staffed by civil servants that eventually became known as general or ordinary post offices (*futsuu yuubinkyoku*), and a vast network of tiny commissioned post offices (*tokutei yuubinkyoku*) run by unpaid postmasters of semi-aristocratic background from the confines of their own homes or businesses. After World War Two, the commissioned postmasters, like their counterparts in the ordinary post offices, were classified as 'general' public servants and began to receive salaries and other benefits, but they remained distinctive in two important ways: they were handpicked by regional bureaucrats from among local residents, and their positions were, in many cases, inherited through family lines. Of the 24,715 post offices in existence in 2003, 1,310 were ordinary post offices, 18,935 were commissioned post offices, and the remainder 'simple post offices' (*kan'i yuubinkyoku*) – tiny postal wickets operated by shopkeepers to dispense stamps and, in some cases, pension checks (Japan 2005). Given their sheer numbers and presence in virtually every community of Japan, the commissioned post offices were widely viewed as the anchor of the postal system at the grassroots level.

Japanese Postal Politics in the Post-war Period

The post-war postal system further resembled the JNR in terms of its contentious labour-management relations. From the moment it was formed in 1946, Zentei, the postal workers union, distinguished itself as one of Japan's most militant labour networks.[5] At the top of its agenda was the complete abolition of the commissioned postal system, which the union regarded as an economically inefficient, semi-feudal institution. Complaining of poor working conditions in the commissioned post offices and their inability to assume postmasterships, postal workers carried out a protracted struggle against the commissioned postal system that lasted well into the 1980s (see Maclachlan 2004, 291–4).

The besieged commissioned postmasters turned to conservative politicians for help, demanding protection from Zentei and its main political ally, the JSP, in return for votes. With their close ties to local communities and their prominent family backgrounds, the postmasters were well positioned to persuade local residents to cast their votes for conservative candidates – particularly in upper house elections. As minister of posts and telecommunications between 1957 and 1958, Tanaka Kakuei solidified the alliance between the newly formed LDP and the postmasters, an alliance that continued into the twenty-first century despite a 1948 law (the National Public Service Law) that banned political activities by civil servants.

Both the LDP and the postmasters went to great lengths over the years to nurture this political exchange relationship. Sympathetic LDP politicians blocked significant reforms to the postal system that might have jeopardized the employment of their supporters (and hence the party's penetration of local Japan), and routinely made appearances at meetings of the National Association of Commissioned Postmasters (*Zenkoku tokutei yuubinkyokuchoukai,* or Zentoku) to pledge their allegiance to the commissioned postmasters.[6] Not a few LDP politicians became advisors or consultants (*komon*) to the association, thereby identifying themselves as spokespersons for the postmasters' interests in the Diet. All the while, the LDP turned a blind eye to the postmasters' more controversial activities, including their electioneering functions and the practice of passing their postmasterships on to their sons. For its part, Zentoku took numerous steps to maintain the ideological unity of the postmasters and their electoral support for the LDP. Zentoku was known to interfere in the selection of postmasters by regional postal bureaus (*yuuseikyoku*), ensuring that only those individuals with conservative leanings and close ties to their communities were tested and interviewed – criteria that favoured the postmasters' offspring and made them beholden to Zentoku. The postal bureaus, meanwhile, did little to open the selection process to 'outsiders' (Nikkei Business 2002, 41–2).

Zentoku also orchestrated the postmasters' election activities by issuing quotas for the number of votes, party, and *kouenkai* memberships that individual postmasters were required to collect. Since their performance within this 'fourth service' was routinely publicized within the organization – along with their performance in the mail, postal savings, and postal insurance services – the postmasters had strong incentives to fulfil these quotas (see Honma 2003, 143–8). Assisting the postmasters in these activities were their wives and retired colleagues, neither of whom fell under the purview of the National Public Service Law. By the mid-1980s, retired postmasters had organized their own, highly secretive network of regional organizations known as *Taiju no kai,* or Taiju. A national, unabashedly political network, Taiju was widely touted as one of the LDP's most loyal and important electoral wings; to wit, Taiju represented as many as 10 per cent of LDP members in some prefectures.[7] Although the electoral might of Zentoku and Taiju was not fully understood, conventional wisdom has it that the postmasters gathered approximately one million votes at the height of their electoral influence during the early 1980s.

By the 1990s, the postmasters' vote-gathering power began to decline as the influence of local opinion leaders in national elections decreased, the number of floating voters increased, and the upper house electoral system was reformed in ways that diluted the power of the organized vote.[8] The postmasters were further handicapped by the gradual weakening of their inheritance practices and the appearance of younger postmasters who rebelled against the profession's conservative customs (see Honma 2003). The period also witnessed a decline in the LDP's commitment to the postmasters as the party's structural reform movement gained momentum – a trend that culminated in Koizumi's ascension to the party presidency in 2001. Despite this shifting balance of power between the postmasters' camp and their reform-oriented opponents, the postmasters remained a significant force in Japanese politics. The myth that the postmasters were still capable of mobilizing one million votes was still widely held by the mainstream media and traditional LDP politicians, many of whom tried to safeguard their electoral futures during the 1990s and early 2000s by strengthening their links with the postmasters. And when all is said and done, the postmasters and their anti-reform allies were still significantly better organized than the proponents of structural reform and postal privatization.

Like NTT, the postal system spawned a 'family' of affiliated small- and medium-sized enterprises that produced and serviced the equipment used by postal facilities and provided supplementary transportation services. These firms enjoyed a secure market for their products and services and functioned as a landing ground for retired bureaucrats from the Ministry of Internal Affairs and Communications (MIC, the post-2001 successor to the MPT) and its regional bureaus. A number of special corporations affiliated with the ministry were also significant destinations for *amakudari* bureaucrats.[9] The Postal Services Center, for example, was a special corporation that marketed and distributed *furusato kozutsumi* (literally, hometown small packages), products indigenous to specific local communities; in early 2001, nearly three-quarters of the Center's ninety staff members were former bureaucrats or postmasters.[10] Also noteworthy were two semi-governmental entities that administered their own national networks of hotels: the so-called Mielparque (formerly known as postal savings halls) and the Postal Insurance Inns (*Kampo no yado*), which offered recreational as well as hotel services. Many of the employees of these networks were former bureaucrats or postmasters.

MPT bureaucrats nurtured a close relationship with NTT, but their linkages with the postal system were even closer. Whereas the state-run telecommunications system enjoyed a semi-autonomous existence following its formal separation from the MPT in 1949, the post offices consistently remained under the ministry's watchful eye. Over time, the relationship between bureaucratic authorities and the postmasters became entrenched in an elaborate – and deeply politicized – institutional structure. During the 1950s, the ministry established a national liaison organization (Tokusuiren) that functioned as a communication channel between bureaucrats and the postmasters, who were carefully organized into groups at the local and regional levels. In terms of its structure and personnel, Tokusuiren closely overlapped with Zentoku, which the post-masters disingenuously referred to as a 'voluntary organization' (*nin'i dantai*);[11] this overlap in turn facilitated behind-the-scenes bureaucratic participation in national elections. This unusual institutional arrange-ment was at the very heart of one of post-war Japan's most powerful – and secretive – 'iron triangles,' not to mention a major impediment to institutional change within the postal system (see Maclachlan 2004).

The state-run postal system distinguished itself from other govern-ment enterprises or public corporations in terms of its many contribu-tions to the state and the 'public interest.' Of particular note were the activities of individual commissioned postmasters. Attracted to the pro-fession by the social status it conferred, early Meiji postmasters saved the state much-needed money by occasionally funding the expansion of postal, telephone, and telegraph services with their personal savings. More important, before 1945, they performed their duties without sal-ary, instead receiving small commissions on postage stamp sales and relying on alternative employment for income. They also encouraged mass incorporation into the polity by serving as the face of the state in isolated rural communities. With the introduction of the postal savings system in 1875, the postmasters helped disseminate the notions of thrift and saving in the absence of a commercial banking system, thereby doing their bit to amass a vast reservoir of deposits for state investment in industrial and military expansion and, after World War Two, rapid economic growth. After the war, many postmasters – particularly those in rural areas – became respected leaders in community development by performing volunteer services for local children and the elderly (see Maclachlan 2004).[12]

Fans of the state-run and corporatized systems also took pride in the many social and economic contributions of the postal services themselves. Chief among these were legal provisions for the state's guarantee of postal savings accounts, a benefit that was not offered to the commercial banks. The postal savings system also offered tax-exempt status to elderly depositors, and the postal insurance system, introduced in 1916, issued life insurance policies that were inexpensive and easy to acquire. The mail collection and delivery service provided a vast array of discounted rates for the handicapped, offered many services in Braille, and encouraged the dissemination of information in society by offering reduced postage rates for newspapers and magazines. The postal savings system facilitated charitable contributions by charging reduced fees for the transfer of funds from postal savings accounts to domestic non-governmental organizations (NGOs) and by establishing special accounts that channelled donations to international NGOs. As Toyoda (in this volume) further illustrates, until 2001, postal savings deposits and life insurance premiums were transferred automatically into the massive Fiscal Investment and Loan Program (FILP) administered by the Ministry of Finance (MOF).[13] After 1 April 2001, although the postal savings and insurance systems now had the freedom to invest deposits and premiums in the private market, the vast majority of these funds continued to flow into the FILP through the purchase of various kinds of FILP bonds. Historically, government institutions used these funds to invest in a host of state-orchestrated projects, including pre-war military expansion, post-war economic recovery, industrial expansion, and support for declining industries and small and medium enterprises. The central government also used FILP funds to issue low-interest loans to local governments for the purposes of local infrastructural and community development, the construction of public housing, industrial development, and the financing of small and medium-sized enterprises (Kobayashi 2001, 130). Community development was also served by the *furusato kotsuzumi* program, which fans of the state-run system widely praised for promoting small businesses and boosting employment within indigenous local industry. Last but not least, the Mielparque and the Postal Insurance Inns together provided local residents with recreational and medical services and served as popular gathering places for the elderly and other local residents.[14]

Early Efforts to Reform the Postal Services

The 'postal lobby' – the postmasters, their LDP allies, posts bureaucrats, and affiliated special corporations – extolled the postal system as a quintessentially 'Japanese' institution that made invaluable contributions to society, contributions that could be offered only by a state-run or public enterprise (see Arai 2003). Critics, on the other hand, branded these services as evidence of 'financial socialism' – inefficient financial practices that promoted social objectives while nurturing vested interests, promoting government mismanagement, and discouraging market competition (Matsubara 1996, 221). Arguing that a postal system need not be a government or public entity in order to serve the public, critics in the LDP, the MOF, Keidanren, and the commercial banking system looked to Sweden, New Zealand, Germany, and the Netherlands, all of which had injected competition not only into their postal savings systems, but also into mail services (see Chuujou 2001, 56–7).

As in the JNR and NTT cases, the movement to privatize the postal services was fuelled in part by fiscal concerns. Postal reform first became an issue for the government in the 1960s, when economists and policy-makers began to argue that Japan's booming industries no longer required injections of FILP funds. Nakasone toyed with privatizing the postal services during the early 1980s, but abandoned the idea once it became clear that political opposition to radical postal reform would be insurmountable. Hashimoto picked up the issue in 1997, only to succumb to opposition from the postal lobby.

It was not until April 2001, when Koizumi became prime minister, that postal privatization and the break-up of the three services rose to the top of the government's agenda and *stayed there*. Like Hashimoto before him, Koizumi was convinced that sweeping postal reform was a fundamental prerequisite to the long-term recovery of Japan's beleaguered financial system. Privatizing and breaking up the services, he maintained, would weaken the need for financial intermediation by the government and invigorate the private banks and insurance companies by encouraging more competition in the financial system. These measures, in turn, would help jumpstart economic growth at a time when Japan's rapidly aging society and shrinking workforce were placing ever-greater demands on the fiscal resources of the state. Strengthening the financial sector through radical postal reform, Koizumi further argued, would do far more to help the economy than any other tool at the state's disposal, including tax increases (Koizumi 1999, 2).

Koizumi and his allies also worried about growing financial and administrative inefficiencies within the postal services. Just as the JNR and NTT had struggled to keep up with competition from new technologies, the mail service began experiencing deficits from the early 1990s as the volume of letter deliveries declined in response to the proliferation of e-mail and mobile phones. These deficits were almost impossible to correct, thanks to the mail service's high fixed labour costs and other financial inflexibilities. Furthermore, virtually all non-urban commissioned post offices were operating in the red, a situation that would be hard to overcome as long as rural and semi-rural populations continued to decline and costly commissioned post offices resisted amalgamation (Matsubara 2001, 39–40, 80). The 2003 corporatization of the postal system was designed to solve some of these problems by subjecting the services to more rigorous accounting methods and stronger incentives to turn a profit, but reformers criticized the plan for allowing postal employees to retain their (costly) status as public servants. Reformers were also concerned that the administrators of each service could still cover the financial losses of specific regions with proceeds from more profitable regions, thereby dampening incentives to introduce cost-cutting reforms to the postal network.

Critics also lambasted the perquisites enjoyed by the postal savings system, all of which continued after 2003. The system was exempted from paying property or corporate taxes, even though it collected deposits, made investments, and paid interest to its customers like any private bank (Matsubara 2001, 85). The system was also authorized to pay higher interest rates on deposits than its private competitors, and its deposits were guaranteed by the state. And while both the postal system and the banks offered ten-year time deposits at fixed interest rates compounded semi-annually, only the postal system allowed depositors to withdraw their funds after six months without penalty. By the late 1990s, as Hashimoto's financial liberalization policies were implemented, the private banks had lost their tolerance of the postal savings system's many privileges and were pressuring LDP reformers to take action. Koizumi was happy to comply.

Before 2001, efforts to reform the postal system were piecemeal at best. Part of the problem was that, with the exception of many bankers and economists, few Japanese sensed that anything was wrong with the system; in fact, most praised the state-backed postal savings system for being far more attentive to their needs than the private banks (Amyx, Takenaka, and Toyoda 2005, 31). Consequently, the postal reform debate during the 1960s and 1970s never progressed past the vague ruminations of government advisory councils that the postal savings system was diverting funds away from the private banking sector and that further research on reform was necessary. In 1987, after failing to put postal privatization on the government agenda, Nakasone managed to cobble together a coalition in the Diet that voted to eliminate the tax-free status of postal savings accounts for all but the elderly, the handicapped, and single mothers. The measure failed to create a level playing field between the banks and the postal savings system, however, since it did nothing to reduce the postal system's comparative advantage in fixed long-term deposits (Rosenbluth 1989, 167, 204, 206). In the late 1990s, Prime Minister Hashimoto included postal privatization in his agenda to liberalize the financial system, but failed to achieve that goal (Mishima 1998, 975). Thanks in no small part to Koizumi, who as minister of health and welfare threatened to resign his portfolio and bring down the cabinet if significant postal reforms were not introduced, Hashimoto managed to score a few smaller victories. First, it was at this time that legislation to transform the state-owned postal services into a public corporation was passed. Second, Hashimoto dealt a heavy blow to the FILP by granting the postal system complete control over the investment of postal savings deposits and insurance premiums, a measure that went into effect in 2001.

Koizumi himself was no stranger to frustrated expectations in his drive to privatize the postal services. In summer 2002, he ushered a series of bills through the Diet that laid out an institutional framework for the new public corporation (Japan Post) and introduced more private sector competition into the mail delivery services. But the law was riddled with loopholes. For example, in a move that mimicked the regulatory empowerment of the MPT following the privatization of NTT, the legislation gave the MIC the authority to control entry into the mail services sector. Potential entrants, moreover, had to agree to erect 100,000 mailboxes around the country – a prohibitive and unnecessary expense for parcel delivery firms like Yamato that were accustomed to servicing their customers door-to-door or in retail shops. Together, these provisions effectively closed the national market to competition.[15]

These loopholes were the handiwork of the postal lobby. In a classic case of interparty collaboration, by the mid-1990s, the lobby had expanded to include not only the postal workers but also, by the end of the decade, members of the Democratic Party of Japan (DPJ), the workers' party of choice following the decline of the Socialist Party. What brought these two left-leaning groups into a loose alliance with the postmasters and the LDP was the fear of what privatization might do to the postal workers' future employment prospects. As Koizumi prepared to submit his reform bills to the Diet in 2002, the anti-reform coalition unleashed a lobbying and public relations campaign that appealed to the public's penchant for financial security and extolled the postal system as a symbol of both Japanese economic modernization and traditional values. The campaign set the ruling party against itself. In contrast to the JNR and NTT cases, in which Nakasone and his allies eventually won united LDP support for privatization, Koizumi – like his predecessors – had far more trouble uniting the party behind postal reform. According to LDP sources, many conservative Diet members opposed reform for fear that it would lead to post office closures and a further weakening of the postmasters' vote-mobilizing functions.[16] Put simply – and in marked contrast to the employees of the JNR and NTT – the postmasters were still important to many LDP politicians as one of the last organized buffers against the electoral whims of the rising floating vote.

The bureaucracy was also divided against itself. In the JNR privatization case, Nakasone successfully brought the Ministry of Transportation in line with Rinchou's reform plan. In the NTT case, MITI wrangled with the MPT for more control over telecommunications, but the pro-reform MPT eventually manoeuvred itself into the driver's seat. Two ministries vied for supremacy in the case of postal reform: the MPT, which from the start was either opposed to or decidedly lukewarm on reform,[17] and the MOF, the more pro-reform ministry that administered the FILP and represented the interests of the banking industry.[18] But, as Rosenbluth points out, there was no policy-making mechanism in place to resolve these bureaucratic differences; instead, the two ministries had to fight it out as equals, hoping at best for a compromise solution (1989, 168). The role of the prime minister in this context was to help broker that compromise, but given the often diametrically opposed interests of the two camps, compromise proved elusive.

In sum, many of the same interest group and institutional dynamics that conditioned the scope of telecommunications and railway reform were shaping the politics of postal privatization. In the JNR case, a divided union movement and a more-or-less unified bureaucratic-party nexus produced a reform package that radically transformed the transportation sector. In the NTT case, a united union movement and a loosely allied bureaucratic-party nexus imposed a moderate organizational overhaul of the telecommunications sector. It should come as no surprise, then, that a fiercely united alliance of interest groups and a divided bureaucratic-party nexus spelled failure for the movement to privatize the postal services – at least until 2004–05.

Koizumi's Gambit

Much to everyone's surprise, Koizumi pulled off a courageous gambit in late 2005 that enabled him to transcend the power alignments of the postal system.

On 5 July, the lower house of the Diet passed Koizumi's bills by a five-vote margin, with thirty-seven LDP members voting against and fourteen others either abstaining from or boycotting the vote.[19] This narrow victory did little to reassure Koizumi and his team as they prepared to push the bills through the upper house, where LDP opposition to postal privatization was especially strong. In an attempt to cow his opponents, Koizumi threatened to call a snap election for the lower house should the bills ultimately fail, vowing to discipline all of those in the LDP who had voted against him. His warnings fell on deaf ears. On 8 August, the upper chamber roundly defeated the bills by a vote of 125 to 108, with thirty LDP lawmakers either abstaining or voting against the government. Against the wishes of most LDP leaders, Koizumi made good on his threats by calling an election for 11 September, which was to be fought as a virtual referendum on postal privatization.

Koizumi refused to offer the party's official endorsement to those who had opposed the legislation, forcing them to run as independents or to form new parties – the most significant of which was the People's New Party (PNP). He then unleashed a slew of young, attractive 'assassins' to run against the 'postal rebels' in their respective constituencies. The LDP went on to score its biggest win ever, clinching 296 of 480 seats. The much smaller Komeitou also did well, bringing the total number of seats won by the LDP-Komeitou coalition to 327. A month later, Koizumi's postal privatization bills sailed through both houses of the Diet with strong majorities; most of the LDP members who had voted against privatization over the summer now supported them.

By going over the heads of his party opponents and appealing directly to the public for support, Koizumi temporarily neutralized the MIC's decidedly cautious stance on privatization and unified the LDP behind reform. In so doing, he put the postal lobby firmly on the defensive. By refusing the LDP's official endorsement of anti-reform politicians, Koizumi forced Zentoku and Taiju to make a difficult choice: support LDP candidates across the board and increase the likelihood that postal privatization would succeed, or side with the opposition parties and risk the further demise of what remained of their exchange relationship with the LDP – a relationship that continued to comprise the heart of the postal lobby. Torn between these equally unattractive choices, Zentoku threw up its hands and instructed the postmasters to vote their consciences. Meanwhile, Taiju chapters around the country announced that they were formally severing their ties with the party, in many cases asking their LDP consultants to resign their positions.[20] But since many Taiju members still felt a strong sense of attachment to the party, the association duplicated Zentoku's policy of allowing members to make their own decisions at the ballot box.[21] And so, on 11 September, many postmasters and their retired colleagues cast their lots with the rebels, while in constituencies without rebel candidates, many cut their ties with the LDP and sided with the PNP or the DPJ. Still others remained loyal to the LDP in the expectation that Koizumi would soon leave the political scene and the exchange relationship between themselves and the LDP would 'return to normal.' Although several rebels were returned to the Diet as independents, the postmasters emerged from the election divided among themselves and with their collective electoral clout significantly diminished.[22]

It is tempting to conclude that these divide-and-conquer electoral tactics were the sole handiwork of a brilliant political strategist. But while Koizumi should be credited for skilfully manipulating the political rules of the game to his advantage, reducing postal reform to only one variable – effective leadership – begs an important question: why did Prime Minister Nakasone not pull the same stunt in the 1980s or Prime Minister Hashimoto in the late 1990s? The answer, I argue, is that Koizumi was operating in a much different institutional setting.

A number of institutional developments warrant attention in this regard, the first of which was the replacement of the Prime Minister's Office with a more powerful Cabinet Office as part of the Hashimoto government's reorganization of government during the late 1990s.[23] Launched in 2001, the Cabinet Office contains a number of new posts designed to enhance the prime minister's leadership capabilities, including five ministers of state in charge of administrative reform, economic and fiscal affairs, and the like (Mulgan 2002, 73). For much of Koizumi's tenure as prime minister, Takenaka Heizou occupied the position of minister of state for economic and fiscal policy, using it to orchestrate the details of a number of reform projects, including postal privatization. Also important was the creation of four standing committees that arguably surpassed even the old Rinchou in stature. Of particular note was the Council on Economic and Fiscal Policy (CEFP), which was designed to give the prime minister more authority in economic affairs. Unlike Rinchou, which was comprised largely of government outsiders, the CEFP was chaired by the prime minister and consisted of the bureaucracy's leading economic ministers, including the minister of internal affairs and communications, the governor of the Bank of Japan, and a handful of private sector businessmen and scholars. As Miura (in this volume) illustrates in the case of labour policy, by pulling the government's key economic and fiscal decision-makers out of their ministerial contexts and into a high-level forum where they were forced to interact with leading thinkers from the private sector, the CEFP reduced bureaucratic localism and interministerial competition – something that the Rinchou ultimately was unable to achieve. Also in contrast to the Rinchou, the fact that CEFP proceedings were open to public scrutiny meant that it was now much more difficult for Koizumi's opponents to sabotage the reform process (see Estevez-Abe 2006, 645). As such, the CEFP's establishment marked a notable step towards strengthening the hand of the prime minister and his cabinet vis-à-vis the career bureaucracy.

With Takenaka at the helm, the CEFP was well positioned to take the lead in the postal privatization process. Despite its many advantages, however, it was not completely immune to interest group pressures. From the start, deliberations were mired in conflict and stalemates as various ministerial members voiced their misgivings about the privatization plan. Asou Tarou, the minister of internal affairs and communications, argued forcibly against breaking up the postal system into its component services, a position that reflected the postal lobby's concerns that privatization accompanied by break-up would lead to bankruptcies within the postal network and hence weaken the electoral influence of the postmasters (Takenaka 2006). The solution to this impasse was to delegate the work of hammering out a blueprint for postal privatization and, later, the privatization bills, to the Postal Privatization Preparatory Office, an organ consisting of scholars and bureaucrats loyal to Takenaka that was located in the Cabinet Secretariat. Circumventing the council in this way enabled Takenaka and Koizumi to further transcend the traditional interest group machinations that continued to plague the reformed policy process. Consequently, the two ultimately were able to produce a plan that removed the three main postal services from under a single institutional roof while subjecting the postal savings and insurance systems to privatization. Koizumi was also sufficiently emboldened by his heightened policy-making authority to submit his bills to the Diet despite opposition from key LDP leaders. This was in marked defiance of LDP custom, which demanded the unanimous (or near unanimous) support of the party leadership before bills were adopted by the cabinet.

In the final analysis, however, the prime minister's enhanced powers to set the policy-making agenda and control the formulation of bills were not enough to get those bills through the Diet in summer 2005. It was at this point that Koizumi took full advantage of changes to Japan's electoral laws. In 1994, Japan shifted from a multi-member-district system, which encouraged LDP candidates to compete as individuals by promising pork-barrel benefits to their constituents, to a hybrid system of single-member (300 seats) and proportional representation districts (180 seats) that provided political parties with incentives to campaign along policy lines. But it took some time for the parties to adjust to the new system. In subsequent elections, policy discussions were disappointingly weak as candidates resorted to tried-and-true tactics to gather the vote. When Prime Minister Hashimoto first pushed for postal reform in 1997, shortly after the first election held under the new electoral rules, he was not in a position to threaten a snap election to push his reform agenda since his party was still recovering from its temporary fall from power in 1993. In 2005, by contrast, Koizumi was in a much stronger position. The new electoral rules had been in place for more than a decade, and the prime minister had less to lose after a lengthy four and a half years in power. Consequently, Koizumi cast the election as a referendum on postal privatization, appealing directly to the population's growing stratum of floating voters – young, well-educated, and largely urban professionals who were far less susceptible than rural residents to the overtures of local opinion leaders such as the postmasters.

In sum, the same sorts of interest group and bureaucratic dynamics that conditioned the NTT and JNR privatization processes were in place in the postal privatization case – so much so, in fact, that one would have expected the opposition of the anti-reform coalition to spell ultimate failure for Koizumi's more diffusely organized privatization movement. What tipped the balance in Koizumi's favour was his skilful use of a new, highly transparent government council and supporting institutions to hammer together a blueprint for postal privatization in defiance of interest groups, bureaucratic actors, and key LDP leaders. Once those special interests caught up with him during the Diet votes of July and August 2005, Koizumi activated the full potential of the new electoral system, appealing directly to the public for support. In a sense, Koizumi resembled Nakasone, who also appealed to public opinion as he struggled to defeat his political rivals. But Koizumi was institutionally positioned to achieve significantly more than his predecessor as he subjected Japan's 'stickiest' public corporation to comprehensive reform and destroyed the exchange relationship between the LDP and the postmasters.

Epilogue: Backtracking on Postal Privatization

Since the mid-1980s, Japanese reformers have scored a few hard-won victories that together pushed the political economy towards a neoliberal capitalist model. As we have seen in the JNR and NTT privatization cases, however, the neoliberal reform process in Japan has tended to leave a number of key traditional institutions and ideological principles intact.

Postal privatization is the most recent case in point. Needless to say, Koizumi's electoral and legislative victories ushered in major changes for the postal system and its associated interest groups. As noted in the introduction, the corporate structure of the old state-run postal system was completely transformed. Government guarantees of new postal savings accounts were abolished. The postal lobby's influence declined as postmasters and postal workers lost their status as public servants and the postal network company began purchasing postal facilities from the commissioned postmasters. Zentei, for its part, became a private sector union, a development that Nakasone – now in his early nineties – must surely be celebrating. Taken together, these changes advanced the liberal economic principles of individual and corporate self-responsibility, competition, and risk taking.

Just as Koizumi's 2005 electoral victory should not be interpreted as a straightforward vote for neoliberal reform, the implementation of postal privatization did not entail the wholesale abolition of more 'traditional' economic principles; rather, the evidence suggests that a significant portion of the population still adheres to the values of state-led capitalism. Consider, for example, the 2005 election returns. The fact that the LDP's share of the popular vote increased only marginally over the previous election suggests that Koizumi's appeal to the values of liberal capitalism did not significantly sway the thinking of ordinary people. The returns also suggest that older political and economic values are still important in the countryside: of the sixteen anti-privatization candidates running in rural areas – areas where clientelistic ties between the old LDP and interest groups are strongest and the social contributions of the postal system most significant – thirteen were re-elected.[24] Koizumi did far better among the floating voters, most of whom live in urban areas. A poll conducted by *Yomiuri Shimbun* in the wake of the election revealed that, of eighty-four suburban constituencies in areas surrounding Tokyo, the LDP captured seventy-one, up from thirty-three in the 2003 lower house election.[25] These results indicate the effects of the significant urban-rural divide in terms of Japanese views of the political economy. While the cities *might* have some sympathy for Koizumi's liberal economic thinking, the countryside is still steeped in the values and ideas of a bygone era.

Nor did the 2005 legislation completely eliminate the postal lobby – to the contrary, that the legislation provided little more than a general outline of privatization gave the lobby ample opportunity to regroup and assert its collective interests as privatization unfolded. Unlike the JNR and NTT privatization processes, which settled most of the relevant reform details *before* legislation was put to a vote, many of the details of postal privatization were left unresolved. One possible reason for this was that Koizumi hoped to avoid conflicts with the postal lobby that could have derailed the overall privatization plan. Similar calculations might have motivated Koizumi's decision after his electoral victory to resubmit his privatization bills to the Diet without amendments – even though he appeared to have a public mandate to eliminate some of the concessions that had been granted to the postal lobby.

Among those concessions was a decision *not* to break up the massive postal savings system into regional corporations, as Koizumi had advocated before becoming prime minister (see Mizuno et al. 2001, 19–25). From the reform camp's perspective, breaking up postal savings would have been the wise thing to do in order to create a more level playing field with the private banking sector, which is organized into regional and city banks. The establishment of a *national* postal savings bank positioned regions that profit from the sale of postal savings accounts to cover for those areas that do less well, thereby preserving a long-standing commitment to universal service and the provision of a stable savings environment for all Japanese – two hallmark values of the old postal system. The survival of a national postal savings system differentiates postal privatization from the privatization of the JNR, which involved a break-up of the old public corporation into financially discrete regional firms.

The government made a number of other concessions to the principles of universal service and, more broadly, equality between rural and urban areas. While at one time Koizumi wished for the complete privatization of the mail service, he eventually succumbed to the postal lobby's pressure to preserve government ownership and the long-standing government monopoly on letter delivery. The rationale behind his decision was to guarantee mail service to sparsely populated (and hence unprofitable) communities.[26] Takenaka took this commitment one step further in a move that was reminiscent of government pledges to maintain universal rail service during the 1980s. During the latter stages of the policy-making process, he repeatedly promised that each and every town and village in Japan would continue to have a post office – a promise that might not have been very cost effective but that nevertheless assuaged the fears of rural citizens that privatization might shrink the postal network and the many social and economic services it provided.[27] Also significant was the government's promise to establish a ¥2 trillion fund to help keep struggling post offices afloat and guarantee their provision of informal social welfare services at the local level. Resembling the management stabilization funds established by the government during the 1980s, the fund would consist of proceeds from the sale of the shares of Japan Post Holdings in the banking and insurance firms. As one scholarly participant in the policy-making process observed, these concessions meshed well with such traditional Japanese values as social equality, risk aversion, financial security, and the integrity of the local community.[28] To be sure, they also served the political interests of the postal lobby, which, as we have seen, enjoys its strongest support in rural and semi-rural communities.

While the postal lobby was significantly weakened during the Koizumi years, it is now regrouping in ways that do not bode well for the long-term privatization process. At first, Zentoku moved to re-establish ties with old LDP allies as part of a broader effort to soften the effects of privatization on the institutions of the commissioned postal system. For the most part, traditionalists in the LDP were happy to play along. In November 2006, in a move to shore up the party's long-term electoral strength, then-prime minister Abe readmitted eleven postal rebels back into the LDP fold. Although the rebels were required to sign a pledge upholding the tenets of postal privatization, many of them went on to link arms with the postmasters on behalf of common goals. Then, the new president of the prototype of Japan Post Holdings, Nishikawa Yoshifumi, discarded a plan drawn up by Ikuta Masaharu, the president of Japan Post until spring 2007, to abolish Tokusuiren and replace it with a new administrative organ connected to the privatized postal firms – a plan that threatened to destroy the postmasters' distinctive occupational identity. Nishikawa agreed to allow the commissioned postmasters to organize themselves after October 2007. While we may never know whether Nishikawa was responding directly to LDP pressures, his actions certainly complemented LDP efforts to mend fences with the postmasters in the lead-up to the July 2007 upper house election.

That said, the postmasters associations refused to return to the LDP fold *en masse,* as the outcomes of the 2007, 2009, and 2010 elections show. In 2007, the postmasters' electoral loyalties remained split: while some Zentoku and Taiju chapters gravitated towards the LDP during the election, others backed the PNP – the party of former LDP 'rebels' – which elected one member to the chamber. By the election of 30 August 2009, however, it was clear that the postmasters were now on the side of the DPJ and the PNP. Campaigning on an anti-structural-reform platform that included a pledge to introduce changes to Koizumi's postal privatization plan, the DPJ attracted a degree of support from the postmasters that must have been the envy of the LDP. In district after district following the dissolution of the Diet on 21 July, the postmasters and their spouses and retired colleagues distributed fliers, participated in rallies, manned the phones at candidates' electoral headquarters, and helped persuade voters to vote for the DPJ and the PNP.[29] And they did so in full view of the media for the first time in more than sixty years, now that they had lost their status as public servants and were thus no longer prohibited by the 1948 National Public Service Law from participating in electoral campaigns. Although the postmasters were far less consequential than the floating voters in bringing the DPJ to power, they continued to support the DPJ and the PNP in the July 2010 upper house election and are likely to continue doing so for as long as these two parties advocate the reform of at least some of Koizumi's handiwork.

As of this writing, the DPJ coalition government has pledged to pass a bill that would do more than reform Koizumi's postal privatization legislation – it would all but reverse it. Spearheaded by the PNP's Kamei Shizuka, a former postal rebel and minister for financial and postal services in the cabinet of former prime minister Hatoyama Yukio,[30] the reform plan includes measures to reorganize the corporate structure of the Japan Post Group, raise the ceiling on postal savings deposits from ¥10 million to ¥20 million, increase postal insurance policy benefits, introduce universal service in postal savings and insurance, and

convert tens of thousands of part-time postal employees into permanent employees. Together, these reforms would increase the comparative advantage of Japan Post Bank in the financial sector, enhance the
postal system's contributions to society, strengthen the hand of government in the services, and dramatically increase costs within the postal
system.

To a significant degree, this political about-face reflects a number of practical problems within the privatization process. Local post
offices have been plagued by long lines as postal workers adjust to the
post-2007 corporate division of labour and a host of new regulatory
requirements. Local residents have complained of a decline in informal social services performed by their postmasters and mail carriers.
Finally, several hundred 'simple post offices' have closed their doors
in anticipation of enhanced competition, and commissioned post
offices are struggling to increase profitability. The fact that these problems appeared in the midst of the post-2008 global economic downturn
and as depopulation and economic decline continues in the countryside has simply strengthened pressures on the powers-that-be to slow
the pace of postal privatization.

More to the point, the coalition government's postal reform proposal
reflects recent changes in Japanese politics. Although the powerful
exchange relationship between the postmasters and sympathetic LDP
lawmakers has been broken and the postal lobby has lost its organizational cohesiveness, the balance of power between the lobby – now
loosely defined – and advocates of structural reform seems to be shifting once again in favour of the former. The DPJ's dependence on the
tiny PNP in both the 2009 lower house and 2010 upper house elections
has positioned the tiny anti-privatization party to influence the parameters of reform proposals significantly. Meanwhile, Koizumi's allies are
out of power, and many conservative politicians implicitly support the
DPJ coalition government's official position that postal privatization
should be reformed. Finally, as the coalition's sweeping electoral victory in late summer 2009 suggests, the Japanese public is rapidly losing
its tolerance for wrenching structural reforms. In short, and to borrow a
phrase from Schoppa (Chapter 1 in this volume), political realignments
have pulled Japan towards a reprioritization of policies that protect the
'little guy.' Against this backdrop, measures to salvage the socially sensitive institutions of the old post office from the 'dehumanizing' processes of privatization make good political sense.

In the final analysis, it is uncertain whether Kamei's anti-privatization blueprint will prevail. The government, after all, is divided on the issue and Prime Minister Kan Naoto lacks the leadership skills of a Nakasone or Koizumi to put together a winning coalition; Kan, meanwhile, seems much less interested in prioritizing postal reform than his predecessor was. The loss of the coalition government's majority in the upper house during the summer 2010 election, moreover, has lessened the odds that radical reform will ever take place. But when all is said and done, there remain strong pockets of opposition to Koizumi's structural reforms within not only the DPJ and the PNP but also the LDP; for as long as such opposition persists, some degree of reform remains a distinct possibility. In sum, Koizumi might have introduced some remarkable changes to the political economy, but Japan has yet to uproot the interests, institutions, and ideas that characterized the state-led postal system and that remain hallmarks of the country's traditional brand of capitalism.

NOTES

1 I would like to thank the two anonymous reviewers for their insightful suggestions for revising this chapter. I am also very grateful to the Shibusawa Foundation for their generous financial support.
2 In March 2001, the postal savings system held ¥250 trillion in deposits, or approximately 35 per cent of household deposits (Doi and Hoshi 2003, 37).
3 Keidanren, the Federation of Economic Organizations, was post-war Japan's most powerful voluntary business association. Now known as Nippon Keidanren, following the merger of Keidanren with Nikkeiren, an association of business employers, the association represents and coordinates the interests of big business.
4 Since 1999, the liberalization of Japanese telecommunications has made significant progress. In response to such trends as international price competition, the rising popularity of e-mail and cell phones, and the declining demand for public telephones, the state has forced NTT, which long monopolized the domestic telephone market, to lease its domestic telephone circuits to competitors. As a result, domestic land-line rates are now dramatically lower than they were just ten or fifteen years ago, and are competitive with comparable U.S. rates.
5 The telecommunications and postal workers were members of the same radical union until the early 1950s, when the former created their own union following the establishment of NTT.

6 Launched in 1953, Zentoku is a 'voluntary organization' of commissioned postmasters that consists of several layers of organizations extending from the national level to the local level. It is the postmasters' primary institutional vehicle for participating in politics.

7 'Yuusei ikka [The postal family],' *Asahi Shimbun*, 13 August 2005.

8 *Asahi Shimbun* (ibid.) estimates that the postmasters gathered only 280,000 votes behind a former MIC official in the 2004 election.

9 The MIC oversaw a number of small public or semi-public corporations that helped implement postal functions. These corporations were prized destinations for bureaucrats following their retirement from the ministry.

10 'Postal unit fined for not declaring income,' *Japan Times*, 29 October 2001; the Center achieved notoriety in spring 2001 for failing to declare about ¥120 million in income over a three-year period.

11 Interview, Zentoku official, Tokyo, 27 March 2003.

12 Of course, not all commissioned postmasters enjoyed the respect of local residents. The historical record is littered with accounts of individual postmasters who illegally pocketed their government allowances and shirked their duties. During the post-war period, however, postmasters were sufficiently concerned about their futures to make a concerted attempt to shore up their reputations as pillars of local Japan.

13 In March 2001, the FILP consisted of ¥418 trillion, the equivalent of approximately 82 per cent of Japan's annual gross domestic product (Doi and Hoshi 2003, 37).

14 Interviews with commissioned postmasters, summer 2002 and spring 2003.

15 The MIC applied its regulatory authority differently in the telecommunications and mail delivery spheres. With regard to NTT, it used its powers to weaken the corporation's stranglehold over the market and encourage competition; in the mail delivery case, however, its ultimate aim was to limit competition. One reason for this discrepancy is that, since the government continues to enjoy a legal monopoly on letter delivery, it could limit private competition to the delivery of flyers, catalogues, certain kinds of magazines, and the like. The government was reluctant to welcome new entrants into the market because of the mail service's inherent vulnerabilities: high fixed costs, the absence of new technologies that might lower those costs, and the already high price of postage.

16 Interviews with LDP Diet members, Tokyo, March 2003 and July 2006.

17 The MIC did not officially oppose privatization. It was, however, very particular about the *kind* of privatization that should be allowed, favouring only limited competition in the three services and opposing the break-up of the postal system into four independent corporations.

18 The MOF's pro-reform stance should not be exaggerated. The ministry actually hesitated to support changes that might weaken the FILP. The banks, for the most part, supported reform in principle but were wary of privatization on the grounds that it might actually empower the postal savings system.

19 'Postal privatization bills squeak by lower house,' *Japan Times*, 6 July 2005.

20 'Min'eikasansei zengiin zetsuenjou [On the severing of ties with former Dietmembers who had voted for privatization],' *Yomiuri Shimbun*, 12 August 2005.

21 'Yuusei ikka,' *Asahi Shimbun*, 13 August 2005.

22 See Reed (in this volume) for a detailed discussion of the electoral fate of the LDP's postal rebels.

23 Hashimoto's efforts to empower the prime minister were in large part a response to growing political concern about the ineffectiveness of prime ministerial leadership during national emergencies and economic crises (Shinoda 2007, 63).

24 I thank Ethan Scheiner for providing me with these observations. Carlson (2008) argues that the electoral success of the rebels is attributable at least in part to the ability of incumbents to hold on to funds amassed before they lost the LDP's electoral backing, as well as to their ability to raise more funds than less experienced 'assassins.' (After the 2005 election, Koizumi introduced changes that would prohibit the transfer of funds from a politician's party branch to other personal organizations upon leaving the party.) These trends point to the lingering importance of money politics and the 'personal vote' in Japanese politics.

25 'Jimintou wa beddotaun de gisekizou [LDP increases seats in suburbs],' *Yomiuri Shimbun*, 12 September 2005.

26 Interview, Professor Yoshino Naoyuki, Keio University, Tokyo, 15 July 2006.

27 Ibid.

28 Ibid.

29 The postmasters' activities on behalf of the DPJ were chronicled in August 2009 in prefecture-specific articles in the My Town series of *Asahi Shimbun*.

30 Kamei resigned from the cabinet in June 2010 on the grounds that the DPJ was dragging its feed on postal reform. He was replaced as minister of postal privatization by Jimi Shouzaburou, a former LDP Diet member and diehard Koizumi foe.

7 Reforming Government Financial Institutions

A. MARIA TOYODA

In the post–World War Two era, policy-based financing was at the centre of Japan's state-led development. Though many nations, ranging from South Korea to France, have employed schemes to direct credit to key sectors, few mobilized private savings for policy-based financing directed at targeted sectors of the economy to the degree that, and as successfully as, Japan did in the second half of the twentieth century. There are simply no parallels to Japan's Fiscal Investment and Loan Program (FILP) in terms of size, scope, and penetration. The FILP system, established in 1953, drew upon private savings primarily through the conduit of the postal savings system, and channelled the capital through a network of government financial institutions (GFIs) that acted as niche lenders to sectors ranging from heavy industry and highways to housing, agriculture, and small business. The high rate of investment enabled by this system helped propel Japan's 'miracle' economy, while also spreading its benefits to farmers and small businessmen who were key supporters of conservative rule.

By the late 1970s, however, this system of policy-based financing was becoming increasingly incongruent with Japan's financial and economic conditions. Though Japan was no longer short of capital or in need of massive investment to stimulate catch-up growth, the FILP and the GFIs remained larger than ever. Shrinking and reforming this sector proved thornier than creating and expanding it, for these institutions had become key instruments of a network that bound together Liberal Democratic Party (LDP) politicians, key voting constituencies and party supporters, postal workers and postmasters, and financial bureaucrats. These concentrated and privileged interests were in favour of perpetuating the institutions of policy-based financing. Through most of the 1980s and into the 1990s, they successfully resisted meaningful reform. Yet, by the late 1990s, the government had resolved to eliminate many of the GFIs, change their funding structures, and privatize postal savings.

This chapter examines how this happened. The puzzle is complex since institutional stickiness created by vested interests and an interlocking set of practices, rules, and expectations is easier to explain than the reform of the government financial system over the past decade. This is especially the case since the potential beneficiaries of change were weaker, less organized, and more uncertain of their gains than were their opponents. So the puzzle this chapter sets out to solve is this: in the face of concentrated, organized, and motivated interests in favour of preserving the FILP and the GFIs, why and how was the system of policy-based financing reformed? How were GFIs eliminated, merged, privatized, and cut off from easy funding through the postal savings system? How was institutional inertia finally overcome?

The chapter unfolds as follows. In the next section, I provide some background on the role that GFIs played in policy-based financing and their relationship to the system of postal savings and the FILP. I also outline the political interests that have coalesced around the system, and highlight the key relationships that would be undermined by reform. I then explain why FILP reform emerged on the agenda, while ruling out simple explanations that might attribute the change entirely to economic necessity – FILP reform has been on the agenda for thirty years, but it has moved forward only in fits and starts. In the third section, I explain how reform became possible as political openings were successfully exploited by Prime Ministers Nakasone, Hashimoto, and Koizumi. I then examine how the diminution of reform energy in the years since Koizumi left office helps to clarify why that prime minister and his reformist predecessors were able to push through reforms. In the last section, however, I emphasize that, despite recent rollbacks under the Democratic Party of Japan (DPJ) government, the reforms of the old policy-based financial system remain a significant change in Japan's political economy.

The FILP System

GFIs are a subset of the special public corporations (*tokushuu houjin*) that were funded directly by the FILP until 2001 and thereafter through a more indirect route.[1] The FILP, in turn, until the 2001 reform, was funded through Japan's Postal Savings System plus some pension reserve funds and through direct transfers from the Ministry of Finance's Trust Fund Bureau. Indeed, Japan's experience with financing through postal savings dates back to 1874, not long after the nation's basic banking system laws were put in place. During the Meiji and Taishou modernization periods, postal savings were mobilized through the 'reserve fund system,' which provided financing for the construction of railroads and communications infrastructure (Miyawaki 1993) as well as for the first Sino-Japanese and Russo-Japanese Wars. During the war years of the 1930s and 1940s, the system was used to accelerate military spending and expansion in China.

In the early post-war period, the system was further institutionalized with the passage of the 1947 Postal Savings Law and the assignment of oversight functions for policy-based financing to the Trust Fund Bureau. Scholars writing about Japan's post-war political economy concur that this system was central to the nation's reconstruction and industrial policy, and served as a key institution for guiding Japan's rapid economic rise in the 1950s and 1960s (see, for example, Johnson 1982; Kato et al. 1994). This system put important levers of power over industrial expansion in the hands of two powerful ministries, the Ministry of International Trade and Industry and the Ministry of Finance. The flow of scarce capital was tightly controlled, and meted out to private banks selectively by the Bank of Japan under the close scrutiny of the Ministry of Finance through 'window guidance.'[2] As was the case for many countries in Europe, postal savings were also mobilized for public use, to build infrastructure and invest in industrial capacity. In the decades following Japan's defeat, this system routing postal savings through the FILP to GFIs played a central role in public finance, closely interlocked with macroeconomic and industrial policies. A few GFIs, such as the Japan Development Bank, the Export-Import Bank, and the Industrial Bank of Japan (which was private, but worked in close coordination with the government), were essential for reconstruction and industrial recovery.[3]

GFIs served not only to direct credit to growth sectors during the decades of Japan's post-war reconstruction; in later years, they also distributed the rewards of high economic growth to LDP supporters, provided finance to prop up fading industries, and helped these industries adjust strategically by exporting their operations to other Asian countries (see Solis 2004). For instance, GFIs provided finance to regional craft and farm cooperatives and to small businesses that did not have easy access to capital through city or regional banks. In doing so, GFIs served a social welfare function, providing these sectors with a financial safety net and helping to spread the wealth. Government finance thus provided some stability during the otherwise volatile period of scarce capital in Japan, helped to cushion the pain of economic slowdown after the oil price shocks of the 1970s, and shielded small businesses and farmers as trade and investment liberalization took effect. In short, GFIs funded through the postal savings system were a central tool of Japanese distributive politics and economic adjustment.

During the period of intense administrative control of capital, policy-based financing gradually began to take on an increasingly political guise as the government created a large number of public corporations (*koueki houjin*), the proliferation of which was funded through growing tax receipts as government expanded following the Korean War (Colignon and Usui 2003, 45) – one estimate puts the total number of such corporations in 2003 at around 26,000 (Carpenter 2003, 2). Public corporations allowed the government to spend money for certain purposes outside the regular budget process, insulated from political interference from either politicians or bureaucrats in competing ministries (Johnson 1978, 25).

Of special consequence to our story, however, is that *koueki houjin* provided benefits not only to politicians but also to bureaucrats, by offering them post-retirement jobs. Since the career ladder employed by government ministries forced most bureaucrats to retire before age fifty-five, post-retirement employment in public corporations – a practice known as *amakudari*[4] – was a major preoccupation of officials seeking to maintain or boost their incomes. The final placement of retiring bureaucrats depended almost entirely on whether their home ministry had administrative authority, formal or otherwise, over the public body. Therefore, each ministry had significant incentives to support the creation of *koueki houjin* that would fall under its jurisdiction.

Tokushuu houjin, or special public corporations, is a distinct category of *koueki houjin,* created by Diet legislation that specified their functions, structure, management, and funding (Johnson 1978). Two classes of special public corporations were authorized to borrow from the FILP: public corporations, such as the Japan Highway Public Corporation and the Forest Development Corporation, that engaged mainly in public infrastructure works, and *tokushuu hojin* that were GFIs (see Table 7.1). These were especially prized retirement destinations for senior bureaucrats.

Table 7.1 Founding Dates and Functions of FILP-Funded Government Financial Institutions

Government Financial Institution	Founding Date	Function
People's Finance Corporation	1949	Credit for small and medium-sized businesses; merged in 2000 to become the National Life Finance Corporation
Government Housing Loan Corporation	1950	Housing loans
Export-Import Bank	1950	Long-term funding to promote exports, imports, and foreign direct investment in Japan; merged with the Overseas Economic Cooperation Fund in 2000 to become the Japan Bank for International Cooperation
Japan Development Bank	1951	Long-term industrial loans; starting in 1988, lending for infrastructure and venture firms; merged in 2000 to become the Development Bank of Japan
Japan Finance Corporation for Small Businesses	1953	Long-term loans for small businesses
Agriculture, Forestry and Fishery Finance Corporation	1953	Long-term loans for farming, forestry, and fishery businesses
Hokkaidou-Touhoku Development Corporation	1956	Long-term financing for industrial development in northern Japan; merged in 2000 to become the Development Bank of Japan
Japan Finance Corporation for Municipal Enterprises	1957	Credit for municipal enterprises to upgrade public services; local government bond purchases for infrastructure and regional industry promotion
Environmental Sanitation Business Finance Corporation	1967	Funds for modernizing public sanitation in small firms; merged in 2000 to become the National Life Finance Corporation
Okinawa Development Finance Corporation	1972	Loans to support industry and social welfare in Okinawa

Source: Japan, Ministry of Finance, Financial Bureau, *Zaisei Touyuushi Ri-pou-to* (FILP Report), various years.

Though the FILP is formally a supplement to the General Account budget, it possesses some unique characteristics compared with other types of budgetary supplements. Before the reforms, FILP budgets were not subject to legislative approval or up for debate, but the consultative process between Ministry of Finance officials and LDP politicians was intensive. One view holds that, in the earlier years of the program, the non-transparent nature of FILP allocations led to greater efficiency in public works spending because they were subject to less political pressure than spending in the General Account, and the mobilization of FILP funding – postal savings – was also less politically sensitive than raising tax revenues (see, for example, Noguchi 1995). In 1973, however, the socialists publicly complained about the secrecy surrounding the FILP and the near-total bureaucratic control over its use. Since then, the FILP and postal savings have become increasingly politicized, as is apparent when one compares the FILP spending pattern over time with that of the General Account. As Figure 7.1 shows, while General Account budget increases normally have been guided by incrementalism, FILP budget increases often have occurred abruptly. Indeed, the growth of the FILP was remarkable. In fiscal year 1955/56, the program accounted for less than 30 per cent of the General Account, but by the mid-1990s, it reached more than 65 per cent.

By and large, the beneficiaries of FILP funds were disproportionately societal sectors that regularly supported the LDP, a pattern that became more evident in the 1970s when allocations made to industrial investments began to decline and attention turned to improving social conditions (see Figure 7.2). The cabinet of Prime Minister Miki Takeo, for example, gave high priority to social welfare, emphasizing low-interest rate loans for housing and passing a Special Measures Law to Promote the Provision of Residential Housing and Land in Major Metropolitan Areas. FILP GFIs such as the Government Housing Loan Corporation were central to these initiatives.

These efforts coincided, however, with the declining electoral appeal of the LDP in a new economic climate. Some scholars note a 'crisis and compensation' pattern to FILP lending to particular sectors such as agriculture and small business during economic downturns and periods of trade liberalization (Calder 1991; Patterson 1994). Consistent with the pattern of political support for the LDP, the FILP heavily favoured rural and low-population areas. In fiscal year 2005/06, for example, FILP allocations for rural Shimane Prefecture were ¥1.38 million per capita, while Kouchi and Tottori Prefectures also posted high per capita FILP

Figure 7.1: FILP and General Account Expenditures, fiscal years 1965/66–2007/08

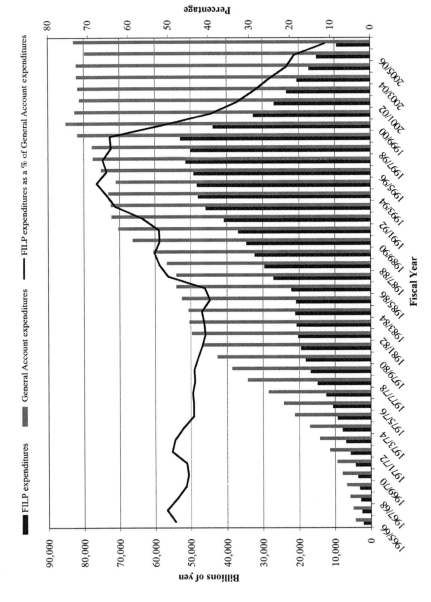

Source: Japan, Ministry of Internal Affairs and Communications, Statistics Bureau, *Kuni no Yousan* and *Keizai Toukei Nenkan*, various years.

Figure 7.2: FILP Expenditures by Category, fiscal years 1954/55–2004/05

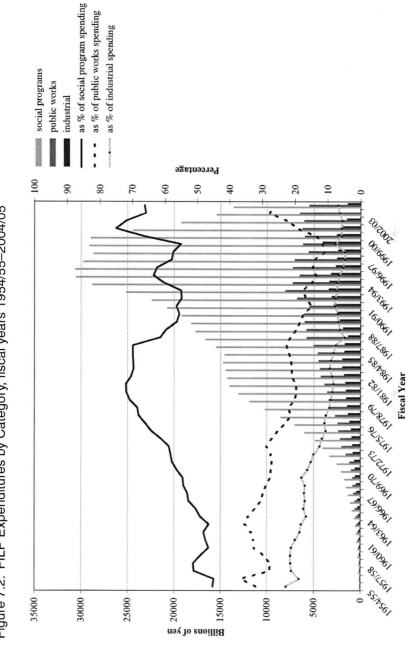

Source: Japan, Ministry of Internal Affairs and Communications, Statistics Bureau, *Kuni no Yousan* and *Keizai Toukei Nenkan,* various years.

receipts; in contrast, Tokyo and the heavily populated neighbouring Saitama and Kanagawa Prefectures received just ¥287,000 per capita.[5] Thus, localities and traditional occupational groups – agriculture, fishing, handicrafts, micro and small businesses – that were strongholds of the LDP stood to lose much from FILP reform.

The effects of reforming the FILP, therefore, have had far greater political consequences than that of the postal system reform in isolation. While privatization of the postal system directly affected the fortunes of postal workers, hereditary special postmasters, bureaucrats in the Ministry of Posts and Telecommunications, and LDP *zoku giin*, or policy tribe members, who depended on the postmasters' political networks (see Amyx, Takenaka, and Toyoda, 2005; and Maclachlan, in this volume), and perhaps led to less intensive service for some rural customers, reform of the FILP directly affected virtually all of the LDP's major constituencies and almost every government ministry.

For this reason, efforts to carry out 'administrative reforms' affecting GFIs funded through the FILP have sparked epic battles in Japanese politics over the past thirty years between politicians and bureaucrats and between different groups of politicians and competing bureaucracies. The battles have been intense because reforms threatened *amakudari* landing spots – amounting to a gutting of pensions of retiring officials[6] – and the related networking and regulatory effects of this practice. They also threatened to weaken the bureaucracy's instruments of control over localities and municipalities, and jeopardized the ability of the ruling LDP to fund items of particular interest to its key constituents, slowing the transfer of wealth and welfare to rural areas, small businesses, agriculture, the fishery and timber industries, and construction.

LDP *zoku giin*, therefore, faced huge losses in the reform game; cuts in public works spending and FILP funding meant fewer political goods to bring home to their districts. Construction *zoku giin* stood to lose important contributions from their backers in this industry, losses that trickled down to local notables who hitched their fortunes to the LDP-driven *doken kokka* (construction state). Even aspects of foreign policy were directly affected as the movement for reform spread to the Japan Bank for International Cooperation, the government bank responsible for official direct assistance to developing countries.

Despite these strong vested interests, reforms were implemented under Prime Ministers Nakasone, Hashimoto, and Koizumi. Why? I begin, in the next section, by dismissing several common explanations before turning to my preferred explanation: that bursts of reform activity occurred when previously infeasible solutions were made possible by periods of political realignment. The most important reforms occurred, I argue, when administrative reforms strengthening the Cabinet Office gave prime ministers the space to propose and drive towards radical changes. Over the course of FILP reform, political realignments mattered a great deal in the shaping of proposals and outcomes. These openings also periodically closed when there was a successful resurgence of opposition, which led to attempts to weaken or water down reform. Ultimately, though, Nakasone, Hashimoto, and Koizumi succeeded in moving reform far enough that complete backtracking was infeasible and, over time, there has been genuine transformation. The evolution of FILP reform, in short, exhibits a pattern of punctuated equilibrium.

Reform Catalysts

Several trends stimulated calls for reform of the FILP. First, the justification for policy-based financing disappeared by the mid-1960s once the post-war Japanese economy was reconstructed and the nation no longer suffered from a shortage of capital. Second, from the early 1980s private banks began to lobby heavily against the crowding out of private investment and their role in lending. Third, financial and interest rate liberalization that began in 1979 had eroded the balance sheet of the Trust Fund Bureau, since a positive yield – the difference between higher long-term lending and lower short-term lending rates – was no longer guaranteed.

While these trends reduced the need for policy-based financing and increased pressure to reduce the flow of money through the FILP to GFIs, post offices continued to collect record savings. Even though their interest rates converged with those offered by private banks, postal savings remained an exceptionally popular savings vehicle. Post offices are ubiquitous and convenient – in metropolitan Tokyo, few people live more than 1.5 kilometres from a post office and, until 1990, postal outlets that accepted deposits outnumbered bank branches of all types of private banks combined (Vittas and Kawaura 1995). Full-service post offices also provided consumers with the convenience of one-stop shopping for banking, insurance, and mail and package delivery service. Postal savings also enjoyed tax benefits and an iron-clad government guarantee against losses in a post-bubble era in which banks were failing. Private savings flooded into the system just when it was becoming clear there was little need for policy-based financing.

Many of these factors, however, were in place long before reform efforts bore any fruit. Why were reforms finally adopted in the late 1990s and not earlier? One common explanation is that there was some sort of 'tipping point' when it became clear to policy-makers that Japan's dire fiscal and public debt situation needed remedying. True, Japan's mounting debt – at 200 per cent of gross domestic product (GDP), it is the largest among the industrialized countries – was a major concern. But policy-makers were long aware of this issue, which has remained salient since the disastrous fiscal year 1975/76, when government revenues declined by 8.5 per cent and borrowing skyrocketed.

Did the 'lost decade' of stagnant economic growth in the 1990s spur policy-makers to act? Average annual real GDP growth during the 1990s was a dismal 1.2 per cent. While Japan registered higher growth in 1995 and 1996 – partially because of increased infrastructural spending after the Great Hanshin Earthquake – the country slipped into a recession in 1997 that deepened in 1998. Those years coincided with a flurry of activity in the Cabinet Office that generated the framework for the reform of postal savings, the FILP, and the bureaucracy. The scale of non-performing loans in both GFIs and private banks was alarming, with the FILP's bad loans totalling three-quarters of its net funds according to one estimate (Doi and Hoshi 2003). The worst offenders were agencies and GFIs that funded public works and social spending, such as loans targeting small and medium-sized enterprises. The Japan Railway Construction Corporation, the Japan Finance Corporation for Municipal Enterprises, the Urban Development Corporation, and the Japan Highway Public Corporation each had net negative capital at the end of fiscal year 2001/02. In all, twenty insolvent agencies required subsidies to remain in business (Doi and Hoshi 2003).

While these economic factors created a sense of urgency, they are insufficient to explain the reform outcomes. As Japan slipped further into recession in 1998, political pressures mounted to *increase* spending, and in November 1998 the government announced a stimulus package valued at almost ¥24 trillion.[7] The alternative sources of revenue for such stimulus spending were the FILP, politically and economically unpalatable tax increases, or the issuance of even more central government debt. Of the three, the FILP was the least politically charged and least transparent to international credit markets. In the end, FILP expenditures actually spiked in fiscal year 1999/2000, and in the following two years so did General Account expenditures and the issuance of total central government debt. In brief, reforms did nothing to address the problem of national debt, and did not affect the use of the FILP to stimulate the economy in the short term.

What about pressure from private banks exerted through the banking *zoku giin* of the LDP and the Ministry of Finance? Here again, the evidence is slim. Private financial institutions were greatly weakened during this period by non-performing loans issued during the bubble economy years. They were the recipients of a major bailout package in 1996 and, from the late 1990s, the Ministry of Finance pressured weak banks to merge with stronger partners. Most were reluctant to lend, but in many cases were forced to do so by the ministry. Banks during the period of reform did seek to remove competition from GFIs, but their arguments were undercut by their weakness and their unwillingness or inability to lend more freely. In contrast, FILP loans served, in the words of the Ministry of Finance, 'cyclical adjustment' functions 'as a flexible and dynamic response to social and economic conditions' (Japan 2003). By the time the government embarked on serious discussion of reform, banks were too weak to influence the outlines of reform. Ultimately, they faced the prospect of competing with newly privatized entities that would be born with considerable advantages such as long phase-in periods of privatization, during which time they would benefit from government guarantees, favourable credit ratings that would lead to lower funding costs, and time to develop new areas of business and expertise.

Let me note one last possibility, which is whether foreign pressure to reform had any effect. Foreign businesses might benefit from the break-up of the financial and insurance behemoth that was postal savings, but foreign pressure did not play a significant role in FILP reform. If anything, U.S. and Japanese bankers and insurers alike were concerned as much with the process of privatization as with its final outcome, fearing that the long phase-in period of privatization for Japan Post would give it time to accrue the advantages of government guarantees. The forces of change and opposition to change were primarily domestic in nature, and foreign pressure did not play a significant role.

The reform story also has been attributed to a number of additional catalysts for change. Among these are the rise of neoliberal ideology among bureaucratic and political actors (Otake 1993); the emergence of an activist prime minister (Hayao 1993); changes in the relationship between bureaucrats and politicians triggered by external factors (Kato et al. 1994); demographic and political redistribution between the centre and the periphery (Muramatsu 1997); and the entrance of foreign capital into the Japanese political economy and the diffusion of new practices (Tiberghien 2007). But Japan has experienced these factors, perhaps in more limited doses, in the past without their significantly changing the underlying patterns of policy-making. Changes in the electoral system, as I note below, played an indirect role in spurring GFI reform by helping to weaken factions that supported the status quo.[8] But the electoral system itself cannot explain why reforms were undertaken. Neither can reforms be explained as the result of reaching a particular tipping point or crisis in terms of either economic or political urgency that followed an extended period of muddling through. Instead, deteriorating circumstances met with solutions that in prior periods were politically infeasible – in particular, the creation and exploitation of political openings through the strengthening of the Cabinet Office.

Invigorating the Kantei: Nakasone, Hashimoto, and Koizumi

Successive efforts at reforming FILP agencies and the special public corporations met with bureaucratic and political resistance throughout the 1980s and into the mid-1990s. It was not until the administration of Hashimoto Ryuutarou (1996–98) that a commitment was made to eliminate many special public corporations and change FILP funding practices.

The Hashimoto administration initiated meaningful reform by pushing through legislation that started the unravelling of the system of policy-based finance. Hashimoto took advantage of public disgust over the wining-and-dining scandals surrounding the Ministry of Finance in 1997 and 1998 to eliminate the role of the Trust Fund Bureau as the direct conduit of postal savings through the FILP to public corporations in 2001. That same year, a Cabinet Office strengthened by Hashimoto's administrative reforms adopted a Reorganization and Rationalization Plan for Public Corporations that eliminated, privatized, and consolidated 163 public corporations. Critics of this first round of reforms point to the fact that postal savings continued to flow into the FILP even after the elimination of the Trust Fund Bureau as middleman. Notably, the FILP was still almost entirely funded through government and government-guaranteed bonds purchased by government agencies, including the postal savings system, which, through its savings, insurance, and pension schemes, purchased 76 per cent of FILP-related bonds in 2001

(Scher and Yoshino 2004, 128). These reforms, however, were the turning point, setting in motion a steady and steep decline in total FILP spending after 1999, with cuts accelerating under the administration of Koizumi Jun'ichirou.

These reforms can be put in historical context by examining how successive rounds of administrative reform have fared since the issue first surfaced. Though reformist politicians are not mainstream in the LDP, the public rhetoric of administrative reform has been a continuous part of Japan's political landscape since the 1970s. The roots of the current reform wave thus can be traced to three earlier episodes, beginning with the 'Rinchou' of Nakasone Yasuhiro, then Hashimoto's administrative reform, and finally Koizumi's postal privatization.

Prior to the 1990s, the most successful period of economic reform was that of 1981–83 led by Nakasone through the formation of a commission for administrative reform, widely known as the Second Rinchou.[9] What prompted this first serious attempt at reform was the massive increase in government debt following the oil price shocks in the 1970s and the subsequent corporate tax hikes. While private firms moved to become more efficient, the public sector remained spendthrift, raising the ire of the business community, which voiced its displeasure through the peak business association, Keidanren, whose chairman, Dokou Toshio, assumed the chairmanship of the Second Rinchou.

Several aspects of this commission stood out. First, Nakasone ensured that the commission would report directly to the prime minister (initially Suzuki Zenkou, then Nakasone himself). Second, the legislation establishing the commission required the prime minister to act upon its findings. Third, the commission members included an unprecedented high number of non-bureaucratic experts and representatives from the private sector. Fourth, a separate party committee was created (administered by Hashimoto) that reported directly to the LDP's executive council, bypassing the normal route of intermediation by the party's Policy Affairs Research Council, where reformist recommendations were likely to be challenged strongly by *zoku giin*. The Second Rinchou's term resulted in the privatization of Nippon Telephone and Telegraph (NTT), Japan National Railways, and Japan Tobacco, and the strengthening of the prime minister's oversight of the bureaucracy through the creation of a Management and Coordination Agency (MCA). Bureaucrats, however, remained at the centre of decision-making, and the subsequent impact on the ministries was minimized as bureaucrats defined for themselves the meaning of deregulation in each sector in their jurisdiction. Thus, while the Second Rinchou constructed the broad framework of administrative reform, the details for carrying out the framework ultimately still rested with the bureaucrats.

In subsequent years, although reform remained on the agenda, further progress did not materialize despite the formation of several new administrative reform councils. The new councils were staffed mainly by bureaucrats, as was the MCA, which took an anti-reformist stance, particularly with respect to any initiatives aimed at weakening the Ministry of Finance. Another attempt was launched in October 1990 under the leadership of Suzuki Eiji, director of the influential Japan Employers' Federation, or Nikkeiren. Upon its closure, Suzuki expressed disappointment with the level of interference from bureaucrats and the *zoku giin*, whose power 'was beyond our imagination.'[10] These *zoku giin* included Hashimoto, who personally intervened to protect the special public corporations that served the interests of agriculture. It was therefore ironic that the next big reform push would occur under Hashimoto in the 1990s.

Hashimoto's challenger in the 1995 LDP presidential race was Koizumi, who ran on the platform of postal savings reform. During that leadership contest, Hashimoto outflanked Koizumi's focus on postal savings reform by calling for even more comprehensive reform of the entire FILP system. Though that effort was ultimately delayed as Hashimoto's team focused on the financial market Big Bang in his first year in office (Noble 2006), the prime minister eventually delivered on some of what he promised. Building on the watered-down Suzuki recommendations, Hashimoto's reform vision was announced just prior to the 1996 general election campaign, during which the prime minister played up 'reform' as a major part of his platform. Then, with an election victory in hand, Hashimoto declared he would pursue reforms even if he were to be 'engulfed in flames.' Though a number of reform committees were already at work, a new body, the Administrative Reform Council (ARC), consisting of fifteen members drawn from the academic and private sectors, was established to consolidate efforts and give them political force. The ARC met from November 1996 to June 1998.

In forming the ARC, Hashimoto took several cues from the Second Rinchou, appointing himself chair and employing tactics to exclude *zoku giin*. For example, his cabinet made efforts to block bureaucrats from using *gosetsumei* – carefully crafted explanations of policy – meant to sway individual politicians and ARC members (Mishima 1998). A subcommittee of the Fund Operations Council convened in February 1997 and chaired by the academic Kaizuka Keimei was charged with looking at the FILP; in July 1997, it called for a huge reduction in FILP spending for fiscal year 1998/99.[11] That did not occur, however, as the recommendation turned out to have been badly timed – Japan was falling further into recession, which generated an upsurge in calls for stimulus spending. The best way forward was to use the FILP and GFIs without raising taxes, since the alternative was to add even more to the burgeoning budget deficit. Thus, there was a huge jump in spending in fiscal year 1999/2000.

Despite the failure to curb spending in the short term, the subcommittee managed to place emphasis on changing funding for the FILP from a passive to an active model.[12] This meant that FILP agencies no longer would be funded passively through the Trust Fund Bureau, which passed along the full sum of postal savings regardless of whether FILP agencies had worthwhile projects to fund. Instead, the agencies would be forced to raise funds actively through bond issuances. The subcommittee's rationale was that this would lead to greater accountability in that funds would be raised based on program needs rather than on the availability of funds.

The 1997 Interim Report of the ARC set the agenda for reforms that were eventually adopted, but in the short term this initial push was stymied. By the time the final report was drafted, *zoku giin* and bureaucrats had regained dominance in crafting compromises that significantly backtracked on the interim recommendations. The consensus is that the ARC failed to make any substantial reforms, though its recommendation to decouple the FILP from passive funding eventually would be put into force through the Amendment to the Trust Fund Bureau Fund Act and Others, passed in May 2000. When the law was put into effect in April 2001, the Trust Fund Bureau was abolished, along with the compulsory deposit of postal savings and pension reserves. The following cabinets of Obuchi Keizou and Mori Yoshirou were quiescent on the issue of reforms.

Nevertheless, Hashimoto's other contributions to changing the political environment were ultimately quite substantial. Many important financial market reform measures would kick in later during the Koizumi era, and his administrative reforms and reorganization began to alter the relationships among politicians, the bureaucracy, and relevant private actors, changing the dynamic between the LDP and the government.

The most significant result of Hashimoto's efforts, however, was to strengthen the prime minister's leadership capacity through the establishment in 2001 of the Cabinet Office, a merger of the Economic Planning Agency and the Prime Minister's Office. The key gains to the cabinet were a greatly expanded, knowledgeable staff in the Cabinet Office and the Cabinet Secretariat[13] and the establishment of an information office to collect data. The prime minister was given legal authority to supervise ministries without first receiving the approval of the cabinet, as well as the power to increase the number of secretaries by executive order. A key measure was the granting of explicit authority to the prime minister and the Cabinet Secretariat to initiate legislation and undertake policy-making. Prior to the enactment of the Hashimoto reforms, the common observation was that the cabinet was viewed as almost completely dependent on the bureaucracy, in part because it was understaffed and not particularly knowledgeable about policy specifics. The absorption of the Economic Planning Agency alone meant a significant leap in expertise on economic matters within the government.

The next reformist push, by Koizumi, relied heavily on the recommendations of a new body within the Cabinet Office, the Council on Economic and Fiscal Policy (CEFP), formed in January 2001 and modeled after the Council of Economic Advisers in the United States.[14] Its purpose was to shift control of the budget to the prime minister, although its function was limited by law to studying and debating the basic principles of the budget and economic management. During the Mori administration, the CEFP was quiescent, but under Koizumi it became the central organ for promoting the reform agenda.

The most influential and vocal members of the CEFP were two from the private sector – Okuda Hiroshi, chairman of Toyota and head of Keidanren, and Ushio Jirou, chairman of Ushio, Inc. – and two academic economists, Honma Masaaki of Osaka University and Yoshikawa Hiroshi of Tokyo University. These four became known as the 'yonnin kai' (gang of four), and formulated most of the radical reform proposals under the coordination of the flamboyant economist from Keio University, Takenaka Heizou (Yomiuri Shimbun Seijibu 2005).[15]

The inclusion of academic economists in the CEFP deserves note. As Ikeo (2003) observes, until the 1990s academics and other private economists were at a disadvantage relative to government staff, who had greater access to information. By the 1980s, however, economists had become more involved in policy as a way of combating U.S. economists on the subject of trade surpluses. In the 1990s, private economists were regularly included in deliberation councils (shingikai), which gave them greater access to government data and an opportunity to voice their opinions. Nevertheless, their impact was limited in comparison with the direct policy-making role some economists were able to assume as members of the CEFP under Koizumi and subsequent prime ministers.

With the CEFP playing a proactive role, egged on by Koizumi (who chaired the CEFP) and Takenaka, the central coordinating role in policy-making moved from *zoku giin* in the Policy Research Council to the Cabinet Office. The CEFP's early success came with the reining in of spending in fiscal year 2001/02. In the following fiscal year, the CEFP proposed a 10 per cent cut in public works, which the LDP ultimately had to accept because of popular support. The climax of the reform period, however, came when Koizumi embarked on his pet project of reforming the postal savings system and FILP-funded GFIs.

Once Koizumi secured a victory on postal reform through his manoeuvres during the September 2005 lower house election campaign, deliberations on reforming FILP lending institutions proceeded at a relatively swift pace. That same month, the CEFP established a framework limiting public financial institutions to making loans in just three areas: loans such as overseas development aid, which could be provided only by the government; loans where a public benefit (such as expanded home-ownership) could be secured only if the government were involved; and projects whose risk assessment was difficult, making private lenders reluctant to become involved. Public financial institutions whose programs did not serve any of these three purposes would be closed, merged, or privatized, so that lending in these areas would be governed by free competition among private lenders. This functionality-based organization thus provided the framework for subsequent deliberations on the shape of consolidation and abolition of some FILP institutions.

In October 2005, the CEFP established a working committee, headed by Minister of Economic and Fiscal Policy Takenaka and consisting of private CEFP members and three outside experts, which turned its attention to the dispensation of eight public financial institutions. With the establishment of the committee, however, the process of coordinating between the government and the LDP had a rough start because of Koizumi's lack of clarity about his preference for how the public institutions should be reorganized.

The CEFP submitted three plans that differed on the structure of consolidation. One plan sought to consolidate the eight FILP GFIs into three entities. Another plan was to merge them into two banks. The third, supposedly favoured by Koizumi, proposed that they be merged into a single entity. There was some confusion, however, about whether

Koizumi's comments on consolidation meant that he favoured the one-entity plan or a multiple-entity plan: did he intend to merge all eight into one institution or merge five of the eight?[16] As it turned out, his position was to merge five of the corporations into one, to privatize the Development Bank of Japan and Shoukou Chuukin Bank, and to abolish the Japan Finance Corporation for Municipal Enterprises (whose functions eventually would be replaced by a locally run entity, although to date the plans are unclear). Koizumi's position was clarified at the end of October 2005 with the ascension of Nakagawa Hidenao as chairman of the LDP's Policy Research Council, who confirmed with Koizumi that he preferred the one-entity plan. Koizumi, on a trip to South Korea in November, reiterated that his plan was to consolidate the lenders into one entity, a position that Takenaka confirmed.

Subsequently, this became the position of the LDP leadership, opposed by bureaucrats, some politicians, and even members of the CEFP. Bureaucrats, in particular, had reason to oppose the one-entity plan, given that it would further loosen their control over municipalities and ties with private industry. The private sector members of the CEFP came into conflict especially with the Ministry of Finance and the Ministry of Economy, Trade and Industry over the consolidation plans. Serious disagreement emerged over the division of functions designated by the council, as well as over the number of final institutions in the proposal. From the two ministries came strong defence of lending to small and medium-size enterprises and for urban renewal and regional economic stimulus. At a meeting of the CEFP in mid-November 2005, Minister of Finance Tanigaki Sadakazu suggested partial privatization, similar to the way the NTT monopoly was broken up. Takenaka, who took a hardline stance on privatization, quickly condemned that approach.[17] Further details emerged at later CEFP meetings, with the proposal that lending be cut in half by fiscal year 2008/09, to be achieved in large part by eliminating loans made by the Japan Financial Corporation for Municipal Enterprises and the Shoukou Chuukin Bank.

Interestingly, at least a couple of the institutions under scrutiny voiced their measured support for the consolidation and privatization plans. Komura Takeshi, president of the Development Bank of Japan, stated that 'remaining a public entity is not an absolute must,' while the presidents of the National Life Finance Corporation and the Japan Finance Corporation allowed that their institutions duplicated those of private institutions. The Japan Finance Corporation head shrugged, 'if the private sector wants to take over everything, that's fine, too.'[18]

Finally, in June 2006, the government adopted its final plan to integrate the Japan Finance Corporation for Small and Medium Enterprise, the National Life Finance Corporation, the Agriculture, Forestry and Fisheries Finance Corporation, and part of the Japan Bank for International Cooperation into one entity in October 2008. The new institution would include international and domestic divisions, with the domestic division further partitioned between small and medium-sized enterprises, agriculture, and small borrower services. The Development Bank of Japan and Shoukou Chuukin were transformed into wholly government-owned stock companies, with eventual full privatization over five to seven years. The Government Housing Loan Corporation was converted into an administrative agency, the Japan Housing Finance Agency. It ceased making loans to individuals for housing, and now focuses on securitizing housing loans to provide private financial institutions with liquidity to allow them to continue providing long-term mortgages. An important part of the restructuring plan (summarized in Table 7.2) is to bar the practice of *amakudari* to the reorganized financial institutions. If successful, this would further weaken the influence of bureaucrats and their interests and stakes in public finance.[19]

Critics, of course, point to the lack of specifics in the FILP institution reform plan and, like the postal privatization plan, there is a lengthy phase-in period that would allow the Development Bank of Japan and Shoukou Chuukin to emerge as powerful competitors of private banks. The Development Bank of Japan, for instance, has cultivated substantial expertise in project financing, restructuring loans, and syndicated overseas lending during the post-bubble period. In the medium term as well, critics also see a problem with the explicit and implicit government guarantees with which the reformed institutions are privileged. For instance, Cargill and Yoshino (2003) have discovered that ratings agencies issue higher scores to government financial agencies when they perceive they are closer to the government. Currently the Development Bank of Japan enjoys a rating of AAA by Rating and Investment Information, though it faces a downgrade after privatization, which would significantly raise its borrowing costs. Still, the steps that have been taken so far mean that, over a longer course of time, FILP institutions will be judged on their merits by the bond markets and ratings agencies.

Senior LDP politicians initially were caught off guard during Koizumi's first year by his resolve to use the CEFP as his main policy weapon. Soon, however, they began to balk at the seriousness with which the

Table 7.2   Reorganization of Public Financial Institutions, October 2008

FILP Institution	Loans Outstanding (¥ trillions, end of fiscal year 2003/04)	Dispensation
Okinawa Development Finance Corporation	1.4	Merged into one entity
National Life Finance Corporation	9.6	
Japan Finance Corporation for Small and Medium Enterprise	7.5	
Agriculture, Forestry and Fisheries Finance Corporation	3.3	
Japan Bank for International Cooperation	20.0	Partial merger with above; overseas aid function to go to the Japan International Cooperation Agency
Government Housing Loan Corporation	55.0	Reincorporated as an administrative agency, the Japan Housing Finance Agency; no longer making direct loans, focusing instead on securitization
Development Bank of Japan	14.3	Privatize
Shoukou Chuukin Bank	9.8	Privatize
Japan Finance Corporation for Municipal Enterprises	25.0	Abolish, then replace eventually with local entity

Sources: Japan, Ministry of Finance, Financial Bureau, *Zaisei Touyuushi Ri-pou-to* (Tokyo, 2005); 'Fiscal Investment and Loans by Agency,' in Japan, Ministry of Internal Affairs and Communications, Statistics Bureau, *Japan Statistical Yearbook 2005* (Tokyo, 2005).

government was pursuing reform of the policy-based finance system. When Koizumi was further weakened by the LDP's poor performance in the 2004 upper house election, this gave an opening to the *zoku giin* to water down the postal privatization bills prior to submission to the full Diet. There were also efforts to undermine plans to cut the number of public employees by bureaucratic proposals that essentially would count retirements as staff reductions without also counting new hires, which would leave the staff count at the same level.

Koizumi played a skilful game of chicken, however, by first threatening and then following through on his threat to expel any party members who did not fall in line. This was an extraordinarily popular move with voters. He subsequently called a snap election to expel thirty-seven 'postal rebels' from their seats by running 'assassin' candidates, many of whom he had hand-picked for the job based on their popular appeal. The 11 September 2005 election resulted in the return of just seventeen of those rebels and a mandate for Koizumi's government to follow through on postal reform and the reforms of GFIs summarized in this section.

Two Steps Forward, One Step Back

In my account of FILP and GFI reforms under Nakasone, Hashimoto, and Koizumi, I have emphasized how stronger cabinet institutions created opportunities for these leaders to push through change. In each case, however, the prime ministers were forced to compromise. Even Koizumi, with all of the new powers available to him through the CEFP, suffered some notable defeats, including a government panel's decision, in the face of very heavy *zoku giin* pressure, not to rein in spending on highway construction despite a decision in December 2003 to privatize the public highway corporations and strictly limit new construction.[20] The LDP prime ministers who succeeded Koizumi barely tried to expand on his reforms and backtracked in some areas. Abe Shinzou, Fukuda Yasuo, and Asou Tarou all suffered from dismal public approval ratings, in part because their commitment to reform appeared lacklustre. Abe, for instance, took an especially hard hit when he agreed to readmit eleven postal rebels to the LDP.

Then there is the new DPJ-led government, which actually has made reversing Koizumi's postal reforms a top policy priority. When Hatoyama Yukio formed his cabinet in 2009, he gave the post of financial services minister, with responsibility for the postal savings system, to Kamei Shizuka from the People's New Party (PNP), which was formed by rebels who had been expelled from the LDP over their refusal to support Koizumi's postal reform legislation in 2005.[21] This party, together with the small Social Democratic Party of Japan (SDPJ), was brought into the DPJ-led coalition in 2009 to provide the DPJ with the votes it needed to pass legislation in the upper house. Almost immediately upon taking up his cabinet duties, Kamei began verbal attacks on the president of Japan Post, Nishikawa Yoshifumi, whom Koizumi had appointed to shepherd through the privatization process; within a month, a new president was installed. Another PNP member, Hasegawa Kentei, a former official in the Ministry of Posts and Telecommunications, was made parliamentary secretary for the Ministry of Internal Affairs and Communication, which administers the postal system.

As of this writing, Kamei has prevailed in forcing the coalition government to adopt measures that will partially reverse the 2007 Koizumi privatization plans. In December 2009, the ruling bloc majority in the lower house passed a law to halt the sale of government shares in Japan Post Holdings, Japan Post Bank, and Japan Post Insurance. The other controversial aspects of the government plan are to double the current cap for individual postal savings accounts to ¥20 million, and to allow its banking and insurance companies more easily to establish new business areas, such as home mortgages and auto loans.[22]

These setbacks to the reforms pushed by Koizumi and his reformist predecessors make it clear that institutions that strengthen the Cabinet Office and other institutional reforms (such as electoral reform) cannot be expected to produce a steady and consistent stream of economic reforms. Instead, reform progress depends on a confluence of additional circumstances that came together for Koizumi but that has not coalesced in the period since he left the scene. For reforms to continue, it is essential that whoever is prime minister perceives there is political advantage to be gained in championing them – institutional changes have created opportunities for prime ministers to exercise leadership in pushing through reforms, but they will only do so if they see opportunities to advance their careers. In 2001, when Koizumi came into office, and again in 2005, when he threw down the gauntlet and challenged his opponents inside the party on postal reform, he saw that voters hungered for 'reform.' They were fed up in particular with government waste and *amakudari,* which had been played up in media reports on banking and bureaucratic scandals during the long 'lost' decade. Koizumi saw an opportunity to link these vague concerns to specific changes in the FILP, GFIs, and the postal savings system.

A variety of opinion polls taken at the time of the September 2005 election make it clear that voters had little idea exactly what was at stake in postal reform. Nevertheless, Koizumi succeeded in using the theatre created by his dispatch of 'assassins' to take on his opponents to turn this policy debate into a litmus test on whether one was for reform or for the corrupt status quo. He succeeded to a degree his opponents never could have expected. Voters flocked to the polls and produced one of the highest voter turnouts of recent elections.[23] One open response poll around the time of the election indicated that postal privatization was the most important issue for 32.9 per cent of respondents, beating out pensions and social security (22.7 per cent).[24]

Moreover, for progress on reforms, it is critical that a prime minister not depend on the votes of anti-reform parties for a majority coalition. In 2005, Koizumi's coalition partner, Koumeitou, supported postal privatization. In 2009, Hatoyama needed votes from the anti-reform PNP and SDPJ in order to pass legislation in the upper house. He was also counting on the PNP to help mobilize votes for DPJ candidates in upper house district races in July 2010. These factors were important enough that they drove Hatoyama's successor, Kan Naoto, to push for an extension of the Diet session to give the PNP and Kamei extra time to pass legislation further watering down Koizumi's postal reforms.[25]

Conclusion

The backward steps that have been taken in the process of reforming Japan's government financial institutions should not lead us to overlook the degree to which the entrepreneurial leadership of Koizumi and his reformist predecessors have changed both policy and politics in ways that make going back to the old ways virtually impossible. Several GFIs, including the giant Japan Housing Finance Agency and the Development Bank of Japan, have either been set on the road to privatization or ceased direct lending. The Trust Fund Bureau of the Ministry of Finance no longer draws up the FILP, and the managers of the postal savings system now have the discretion to decide how much – if any – of their funds go into the remaining GFIs and public corporations such as Japan Highway. As the postal savings unit of Japan Post begins to make home mortgage and auto loans and to expand into other areas of direct finance, it will have less money to send to these government bodies, which will be forced to depend even more on their ability to float bonds on the open market – rather than on the ability of constituencies benefiting from favourable GFI financing to influence politicians.

None of these reforms is at risk of being reversed by the DPJ-led government, despite the participation of the PNP in this government. Future governments that do not include parties such as the PNP or that rely heavily on postal workers and postmasters will feel hard pressed to ignore mounting pressure from both international and domestic actors that support further privatization of GFIs and the conversion of the postal savings system into what amounts to a private bank. A future prime minister who sees electoral advantage in taking up the reform banner, and who secures a single-party majority or does not depend on anti-reform coalition partners, will be able to turn to the same cabinet institutions that empowered Koizumi to push through this next set of reforms.

NOTES

1 Since 2001, the special public corporations have been funded indirectly through a combination of FILP agency bonds and a pooled FILP loan fund backed by bonds issued through the regular financial markets. For details, see Iwamoto (2002); and Amyx, Takenaka, and Toyoda (2005).
2 For descriptive accounts of how the systems of 'over-loans' by the Bank of Japan to the city banks and 'over-borrowing' by Japan's key industries were crucial for meeting the high demand for capital during this period, see Johnson (1982); Zysman (1983); Aoki and Patrick (1994); and Calder (1995).
3 During the U.S. Occupation, Joseph Dodge mandated that the proceeds of domestic sales of U.S. aid goods be deposited in a counterpart fund separate from the general budget. This fund eventually was used initially to capitalize and form the Japan Development Bank.
4 Since those retiring into public corporations do not technically leave government service, this practice is more accurately captured by the Japanese term *yokosuberi* (side-slipping).
5 'Opinion: Indifferent Tokyoites behind distorted income redistribution,' Nikkei Net Interactive, 11 July 2005. Japan possesses a highly centralized and distributive system of taxation. Some two-thirds of public spending is local, while only about one-third of the taxes are collected at the local level. The structure of taxation and spending has made it difficult to control public works spending, which disproportionately benefits the less-populated areas of the archipelago. Some changes have already been made, but future reform measures now being discussed involve more extensive restructuring of local and regional subsidization.
6 I am indebted to an anonymous reviewer for this turn of phrase.
7 Japan, Ministry of Foreign Affairs, Press Conference by the Press Secretary, Tokyo, 17 November 1998; available online at http://www.mofa.go.jp/announce/press/1998/11/1117.html.
8 Koizumi's anti-factional politics would not have gained much traction without the 1994 electoral reforms that reduced the incentives produced under the multi-member-district system to engage in the highly personalistic

electioneering that reinforced the power of factions. Horiuchi and Saito (2003) offer evidence that the new electoral system encouraged policy change both by redrawing district boundaries, and by reducing inequalities in representation across districts.

9 Rinchou is the Japanese abbreviation for Rinji Gyousei Chousakai, or Ad Hoc Research Committee on Administrative Reform. The first Rinchou was held between 1962 and 1964 and is generally regarded as inconsequential. For an expanded discussion of the second Rinchou, see Maclachlan, in this volume.

10 Elaine Kurtenbach, 'Japan considers reinventing its own government,' *Associated Press*, 28 October 1993.

11 'Panel to urge major cut in gov't 2nd budget,' Japan Economic Newswire, 8 July 1997.

12 'Government panel releases drastic Zaito reform proposals,' Jiji Press Ticker Service, 27 November 1997.

13 The 2001 revision of the Cabinet Law granted the Cabinet Secretariat the additional functions of planning and drafting proposals and legislation, as well as comprehensive coordination. These newly articulated functions were meant to strengthen the leadership of the prime minister.

14 The creation of the Cabinet Office, however, has not completely mitigated issues of factionalism and ministerial pressure. Two-thirds of the roughly 300 staff in the Cabinet Office come from the former Economic Planning Agency. The rest are seconded from other government ministries and agencies, and retain loyalties to particular cabinet ministers, while much of the lower-order work is farmed out to junior staff at the home ministry. Yet they are expected to work on policy that transcends the particular interests of their home ministries. Still, under Koizumi, the trend towards including private experts accelerated to the point where more radical policy measures were proposed by the government.

15 Alternate reminiscences suggest that Takenaka and his own staff finalized policy drafts prior to Council meetings, and these were then presented as if they were the policy proposals of the private sector members of the Council.

16 One sticking point with the one-entity plan lay with how the Japan Bank for International Cooperation would be merged. It posed a problem because of its overseas lending and diplomatic and strategic operations lending. Under the one-entity plan, the bank would be split up, with lending operations transferred to the new entity and its other aid operations brought under either the Japan International Cooperation Agency or the direct control of the prime minister.

17 'Takenaka at odds with Tanigaki over public financing reform,' Nikkei Net Interactive, 27 November 2005.

18 Nikkei Net Interactive, 26 October 2005.
19 In December 2008, the Asou administration set up the Center for Personnel
   Interchanges between the Government and Private Entities, a job placement centre that reports to the Cabinet Secretariat. Both Asou and the DPJ
   campaigned in favour of barring ministries from arranging *amakudari* posts
   for their own retirees. The Center, whose claim of independence from the
   ministries remains suspect, is meant to weaken the direct personnel links
   between regulators and the regulated.
20 I thank Chao Chi Lin for reminding me that highway privatization and
   spending proposals did not emanate from the CEFP but from a separate
   committee in the Cabinet Office. Still, I keep the example because it is
   consistent with the CEFP's desire to rein in spending and rationalize the
   public institutions.
21 The PNP was formed by some of the postal rebels Koizumi expelled from
   the LDP.
22 Incidentally, in 2005, the DPJ's postal privatization proposal recommended
   that the postal savings cap be *halved* to ¥5 million. Current plans do not
   require Japan Post Bank to pay deposit insurance premiums on amounts
   over ¥10 million, suggesting that there is a tacit government guarantee
   for the additional ¥10 million that depositors would be allowed to hold in
   their postal savings accounts.
23 The 2005 elections were what Mayhew and Arnold (2006) call a 'show-
   down vote,' with a single salient issue, high level of attention by the media,
   and suspense about the final results.
24 'Dai-44 no shuugiin sousenkyou ni kansuru anketo,' *Dimusu doraibu o-pun
   deeta Timely Research,* 15 September 2005; available online at http://www.
   dims.ne.jp/timelyresearch/enq/050915/. The results could be skewed given
   that the respondents answered the survey on the Internet. Only 5.5 per
   cent of respondents were in their sixties. Still, it is surprising that, in that
   age cohort, only 18.9 per cent of women answered that pensions and social
   security were the most important issues, about the same percentage as that
   of men in their twenties.
25 'Kan to discuss extending Diet session,' Nikkei.com, 8 June 2010.

8 The Impact of Two-Party Competition on Neoliberal Reform and Labour Unions in Japan

MARI MIURA

The role of organized labour appears to be diminishing in Japan. The unionization rate has been steadily decreasing, falling from 34.4 per cent in 1975 to 18.8 per cent in 2005. The number of unionized workers, too, has been decreasing since 1994. By 2005, there were only ten million unionized workers in the country.[1] Wage levels have been reduced since 1998, and wage discrepancies among different categories of workers have increased. The presence of labour unions in national politics and policy-making process is also diminishing. The Koizumi cabinet (2001–06) labelled unions one of the 'resistance forces' to reform and excluded union representatives from key policy deliberations, an exclusion that continued through the end of the Asou cabinet in 2009.

While these developments point to a very real erosion in the power of organized labour in Japan, the recent record is not entirely bleak. Although the unions have been excluded from important policy deliberations, they have been able to block major labour market reforms in the Diet by pushing through amendments that have eviscerated the intended changes. Thus, in 1998, when the government attempted to reduce overtime costs for employers by significantly expanding the category of workers assigned to 'discretionary work hours,' the unions succeeded in attaching onerous conditions that made the new rules virtually useless to employers. Similarly, in 2003, the unions and the Democratic Party of Japan (DPJ) worked together to beat back a government attempt to ease restrictions on the ability of employers to dismiss permanent employees. While firms facing bankruptcy have laid off workers in increasing numbers, this victory has helped preserve 'lifetime employment' protections for core employees of firms that are not facing dire economic conditions.

Taken together, these two sets of developments – the marginalization of labour unions in the policy deliberation process and the ability of labour to defend its core interests in the Diet – pose a real conundrum. Why exactly have the labour unions been pushed to the sidelines of the policy process? Is their experience simply the local manifestation of what some have described as a worldwide phenomenon in an era of 'globalization'? If so, how is it that labour unions have been able to hold their own in the Diet? Alternatively, do labour's recent problems simply confirm the conventional wisdom on Japan's political economy captured by such expressions as 'labour exclusion' or 'corporatism without labour'? This interpretation, too, has difficulty accounting for the recent success of labour in the Diet, as well as its substantial incorporation into policy deliberations during the 1980s and early 1990s.

In this chapter, I attempt to make sense of this pattern by emphasizing the effects of recent changes in *ideas* and *institutions*. Labour's exclusion from the key policy deliberations, I argue, both reflected and reinforced a paradigm shift that took place in Japanese management. Before the mid-1990s, employers by-and-large had bought into the view that Japan's unique system of labour-management cooperation (enterprise unions, lifetime employment) was a significant source of Japan's competitive advantage. Given this cognition, it was quite natural for management to work with unions in national-level policy deliberations to pursue common interests in a largely cooperative manner. As the 1990s wore on, however, the economic shock of the 'lost decade,' combined with the effects of 'globalization,' caused most managers to change their minds about the costs and benefits of Japan's labour market structures. They began to discern that a flexible labour market would be more beneficial and, therefore, started to advocate labour market reform. Their failure to secure all of the changes they sought, I argue, can be explained by changes that were made around this same time in Japan's political institutions. The intensified party competition between the Liberal Democratic Party (LDP) and the DPJ that arose after electoral reforms were adopted in 1994 significantly increased the importance of urban voters, many of whom are salaried workers, and their families. Eager to court these voters, the DPJ energetically represented the interests of salaried workers when labour market reforms came before the Diet. Faced with the risk of losing votes from this constituency, the LDP backed down and accepted amendments. As a result, neoliberal labour market reforms suffered setbacks and compromises so that the LDP would not lose the support of such voters. The questions of who represents the interests of salaried workers and how these interests are defined thus became critical issues in Japanese democracy.

This chapter is organized as follows. In the first section, I explore the various ways in which labour has been pushed onto the ropes in its struggle to maintain a voice in national politics and policy-making. I start with an examination of how labour's position has been weakened in terms of the dynamics of industrial relations and the process of wage setting; I then look at how this exclusion has spread to the national level, where labour representatives have been kept off key, newly created deliberation councils. In the second section, I document the one exception to this pattern: labour's success in blocking labour market deregulation initiatives in the Diet. Then, in the third section, I attempt to make sense of this puzzling pattern. I look first at changes in the dominant discourse on labour issues among corporate managers. Sometime around the mid-1990s, cost cutting became the most important management goal, eclipsing the previous focus on labour-management cooperation. I argue that the paradigm shift to neoliberalism helped shape a new policy-making process that had the effect of shifting the balance of power between labour and managers. Top-down decision-making, which bypassed bureaucratic coordination, enabled labour market deregulation measures to dominate the structural reform agenda and reach the floor of the Diet. At the same time, this transformation of the policy-making process resulted in the Diet's – the final veto point in the Japanese political system – becoming the locus of real decision-making. The labour unions that were marginalized in the prior coordination stage of policy-making were compelled to voice their opposition to government reform plans in the Diet, where the LDP revealed a surprising willingness to resist pressure from the business community and make compromises in order not to lose support from salaried workers.

Labour on the Ropes

The challenge labour unions face in attempting to maintain their influence in the political arena begins with the basic fact that union membership has been declining now for some time. Membership has declined every year since 1994, with the unionization rate dropping from 24.1 per cent in 1994 to 18.7 per cent in 2005.[2] The major factor behind this rapid decline was the restructuring of large companies (Nakamura 2005, 29–32). Since unions are most organized in large companies due to union-shop agreements, the shrinking number of employees in large companies directly affected Japan's unionization rate. The political power of unions, however, does not depend solely on their organizational resources; political opportunity structures surrounding unions are also significant (Kume 1998). Nevertheless, a decrease in the unionization rate cannot be anything other than a negative influence on union political power.

The drop in the unionization rate created a sense of crisis among the unions. As the numbers and proportion of non-regular workers, such as part-time and temporary workers increased, unions began to include non-regular workers as targets of their unionization efforts. Rengou (the Japanese Trade Union Confederation) modified its policy in 2001 to emphasize the importance of organizing non-regular workers (Rengou 21-seiki e no Chousen Iinkai 2001). Some industrial federations, such as UI Zensen (the Japanese Federation of Textile, Chemical, Food, Commercial, Service and General Workers' Unions), energetically organized part-time workers in the retail sector and achieved relative success. Indeed, in 2009, the unionization rate actually rose by 0.4 of a percentage point from the previous year, reaching 18.5 per cent, which can be attributed to the increase in unionization of non-regular workers. Nevertheless, such efforts to recruit non-regular workers were not enough to offset the massive wave of restructuring.

A second challenge to the power of Japanese unions grew out of the breakdown in coordinated wage bargaining structures. After all, unions are organizations that function first and foremost by *collective* bargaining. While Japan's wage bargaining has always been more decentralized than wage bargaining in northern European nations, industrial-level coordination has been pursued through a mechanism known as the 'spring offensive' (*shuntou*), whereby enterprise-level collective bargaining in each industry is scheduled at around the same time period, usually March, to coordinate wage increase levels. Unions conceived of this strategy to compensate for the weaknesses of enterprise unionism. After the initiation of the spring offensive in 1955, wage levels had a significant influence on other sectors, including small business, where unions did not exist, and in the public sector, where collective bargaining was forbidden. Until 1975, the spring offensive contributed to wage standardization across industries, which, in turn, served to increase domestic demand. Large-scale wage increases ended in 1975, and since then the spring offensive has worked instead to restrain wage increases. Nevertheless, although the pace of wage raises began to slow after 1975, wage standardization across industries and sectors was achieved until the late 1990s.

The turning point in the fortunes of the spring offensive came in 1995. Nikkeiren (the Japan Federation of Employers' Associations) aggressively sought 'structural reform of the spring offensive,' pushing for retrenchment of total labour costs, the demolition of horizontal wage standardization, and widespread adoption of performance-based payment. In 1998, Rengou, pushed into a defensive position, agreed to a freeze of the basic wage rate in exchange for employment protection. Indeed, between 1998 and 2006, the wage level negotiated at the spring offensive actually decreased.[3] The most important function of the spring offensive was to level wages across companies and industries rather than to obtain wage increases in and of themselves. After 1998, wage gaps finally began to widen, manifesting the end of the 'spring offensive level' (Nakamura 2005, 12–13). In 2002, Rengou at last gave up on calling for a unified basic wage rate raise, which until then had been an effective strategy for realizing wage standardization. In 2003, employers publicly declared the *shuntou* system dead: 'the spring offensive, in terms of unions calling for wage increases and using forceful means in their "struggle" to achieve social levelling, has ended' (Nihon Keizai Dantai Rengoukai 2003, 61).

The individualization of industrial relations can also be identified in the realm of labour disputes. The number of collective labour disputes between unions and employers has declined, whereas individual labour disputes between individual workers and employers have been increasing. For instance, while employment restructuring rose in 1999 and 2002 to the level seen in 1975, collective labour disputes did not increase sharply, as they had in 1975. The major reason for this resides not in union weakness but in the deepening of information sharing between unions and employers, as well as the establishment of rules regarding changes in working conditions due to the accumulation of precedents (Outake and Okudaira 2006). The increase in individual labour disputes suggests, however, that unions are not capable of dealing with the various problems individual workers face.

What do these changes in the role and influence of unions in industrial relations mean for labour's role in politics? First, it is important to remember that, despite these setbacks, labour enjoys certain advantages at the plant level that do not necessarily translate into influence in Tokyo politics. At the plant level, it is possible that labour could reassert itself when and if the economic turnaround occurs and demographic forces lead to labour shortages. Union cooperation is still necessary for employers to redesign personnel systems successfully, as an overtly unfair system is likely to become dysfunctional. Specialists in industrial relations claim that fuller participation by unions in management is indispensable for employers to operate fair and sustainable performance-based systems (Nakamura 2006). Moreover, the introduction of an industrial tribunal system in 2006 could give unions a new role. Individual labour disputes are expected to be settled by a three-member industrial tribunal commission comprising a district court judge and two labour relations referees from management and labour, respectively.

Having lost the ability to disrupt economic activity through strikes and the ability to insist on wage increases, unions have also lost some of the most important levers of power they once enjoyed. Wage constraints and even decreases have already been implemented with tacit support from the unions, and employers no longer need to fabricate corporatism as they did in the 1970s.[4] Although there is room for unions to expand their influence again at the micro level, their presence at the macro level is restricted.

Nowhere is this decline in union presence in macro politics clearer than in Rengou's disappearance as a major player in party politics in recent years. In the period after it was founded in 1989, this giant labour union federation played a leading role in sparking and shaping successive rounds of party realignment, helping to bring together the disparate coalition that briefly ousted the LDP from power in 1993–94 and serving as midwife to the birth of new parties that replaced the Japan Socialist Party as the leading alternative to the LDP in the years that followed. Rengou's strategy was to create a viable opposition to the LDP in order to achieve alternation of power, with the ultimate aim of unifying all social democratic forces within a single moderate progressive party. By prioritizing the goal of unifying all anti-LDP, non-communist forces in order to hasten power alternation, however, Rengou ended up sacrificing its second goal (Nakakita 1999). Since 1996, the interests of social democracy have been divided between the Social Democratic Party of Japan, which has been marginalized under the new electoral system, and the DPJ. Rengou's active role in the process of party realignment in the mid-1990s was probably rather exceptional, and most likely facilitated by the extraordinary fluidity of Japanese politics at the time. Once the party system was stabilized to an extent by the consolidation of the smaller centrist parties under the DPJ in 1998, Rengou's role was more or less limited to that of a pressure group. Moreover, although the DPJ has become a powerful party, winning more seats than the ruling LDP-led coalition in both the 2007 upper house election and the

2009 lower house election, Rengou's voice within this party has been reduced to one among many in the disparate social coalition that makes up the party. In stark contrast to the intimate relationship that Souhyou (the General Council of Japanese Trade Unions) enjoyed with the Japan Socialist Party, Rengou has encountered severe difficulties in persuading the DPJ to accept its favoured policies.

The increasing distance between Rengou and the DPJ was predictable from the logic of the electoral system. Under the new electoral system, in which a candidate needs to appeal to a wider range of interests to win a constituency, Rengou's support is necessary but not in itself sufficient for DPJ candidates. Indeed, the DPJ has constantly sought to overcome its dependence on the unions. Insofar as the DPJ perceived that union support gave voters the damaging impression that it could not undertake fundamental reform, it was unlikely to be responsive to Rengou's policy demands. Therefore, the distance between Rengou and the DPJ has depended on the DPJ leadership as well as on the issue at stake. For instance, the distance was probably at its largest when Maehara Seiji was the DPJ leader between September 2005 and April 2006. Maehara repeatedly claimed that the DPJ should not rely on unions to revitalize the party, which had suffered a heavy defeat in the 2005 general election. In contrast, when Ozawa Ichirou succeeded Maehara, he restored the party's relationship with Rengou, which led to the launching of a joint campaign emphasizing the negative consequences of Koizumi's structural reform.

The inability of Rengou to mobilize sufficient numbers of voters can be seen in the results of recent upper house elections, which give us an opportunity to gauge its ability to mobilize voters. In the 2001 election, nine union leaders ran on the DPJ list, seeking to obtain 700,000 votes per candidate, or a total of 6.3 million votes. Yet only six candidates were elected, with a total of 1.7 million votes. Rengou admitted that this outcome was a 'total rout' (*zanpai*), and many within the DPJ commented on the necessity of distancing the party from the labour federation. The number of votes for individual candidates in itself, however, might not accurately reflect Rengou's mobilization capacity, since Japan's upper house rules allowed voters to cast a vote either for an individual candidate or for a party list. While Rengou asked its members to write down individual candidates' names, it is quite possible that many members instead simply voted 'DPJ.'

In the subsequent election of 2004, Rengou worked harder to make it clear to its members that they needed to vote for individual labour *candidates* rather than a party, since this was the key to demonstrating to the DPJ leadership how many voters the union could mobilize and since votes for specific candidates determined which candidates from the DPJ list would get seats in the Diet. This time, all eight of its candidates were elected, and Rengou claimed that its support contributed to the DPJ's great leap forward, with the party winning fifty seats compared with the LDP's forty-nine. Rengou's total votes, however, numbered only 1.73 million.[5]

The result of the 2007 election was even more favourable for Rengou. The DPJ gained sixty seats, becoming the majority party in the upper house. All seven of Rengou's candidates were elected, with a total of 1.82 million votes. The biggest contributor was a candidate from the All-Japan Prefectural and Municipal Workers Union (Jichirou), who gained 340,000 more votes than did that union's candidate in 2004.[6] Although Rengou has steadily increased the number of votes it has won in the past three upper house elections, its mobilization capacity has been limited each time to no more than 1.7 to 1.8 million. Most candidates collect around 200,000–300,000 votes, far from the organization's initial goal of 700,000.

With evident limitations on the ability of labour to mobilize *workers* in the industrial relations process and *voters* at election time, one probably should not be surprised that unions have been sidelined in the policy deliberation process. The decline of labour was most evident under the Koizumi cabinet, which made the Council on Economic and Fiscal Policy (CEFP) the locus of decision-making. The CEFP was originally conceived as part of Prime Minister Hashimoto Ryuutarou's administrative reform, which aimed to strengthen the function of the Cabinet Office and was set up in January 2001 under the Mori cabinet (2000–01). Prime Minister Mori Yoshirou did not make much use of this new organ, but Prime Minister Koizumi Jun'ichirou clearly understood its usefulness for his power struggle against his own party. Under his cabinet, the CEFP became the locus of decision-making on budget, economic, and fiscal policy, taking power away from the LDP's *zoku* politicians (Shiroyama 2003; Makihara 2005).[7] With both the Ministry of Finance and the CEFP committed to fiscal retrenchment and *zoku* politicians pushed aside, ministries vying for budget allocations were compelled to make compromises on budget and policy. The influence of the CEFP was most evident in areas such as postal reform (see Maclachlan, in this volume), but it also had a major impact in pushing through budget cuts for local governments (the so-called trinity reform), reductions in health care expenditures, and the reform of special public corporations. In these policy areas, Koizumi's strong leadership was decisive in settling conflicts within the government and between his cabinet and the LDP.

In view of the CEFP's influence, its composition and membership were crucial to the direction of general policy. The CEFP comprised fewer than eleven members, including the prime minister as chairman, the chief cabinet secretary, the minister of state for economic and fiscal policy, and at least four representatives from the private sector. Between the birth of the CEFP in 2001 and the end of the Koizumi cabinet in 2006, the same four individuals served as private sector members. Two were economics professors (Honma Masaaki from the University of Osaka and Yoshikawa Hiroshi from the University of Tokyo) and two were business leaders (Okuda Hiroshi, chairman of Toyota Motor Corporation and president of Nippon Keidanren, and Ushio Jirou, chief executive officer of Ushio Inc. and former president of Keizai Douyuukai, the Japan Association of Corporate Executives).[8]

During the Koizumi years, the four private sector members regularly held meetings, submitting bold recommendations to the CEFP. They consistently sought the realization of a small government, including the prevention of tax and social contribution increases, the contraction of public financing, and the restructuring of the public sector. Interestingly, they were nominated by Prime Minister Mori, who chaired the CEFP for the first four months. Koizumi inherited these four members, although he could have changed them had he wanted. Takenaka Heizou, minister of state for economic and fiscal policy and former Keio University economics-professor-turned-politician under Koizumi's patronage, provided them with political support, seconded by Koizumi, urging them to present their proposals or 'private sector papers.' These private sector members played an important role in setting the CEFP's agenda (Outa 2006).

No labour representative, however, served on this important policy-making body. Given their influence in the CEFP, the absence of labour representatives in pursuing Koizumi's structural reforms was striking, and in stark contrast to the administrative reforms of the 1980s. The equivalent body to the CEFP at the time was Rinchou (the Second Provisional Commission on Administrative Reform), the driving organization behind the administrative reforms, which included privatization of the national railway and public telephone company. Among its nine members, Rinchou included two labour representatives from the two rival labour confederations, Souhyou and Doumei, respectively. All the subsequent administrative reform commissions, modelled on Rinchou, also included at least one labour representative until the advent of the Koizumi cabinet. Labour exclusion, therefore, is indeed a conspicuous feature of Koizumi's structural reforms.

When Koizumi left office in September 2006, the four private sector members also resigned from the CEFP. To replace them, Prime Minister Abe (2006–07) appointed two economists (Itou Takatoshi of the University of Tokyo and Yashiro Naohiro of the International Christian University) and two business leaders (Mitarai Fujio, president and chief executive officer of Canon Inc. and chairman of Nippon Keidanren, and Niwa Uichirou, chairman of Itouchu Corporation and a board member of Keizai Douyuukai). Whereas the business organizations continued to send their presidents to the CEFP, labour exclusion from the council remained the status quo, although Professor Yashiro, a prominent advocate of a flexible labour market, proposed a 'labour big bang,' a fundamental labour market reform. However, neither Abe nor his successor Fukuda Yasuo (2007–08) prioritized economic issues or fiscal restraint to the extent Koizumi did. Thus, even though the business-friendly composition of the CEFP prevailed, its importance in policy-making waned after Koizumi stepped down. This tendency continued under Prime Minister Asou (2008–09), who renewed the composition of the private sector members without changing the predominance of business representation, but shifted the policy priority from structural reforms to fiscal stimulus, thereby downplaying the role of the CEFP.[9]

Let us now consider the role labour has played within the policy deliberation process on specific issues that have been of greatest concern to workers and the unions. What is striking is how the exclusion of labour has extended even to these areas, where tripartite bargaining (with labour, management, and government all at the table) was the norm until the 1990s. The main locus of this tripartite bargaining used to be the Ministry of Labour's advisory councils, such as the Labour Standards Council (Schwartz 1998). Under this system, while the ministry led deliberations and proposed a framework for a deal, it was usually careful to seek a consensus among the conflicting parties. While these councils have not been disbanded, they – and labour unions – have been pushed aside because of the way policy-making has been reorganized as more of a top-down decision-making process. All of the major policies on the deregulation agenda were first proposed by ad hoc deliberative commissions and then approved by the cabinet, thus constraining the ability of the Ministry of Health, Labour and Welfare – the merged ministry that took over the functions of the Ministry of Labour – to negotiate with employers and unions once the issue was handed off to it. I have called this new mode of policy-making the 'new politics of labour' (Miura 2002) and later the 'majoritarian policy-making process' (Miura 2007).

Under the new politics of labour, as the ad hoc deregulation panels set the agenda and when the advisory councils were not able to reach a consensus, the locus of bargaining shifted to the Diet. This kind of adversarial process was evident in the cases of the Labour Standards Law in 1998 and 2003 and the Dispatching Manpower Business Law in 1999 and 2003, discussed in more detail in the next section.

The key players in the new politics of labour are ad hoc deregulation panels, a series of deliberative bodies that date back to the arrival on the scene of the first non-LDP prime minister since 1955, Hosokawa Morihiro (1993–94). Hosokawa proposed the establishment of an Administrative Reform Committee to promote deregulation and information disclosure. This committee, subsequently established under the government of Murayama Tomiichi (1994–96), gave birth in 1995 to the Deregulation Subcommittee, which advocated bold reform plans, including labour market reform. Initially instituted as an ad hoc commission with a three-year mandate, it has survived several reorganizations to remain in existence under LDP governments, renamed first as the Deregulation Committee (1998–2001, then as the Regulatory Reform Committee in 1999), the Council for Regulatory Reform (2001–04), the Council for the Promotion of Regulatory Reform (2004–07), and, most recently, the Council for Regulatory Reform (2007–10).

While the name of this panel has changed over the course of the past ten years, as have its legal standing and administrative staff, the chairmanship was held by Miyauchi Yoshihiko, chairman of Orix Corporation and an important champion of Japan's deregulation and privatization of public services, without interruption from 1996 until 2006. The deregulation panel, under whatever name, consisted of approximately fifteen members, most of whom were neoliberal economists and entrepreneurs. Labour representatives held one post in the initial Deregulation Subcommittee and the Deregulation/Regulatory Reform Committee, but had no representation in the Council for Regulatory Reform or subsequent bodies. Just as the CEFP excluded labour, so did the deregulation panel under the Koizumi government. Consequently, the representation of social interests on the deregulation panel differed completely from that on the Ministry of Health, Labour and Welfare's advisory councils, where labour secures a third of the membership, or at least stands on an equal footing with employers. The shift of agenda-setting power to the deregulation panel thus tilted the balance of power in favour of business. Moreover, as far as labour market reform is concerned, it is important to note that temporary staff agencies (also known as manpower dispatching companies) were able to gain access to the policy-making process, from which they were excluded under the ministry's advisory councils.[10]

In the final section of the chapter, I return to the question of *why* labour has been marginalized in the policy deliberation process. In seeking to understand the reasons for this trend, it is critical to recognize that the change in policy-making institutions just described was not a random event or an accident, but was welcomed – indeed, sought – by managers, who repeatedly condemned consensus-oriented policy-making in advisory councils that slowed down decisions and favoured vested interests, and they exerted strong pressure to establish the Deregulation Subcommittee. The changing business environment prompted managers to press for changes to the domestic legal system – particularly with respect to corporate governance and the commercial code – so that they could feel better able to compete against foreign firms on a fair or better footing. Since conventional policy-making takes time, managers called for the creation of ad hoc commissions that would be able to influence cabinet decisions and bypass bureaucrat-led advisory councils. At the same time, they vigorously lobbied the LDP to propose politician-sponsored bills, which was another way to bypass the bureaucracy. Their efforts in the former regard resulted in the creation of not only the Deregulation Subcommittee but also the Industrial Competitiveness Council and, in the latter regard, in the commercial code reforms that were conducted every year between 1997 and 2001 through politician-sponsored legislation.

Why did managers push so hard for changes in policy-making procedures? I return to this question once I have examined the one exception to the pattern of marginalization of labour: its success in the Diet.

Labour Unions and Workers in the Diet

The simple fact of labour's exclusion from policy deliberations within the government in itself did not mean that the unions gave up or that workers were powerless to affect policy outcomes. In the case of labour market reform, Rengou ultimately was able to lobby the DPJ to propose amendments to the government's legislation on the Diet floor. It was then able, in several cases, to extract compromises from the LDP. Of the four major enactments of labour market reform legislation between 1998 and 2003, only the 2003 Dispatching Manpower Business Law survived the Diet process unamended. The other three pieces of legislation were subjected to substantial modifications proposed by the DPJ, and basically based on Rengou's demands. Thus, the ruling coalition's setbacks on the floor of the Diet significantly limited the degree of Japanese labour market reform. Since, under a parliamentary system such as Japan's, the government, supported by the parliamentary majority, is usually able to pass its bills without conceding to the opposition, one needs to ask what political conditions allowed such ostensibly unexpected outcomes.

Rengou opposed the bills mainly for the following reasons. First, the 1998 amendment of the Labour Standards Law aimed to introduce discretionary working-hour rules under which certain hours set by employer-employee negotiation would be counted as working hours regardless of the actual hours workers took to accomplish a task.[11] This rule was expected to reduce overtime payments, which constitute a significant portion of workers' pay during certain seasons in certain professions even though, in reality, many workers already undertake 'service overtime work' for which they do not claim overtime payment. Nominally, employers were successful in greatly extending the coverage of the rules, but succeeded in inserting detailed conditions for the introduction of discretionary working-hour rules that made the new rules practically unusable.[12]

Second, the ruling coalition attempted to use the 2003 amendments to the Labour Standards Law to introduce rules that would have made it easier for employers to dismiss redundant employees. In Japan, dismissal rules are based on case law precedents, which traditionally have made dismissal difficult and costly (Foote 1996). In the Diet, however, the DPJ and Rengou succeeded in modifying the proposed legislation by erasing the phrase that stated that employers had the right to dismiss workers, and so succeeded in securing the existing level of employment protection for Japanese workers.

Third, rules were proposed that would have restricted the scope of jobs that could be filled legally by temporary agency workers. Previously, the law had allowed temporary agencies to fill jobs in only a few specialized areas on a 'positive list.' The proposed revision of the Dispatching Manpower Business Law in 1999, however, introduced the 'negative list method' by which only jobs where temporary agencies were *not* allowed to fill slots would be specified – a potentially significant change that could have opened the door wide to this low-cost and flexible labour force, thereby further weakening the ability of unionized core workers to defend their privileges. Among the numerous controversial issues, Rengou most vehemently opposed the introduction of dispatched labour to the manufacturing sector, where unions are the most organized. When this legislation was discussed at the relevant Ministry of Labour advisory council in 1999, Rengou succeeded in placing manufacturing jobs explicitly on the negative list.[13] Rengou also lobbied the DPJ to amend the government bill in the Diet to add protective measures for temporary agency workers. Most of Rengou's demands were realized as the LDP conceded to the DPJ and other opposition parties.[14]

Another example of an LDP concession was the case of the white-collar exemption system, which would have allowed *some* white-collar workers to be exempted from work-hour regulations, thereby barring them from receiving overtime payment. Employers had been advocating the introduction of such a system since the mid-1990s, and a bill to this effect was on the point of being drafted in 2006. Since executives were already exempted from the working-hour regulations, the crucial question was who else would be exempted. At one point, Nippon Keidanren proposed that workers who earned over ¥4 million in annual salary should be exempted, a threshold that would have excluded almost all white-collar workers from receiving overtime payment. Since Rengou strongly opposed the white-collar exemption system from the beginning, it was very likely that the DPJ would seek to amend the government bill if it were proposed to the Diet. This time, workers gained a significant measure of help from the mass media, which covered the deliberation process to an unprecedented degree – they usually pay scant attention to labour law formulation – and named the bill 'the no overtime payment law,' emphasizing the fact that employers supported it as a means of cutting labour costs. Consequently, the LDP gave up on proposing the bill to the Diet in early 2007 out of fear the media's framing of the issue would have a negative effect on the party's performance in the upper house election scheduled for six months later.

The only exception to the pattern of success by Rengou and labour on the Diet floor came in 2003, when the government again attempted to modify dispatching manpower business regulations. This time, the legislation that reached the floor took manufacturing jobs off the negative list, opening up the sector to temporary work agencies. Rengou, however, was unable to force modifications on the Diet floor, despite its success in winning DPJ support. I return to these cases in the next section, where I try to make sense of the overall pattern of labour marginalization, tempered by occasional success in the Diet.

Corporatism without Labour?

The increasing marginalization of labour unions since the mid-1990s makes it tempting to conclude that Japan has simply reverted to a condition it was said to occupy until the 1970s: 'corporatism without labour,' a concept first presented by T.J. Pempel and Keiichi Tsunekawa (1979), who argued that labour was systemically excluded from policy-making processes in Japan. Pempel later asserted that this concept remained valid in Japanese politics (1997, 340).

The role of Japanese unions is indeed subject to differing interpretations. Critical views, including those of Pempel and Tsunekawa, emphasize the organizational weakness of unions and their consequent exclusion, whereas revisionists positively evaluate union participation at both the firm level and the political level. For instance, Kume (1998) stresses the fact that large-firm private sector unions cooperate with their managers at the firm level, which strengthens their political power at the level of national politics. Union leaders, in fact, were invited to join numerous government committees, including high profile panels such as Rinchou, as discussed above.

Recent developments, driven by globalization, seem to support the 'corporatism without labour' view. As Pempel emphasizes in his more recent work (1997), a globalized economy shifts the balance of power from labour to capital or, more precisely, from immobile-asset holders to mobile-asset holders. Thus, for him, the recent decline of unions is evidence of labour's continuing marginalization. Japanese unions, already weak, diminished further as globalization accelerated the concentration of power in the hands of managers. On the other hand, revisionists have difficulty providing a consistent explanation of this change. If union participation were so important to Japanese firms' competitiveness, why would managers suddenly commit corporate suicide by changing the rules? Kume attempts to square this circle by blaming Rengou for adopting an adversarial attitude that pitted unions against managers and the government to an unnecessarily antagonistic extent (2005). If only unions had been more cooperative, he suggests, they could have held onto the old system and their old power.

Although the exclusion of labour from the CEFP and policy deliberation councils and its diminished role in industrial relations seem to testify to the validity of the critical ('corporatism without labour') view, the characterization of recent developments as merely a continuation of past patterns fails, in my view, to appreciate the very real ways in which labour had carved out a position of influence for itself prior to the mid-1990s and asks us to ignore the changes in labour's position in recent years. One can make sense of recent developments only if one appreciates the level of power labour once enjoyed and focuses on why it has fallen on such difficult times. The two opposing views can be reconciled to a degree, and it is only by means of such reconciliation that the meaning of the recent changes can be understood.

To begin, it is useful to separate the macro and micro levels as well as public and private unions. The conservative governments of the LDP consistently sought to undermine the power of the public unions, while occasionally attempting to co-opt moderate, 'realistic' unions, which usually reside in the private sector (Garon 1987). Moderate private sector unions were not only willing to participate in decision-making at the firm level; they also sought to participate in government processes. Thus, in the context of private sector unions, labour appeared to be incorporated at both the micro and macro levels. Yet, such incorporation came at the expense of the exclusion of public sector unions, and thus it would be misleading to state that class compromise was institutionalized in Japan (Pontusson 2005). In short, though I recognize the micro-level labour participation that revisionists emphasize, as well as Rengou's participation in government processes, I maintain that Japanese unions as a whole remain organizationally and politically weak.

What is still unclear is why private sector unions, which used to be regarded as one of the foundations of Japanese competitiveness, have continued to wane organizationally as well as politically. To the extent that unions provided cooperative industrial relations and high productivity, their decline presents a new problem rather than a solution to employers. I argue that a paradigm shift in Japanese management occurred in the 1990s that changed the context in which labour politics is played out.

The phenomenon of labour decline cannot be understood without analysing the preferences of managers, because it was they, not unions, who had as a clear objective the transformation of existing institutions. Since the 1990s, managers have become much readier to cut production costs – notably labour costs – in order to maintain, increase, or maximize profits. In this regard, managers' cost consciousness differs completely from their previous inclination towards long-term commitment and the interests of stakeholders.[15] Accordingly, in the mid-1990s, managers began in earnest to dismantle Japan's high labour cost structure. In 1995, Nikkeiren proposed grouping employees into three categories: a core category of workers who would receive in-house training and employment protection, and highly skilled or professional workers and unskilled workers who would be supplied from the external labour market. This stratification would have required not just a change in human resource strategy at the company level but also policy reform at the national level, and triggered attempts to push through drastic labour law changes beginning in the late 1990s.

Similarly, the other business association, Keidanren, advocated a transformation of the policy paradigm from an emphasis on employment stability within companies belonging to the same group to the guarantee of employment opportunities at the level of the whole of society. For that goal to be achieved, Keidanren argued, smooth job transfers stemming from a worker's own volition should be encouraged through far-reaching reforms of labour-related regulations and the transformation of the current enterprise pension system, which inhibits job transfers.[16] As evidenced by its use of the term 'paradigm shift,' Keidanren adopted a much more drastic stance than Nikkeiren, as its proposal aimed to release employers from a responsibility to offer employment security.

A perception on the part of managers that Japan's labour costs were internationally high laid the foundation for Nikkeiren's proposal. In fact, every year since 1995, Nikkeiren/Nippon Keidanren, in its annual report on management-labour policy, has emphasized the need to reduce total labour costs in order for Japanese firms to compete in the midst of intensified global competition. According to Nikkeiren, as of 1993 Japan's labour costs in the manufacturing sector were the highest of any of the advanced industrialized countries – twice as high as those in the United Kingdom or France and 1.4 times higher than those in the United States. Nikkeiren remains concerned that the Japanese level is consistently among the highest, surpassed in 2003 only by the United Kingdom, whose labour costs had climbed to 10 per cent higher than those in Japan.[17] According to the Japan Institute for Labour Policy and

Training, however, a different picture emerges. It argues that, when the Japanese manufacturing sector's labour costs are set at a constant of 100, costs for the U.S. counterpart were 185 in 1985 but dropped sharply to 71 in 1995, while aggressive cost cutting by Japanese managers (and exchange rate movements) have led to a convergence of U.S. and Japanese labour costs since 2001.[18]

Nikkeiren sought to justify its aggressive pursuit of labour cost reductions from the viewpoint of Japan's international competitiveness. Indeed, Japan has experienced significant effects of increasing globalization. For example, in 1996, overseas profits of Japanese firms began to surpass Japanese exports.[19] Japanese imports from China surpassed those from the United States in 2002 and were double the U.S. level by 2005;[20] moreover, most imported items from China are consumer goods such as textiles and home electronics, which hit Japanese industries and jobs. But at the same time, increasing imports from China have been offset by mounting exports from Japan, and China has been Japan's largest trade partner since 2004. The integration of the Japanese economy into the world economy thus has grown in magnitude and widened in scope. If the relatively isolated position of the Japanese economy meant that the discourse of globalization was rarely heard in Japan prior to the 1990s, today's level of globalization provides justification for those who claim that Japan needs to implement further labour cost reductions.

Interestingly, neither Japanese managers of large manufacturing companies nor mainstream unions have rung alarm bells calling attention to the trade-off between overseas production and domestic jobs (Schoppa 2006b, 107–10). The main reason for this is that there is a trade-off between jobs and wages in the Japanese labour market, which diminishes the scope for a trade-off between globalization and domestic jobs to emerge and thus to be recognized. In other words, the impact of globalization appears not in the level of employment but in the level of wages in Japan.

In sum, Japanese management, which has become much more cost sensitive over the past decade, is in the midst of a paradigm shift. While one might assume cost-conscious management to be a universal strategy, it was foreign to Japanese management philosophy until the 1990s. The 'politics of productivity' had prevailed since the mid-1950s, as a result of which cooperative industrial relations were forged as a social norm.[21] Japanese managers began to abandon the politics of productivity in the political context of leftist decline and the economic context of globalization and deindustrialization, introducing performance-based payment, replacing regular workers with cheaper non-regular work-ers, demolishing the spring offensive, and championing policy reform that would allow further flexibility in management. They also worked to reduce social contributions, a non-negligible component of labour costs. Corporate governance has also been transformed partly due to Keidanren's continuous pressure, shifting power from stakeholders to stockholders. While it remains easy to identify differences between the United States and Japan, or the Anglo-American model and Japan, as far as labour is concerned, the 'evaporation' (Dore 2006) of labour unions is a striking phenomenon hitherto unseen in Japanese capitalism.

This story of a paradigm shift among managers fits well with the chronology of institutional and policy change documented in the first section of this chapter. Political institutions began to change in the mid-1990s as a result of the emergence of a new political space for neoliberal politicians to pursue deregulatory reforms, just when managers arrived at the conclusion that Japan's high labour costs in an era of globaliza-tion 'forced' them to bring these costs down. And when one looks for fingerprints to see *who* pressed for changes in policy-making structures governing labour market reform, one sees that it was a cohesive group of business leaders and neoliberal economists. This same group then used the new institutions of the CEFP and deregulation panels to press for far-reaching liberalization of Japan's labour market.

That leaves, then, the question of why, despite all this paradigm shifting and change in policy-making institutions, labour ultimately was successful in stopping key government initiatives on the Diet floor. Critically, institutional change in Japan was not limited to changes in the powers of the Cabinet Office and the CEFP: the 1990s also saw Japan adopt a major change in its electoral rules, which helped trig-ger a major change in its party system (see the chapters by Schoppa and Reed, in this volume). The emergence of the DPJ as the leading rival to the LDP after these reforms, with the two parties competing for the votes of urban, salaried, unaffiliated voters, has introduced a new political dynamism that is beyond the control of neoliberal economists and their business allies. Although the DPJ is peopled by neoliberal-minded politicians, it tends to pursue progressive positions on social issues, including labour market reforms, to differentiate itself from the LDP (Miura, Lee, and Weiner 2005). At the same time, the LDP has also courted salaried workers in order to limit DPJ gains, especially when it has been weak. A close look at the timing and circumstances of the five cases of labour market reform legislation discussed above reveals a number of patterns.

First, the LDP has tended to make concessions when it has lacked a parliamentary majority. From July 1998, when the LDP lost the upper house election, until October 1999, when the government of Obuchi Keizou (1998–2000) allied with Koumeitou, the LDP lacked a majority in the upper house. That weakness compelled the LDP to concede in the case of the 1999 Dispatching Manpower Business Law. In contrast, the LDP's coalition with Koumeitou allowed it to take a hard-line stance vis-à-vis opposition parties, as seen in the case of the 2003 Dispatching Manpower Business Law. In 1999, unions were able to block the legislation that would have allowed temporary work agencies to dispatch workers in the manufacturing sector, but in 2003 they were unsuccessful.

Second, the LDP has been especially leery of taking positions that might be viewed as hostile to the interests of salaried workers. Of the five cases, three were not favourable to salaried workers, to the extent that they might even have incited mass demonstrations: the discretionary working-hour rules (the 1998 Labour Standards Law), the dismissal law (the 2003 Labour Standards Law), and the white-collar exemption system discussed in 2006–07. Since the LDP had secured a majority in both houses when these pieces of legislation were mooted, it could have passed the bills without amendments.[22] It did not take such an uncompromising position, however, mainly because salaried workers had gained importance as a voting bloc. Since cities were the DPJ's stronghold and two-party competition was quite tight, it was not politically expedient to provoke the ire of salaried workers.

The contrasting outcomes of the dismissal law and the Dispatching Manpower Business Law could not have been more striking. The Diet passed these two bills at around the same time, in 2003, but the LDP compromised only in the case of the dismissal law. The fact that Rengou concentrated its resources in order to oppose the dismissal law certainly affected the divergent result. However, the LDP also appears to have accepted a compromise because this rule change affected *all* salaried workers, including the urban salaried workers whose status as swing voters in the competition with the DPJ made them a group the party could not afford to offend. In contrast, the LDP resisted pressure to compromise on the amendment of the Dispatching Manpower Business Law because this change affected only temporary work agency workers. Indeed, the LDP's distinguishing between salaried workers and non-regular workers contributes to the further stratification of the labour market in ways that shift the burden of reductions in labour costs to workers on the periphery. For instance, a 2005 amendment to the Construction Workers' Employment Improvement Law in effect allowed the use of temporary agency workers to be introduced into the construction sector despite the DPJ's opposition. This legislation looks likely to increase the number of contingent workers in the construction sector, unless appropriate countermeasures are taken.

The other interesting comparison is between the Labour Standards Law amendments in 1998 and 2003, on the one hand, and the white-collar exemption system, on the other. The former cases were amended in the Diet, allowing the DPJ to claim the credit, whereas in the latter case the LDP had already made a concession in favour of salaried workers before the parliamentary deliberations began. If the LDP did care about workers as potential constituencies, surely it would have been more profitable to amend the bills while they were still being drafted. This way, the LDP would have been able to claim credit. That the LDP was slow to respond to union critiques and challenges in the former cases suggests that it was the attention of the mass media that triggered the LDP's unusual degree of concession in the latter case. Even though salaried workers are gaining importance as a constituency for the LDP, the party puts a priority on business interests unless sensational media coverage threatens its electoral prospects.

Lastly, it should be noted that the relationship between the LDP and Rengou is much more diverse than the notion of 'corporatism without labour' implies. Even under the Koizumi cabinet, Rengou was not excluded from deliberations on the full range of policy issues on the agenda.[23] In fact, Koizumi took steps early in his administration to re-establish what was at that point a broken relationship between the LDP and Rengou. After it was established in 1989, Rengou held regular meetings with the prime minister until 1999, when Prime Minister Obuchi refused to meet the leader of Rengou, expressing his irritation about the union federation's adamant opposition to the LDP's pension reform plan. Obuchi's successor, Mori, did not re-establish the relationship with Rengou. In contrast, Koizumi attended the May Day Central Convention in 2001, which prime ministers had avoided for the previous five years. Official government-labour meetings also were resumed in August 2001. Corporatist meetings of the prime minister, the leader of the business community, and the labour leader, first organized under the Hashimoto cabinet (1996–98) and suspended during the Obuchi and Mori administrations, also resumed in June 2001. In March 2002, the government, business, and labour agreed on the 'Five Principles of

Japanese-type Work Sharing,' the first social agreement on employment issues among these three parties. In November 2002, Koizumi solicited Okuda Hiroshi, chairman of Nikkeiren, and Sasamori Kiyoshi, president of Rengou, to offer their cooperation on unemployment problems.[24]

Another example of labour inclusion is the Committee on Social Security Review, set up in 2004 by Koizumi in response to Rengou pressure and charged with reviewing the overall social security system. A private deliberation body of the Cabinet Chief Secretary, its five members included a labour representative (Sasamori) and a business representative (Nishimuro Taizou, vice-president of Nippon Keidanren and senior advisor of Toshiba). The committee was not an influential institution on the level of the CEFP, but its establishment at least suggests that Koizumi did not intend to exclude Rengou completely from the government process. Likewise, Prime Minister Abe created the Roundtable for Growth Strategy in 2006, and invited labour representatives and business leaders to attempt to forge a consensus on the increase in the minimum wage. The Asou cabinet also set up an advisory panel to realize a 'safe society,' inviting the participation of both labour and business leaders.

The above examples illustrate how the LDP has tried to incorporate Rengou whenever it perceives political benefits from such an approach. 'Corporatism without labour' thus underestimates both the novelty of labour's having become excluded from labour market issues and the fact that labour can be invited to the policy table at any time, depending on the political calculations of the ruling party. Furthermore, this macro-level concept fails to account for labour's occasional successes in the Diet. Instead, the dynamics of interparty competition play an important part in shaping recent developments in Japanese labour policy. The ending of LDP hegemony allowed the establishment of the deregulation panels, which hastened the speed of labour market reforms by setting the agenda in favour of business. The new policy-making process, however, invited opposition from labour unions, which lobbied the DPJ to amend the government bills in the Diet. The LDP's strength in the Diet and its need to appeal to salaried workers affected the ultimate fortunes of the bills.

Conclusion

In this chapter, I analysed the decline of labour at the level of Japanese national politics and in collective bargaining, and I argued that the paradigm shift in Japanese management drove such changes. In the new business environment, managers have sought aggressively to cut labour costs, which have aggravated distributional conflicts between capital and labour. A classic, but new, class conflict has been translated into law-making processes. On the one hand, a top-down policy-making process has emerged to bypass tripartite decision-making traditionally coordinated by the bureaucracy. On the other hand, in a counter movement, unions and the DPJ have voiced their opposition and, in many cases, have been able to modify government bills in their favour on the floor of the Diet. Thus, the liberalization of the Japanese labour market has proceeded to a certain extent, especially regarding non-regular workers, but employment protection for regular workers remains intact, if not in a stronger position.

These trends came to a particular head during the Koizumi years, although the examples in this chapter make it clear that the basic pattern began earlier and continued until the election of the DPJ government. A key development during the Koizumi years was the emergence of the CEFP – dominated by business leaders and economists and lacking even a single labour representative – as the dominant top-down initiator of economic reform. The CEFP, with the strong backing of the then-minister of economy and fiscal policy, Takenaka Heizou, pressured banks to increase their efforts to write off and restructure non-performing loans, thus accelerating corporate reorganization and diminishing the organizational bases of labour unions. Deliberative commissions set up under Koizumi and his immediate predecessor also excluded labour representatives and pushed for labour market reforms. Unlike Nakasone's administrative reforms, Koizumi's structural reforms did not take direct aim at militant unionism in the public sector or seek the absolute defeat of the union movement. Yet his policies, whether as an intended or unintended consequence, undermined the overall strength of the unions.

It should also be noted that these anti-labour policies were not the only ones pursued by the Koizumi cabinet. On his watch, the LDP aimed to appeal to urban voters, which both intensified competition between the LDP and the DPJ and curtailed the extent of labour market reform. The LDP's policy u-turn under Koizumi's prime ministership was induced by urban voters who lacked clear party loyalty. Their support was crucial for Koizumi to undertake his neoliberal reform, which reduced financial assistance to the LDP's traditional constituencies. In order to compensate for the lost support of the LDP's former clients, Koizumi needed to keep public opinion on his side. To that end, he skilfully avoided politicization of issues that would hurt the interests of salaried workers, many of whom supported his government. The case of the 2003 Labour Standards Law testifies to the dynamism of Koizumi's social coalition, as does his attempt to re-establish the broken relationship with Rengou and the fabrication of the social agreement.

The importance of urban voters was already well recognized by the LDP in the 1980s, when Nakasone aimed to shift the LDP's support base towards urban and suburban areas – indeed, the slogan of 'fiscal reconstruction without tax increases' targeted salaried workers. Koizumi further strengthened this trend: immediately after the establishment of his cabinet, Finance Minister Shiokawa Masajuurou asserted that the cabinet would emphasize urban areas.[25] The fact that urban voters also supported the DPJ made the LDP far more sensitive to them than in the 1980s.

How will the election of the DPJ government in 2009 and its defeat in the upper house election in 2010 ultimately affect the trends I have analysed in this chapter? It is worth pointing out several important decisions it has made that might provide hints as to the future of labour politics in Japan.

First, the Hatoyama cabinet decided to abolish both the CEFP and the Council for Regulatory Reform, the two main vehicles of neoliberal market reform during the time period discussed in this chapter, with the result that general deregulatory items will now be discussed under the Government Revitalization Unit headed by the minister of state for government revitalization. Labour representatives are not included in this organ's subcommittee on regulatory reform. Even though the DPJ is backed by Rengou, with respect to regulatory reform it appears that the DPJ intends to proceed without including labour.

Second, however, labour issues will be deliberated under the advisory councils of the Ministry of Health, Labour and Welfare. If the Government Revitalization Unit chooses not to discuss labour market rules, its exclusion of labour might not matter much in the eyes of organized labour. Since Rengou is ardently opposed to any erosion of the ministry's advisory councils, it has pressured Minister Nagatsuma Akira to respect them. Since the DPJ places a high priority on realizing strong cabinet leadership vis-à-vis the bureaucracy and backbenchers, preservation of the advisory councils in their current form clearly contradicts that stance; nonetheless, Nagatsuma has accepted Rengou's demands.[26] Therefore, it is perhaps more likely that bureaucrats will regain the initiative in labour market reform under the DPJ government.

One caveat is that workers have become much more diversified as a result of the labour market reforms since the late 1990s – over a third are now non-regular workers. Organized labour still has the potential to aggregate diverse interests from among different categories of workers, but it is nonetheless true that they predominantly organize regular workers. If social concerns about poverty and the working poor were to increase to the extent that a political response became inevitable, it would be difficult for Rengou to defend the virtues of interest coordination at the advisory councils. This is because, at the advisory councils, where both labour and business make concessions in order to forge a consensus, final decisions are always moderate: particularly detrimental neither to union interests nor to business interests.

If, however, the general public were to demand further regulation to address issues relating to the working poor and if the DPJ government were to respond to such demands, Rengou's concessions to employers might be viewed as unacceptable, if not downright treacherous, by non-regular workers.[27] Rengou, ironically, now finds itself in a *more* difficult position under the DPJ government it supports than under the LDP government it opposed. In many ways, it was relatively simple for Rengou to maintain an oppositional stance vis-à-vis the LDP's pursuit of labour market liberalization, but if the DPJ defends the interests of non-regular workers to a greater extent than does Rengou, Rengou would be hard pressed to justify its apparent lukewarm stance. Conversely, if the DPJ pursues reform that is likely to have negative repercussions for non-regular workers, Rengou's stance of neither opposing nor criticizing the DPJ might become untenable. Thus, the real challenge for Rengou is how to mediate the clash of interests between regular workers and non-regular workers.

NOTES

1 By way of reference, it should be noted that the decline in the unionization rate is not a universal phenomenon. Between 1970 and 2003, among the twenty-four member countries of the Organisation for Economic Co-operation and Development, eight experienced a decline in unionization rates of over ten percentage points: New Zealand (–33.1), Australia (–27.3), the United Kingdom (–15.5), Japan (–15.4), the Netherlands (–14.2), France (–13.4), Switzerland (–11.2), and the United States (–11.1). Four others witnessed an increase in unionization rates of over ten percentage points: Finland (22.8), Belgium (13.3), Sweden (10.3), and Denmark (10.1) (Visser 2006).
2 The data are based on 'Roudou Kumiai Kiso Chousa,' surveys conducted annually by the Ministry of Health, Labour and Welfare.

3 In the spring offensive of 2006, unions succeeded in securing wage increases in certain industries such as the automobile and electronics industries, ending five consecutive years of wage decreases.

4 The 1975 spring offensive produced wage restraints, whereby many scholars noticed the formation of a kind of corporatism.

5 Not all union members affiliated with Rengou support the DPJ. A not-insignificant number of them actually express support for the LDP, which is a matter of concern to the Rengou leadership. A statistical analysis of the 2001 election, however, reveals that union membership has a positive impact on voting for the DPJ (Bessho and Hara 2005).

6 The number of votes cast for the candidate from the All-Japan Prefectural and Municipal Workers Union tripled between 2004 and 2007. The major factor behind this mobilization power was that repeated scandals involving the Social Insurance Agency pushed the demolition of the organization onto the political agenda, creating a sense of crisis among the union members.

7 *Zoku* politicians, or policy tribes, are middle-ranking LDP politicians who ally with a certain ministry or agency in order to appropriate budgets or the like and in return wield a strong influence over policy on a day-to-day basis

8 Nippon Keidanren (the Japan Business Federation) was reorganized in 2002 by the amalgamation of Keidanren (the Japan Federation of Economic Organizations) and Nikkeiren (the Japan Federation of Employers' Associations). Okuda Hiroshi was the chairman of Nikkeiren when he was first appointed as the CEFP's member and became the first chairman of Nippon Keidanren.

9 Prime Minister Asou appointed two economists (Yoshikawa Hiroshi, professor at the University of Tokyo, and Iwata Kazumasa, former professor at the University of Tokyo and former deputy governor of the Bank of Japan) and two business leaders (Chou Fujio, chairman of Toyota Motor and vice chairman of Nippon Keidanren, and Mimura Akio, chairman of Nippon Steel and vice chairman of Nippon Keidanren).

10 At the ministry's advisory councils, representatives of employers are allowed to attend, but not representatives of a particular business. Since temporary staff agencies constitute a type of business, they are not qualified to participate in the advisory councils, but they now attend the meetings as observers.

11 Discretionary working-hour rules were first adopted in 1987 for professionals such as designers, producers, directors, information technicians, and research and development engineers. Another six job types were

added to the list in 1997, but again these were professional. In contrast, the 1998 amendment enabled employers to apply the discretionary working-hour rules to white-collar workers involved with management in a core division of a company.

12 On the detailed preconditions for introducing the discretionary working-hour rules to planning divisions, see Sugeno (2000, 296–9). Both Rengou and Nikkeiren admit that the new rules based on the 1998 amendment would not spread the introduction of discretionary working-hour rules (interview with Kenichi Kumagai, Division Director of Labour Law Division, Rengou, Tokyo, 21 July 2000; interview with Nikkeiren's Labour Law Department, Tokyo, 7 September 2000).

13 While the main text of the law did not place the manufacturing sector on the negative list, an exception clause allowed the sector to be exempted.

14 As Weathers (2004) shows, the 1999 Dispatching Manpower Business Law does not provide enough protection to temporary agency workers. But, compared to the original government bill, the amendment at the Diet improved some of the protective measures therein.

15 Regarding Japan's past management model, see Dore (2002).

16 Keidanren, 'An Attractive Japan: Keidanren's Vision for 2020,' often called the 'Toyoda Vision,' 1996.

17 For the data on 1993, see Nihon Keizai Dantai Rengokai (1995). Other data can be found in the various annual editions of the same report.

18 See Japan Institute for Labour Policy and Training, *Deitabukku Kokusai Roudou Hikaku* (various years).

19 See Japan, Ministry of Economy, Trade and Industry, *Kaigai Jigyou Katsudou Kihon Chousa*; available online at http://www.meti.go.jp/statistics/tyo/kai gaizi/index.html.

20 See Japan, Ministry of Finance, *Trade Statistics*; available online at http://www.customs.go.jp/toukei/info/index_e.htm.

21 The rationale behind the politics of productivity was that constructive industrial relations would enhance productive efficiency, which would lead to capital formation as well as economic growth. A fair distribution of shares among capital, labour, and consumers would alleviate or sideline class struggle, which, in turn, would serve to further increase productivity. See Nitta (2003) and Miura (2008).

22 In the case of the 1998 Labour Standards Law, the Social Democratic Party allied with the LDP without participating in the cabinet, which made it necessary for the LDP to compromise in the first place.

23 It should also be noted that the advisory councils under the Ministry of Health, Labour and Welfare continue to be the main deliberation arena for

labour issues. No relevant government bills can be drafted without at least securing the nominal support of these councils.

24 This top-level tripartite meeting has been suspended since December 2002. Koizumi's openness to meeting with union leaders early in his tenure suggests that he did not come into office with a completely anti-union attitude.

25 'Shushou "Toshi Juushi" Senmei ni' [Prime Minister asserting "priority on urban areas"], *Nihon Keizai Shimbun*, 23 May 2001.

26 In contrast, the DPJ changed the membership of the advisory council on medical insurance issues in order to implement its policy in this area.

27 The process of amending the Dispatching Manpower Business Law under the Hatoyama cabinet is relevant to this point, but is beyond the scope of this chapter.

9 Conclusion: The Evolutionary Dance Continues with the DPJ Victory in 2009

LEONARD J. SCHOPPA AND AIJI TANAKA

In Chapter 1, the process through which policy and party politics have been changing in Japan was likened to an 'evolutionary dance.' The contributions to this volume describe a set of changes in the environment shaping Japanese politics, all taking place in the period from 1993 to 1996, that add up, in effect, to an abrupt change in music. Extending this metaphor a bit, it is as if a disk jockey suddenly had shifted from playing the doo-wop sounds of 1950s-style rock and roll to the synthesized percussion beat of modern hip hop. With such a dramatic change in music, we should not be surprised to see the dancers (the parties) struggling to adapt to new rhythms. Just as most dancers, faced with an abrupt change in music, likely would stumble before perhaps adapting to the new sound, the process of adjustment by Japanese parties since the 1990s has not been a pretty sight.

Under the 1955 System, the background music shaping Japanese politics included an electorate primed by the street battles of the 1960 Security Treaty Crisis to focus on parties' differences over national security policy (even as the vast majority of voters came to accept the compromise of the Yoshida Doctrine), electoral institutions that encouraged intra-party competition and clientelism, political institutions that made it difficult for prime ministers to exercise leadership, and rapid economic growth that validated Japan's version of state-led capitalism. Dancing to the predictable rhythms of this music, the parties developed stable ways of appealing for votes and making policy.

The Liberal Democratic Party (LDP) – always in the lead – developed an extensive network of ties to interest groups that benefited from the subsidies, loans, and regulatory protection the party offered in the name of helping the Japanese economy grow, all the while winning election after election by warning voters that the Cold War environment made it too risky to put the Socialists in charge. As Reed describes (in this volume), the party also developed electoral strategies – allowing victorious 'independents' who had just defeated LDP nominees into the party after the election – that made perfect sense under the old electoral rules.

Meanwhile, the Socialists, too, got quite comfortable dancing to this beat. They were never able to win, but appeals based on pacifism and their ties to organized labour were sufficient to guarantee them about 120 seats at every lower house election. Their noisy defence of the Constitution was sufficient to prevent significant departures from the Yoshida Doctrine, and the party's appeal to workers, farmers, and small business was threatening enough to keep the LDP attentive to these constituencies. By refusing to offer the voters a neoliberal alternative, the parties in effect conspired to maintain the nation's convoy system of protecting the weaker elements in society.

Then, in the 1990s, the music suddenly changed. The abrupt end of the Cold War took security issues (temporarily) off the table, just as the prolonged economic slump made voters question the established economic model and search for an alternative. New electoral rules adopted in 1994 just as suddenly changed the incentive and opportunity structure facing the parties. They now had an opportunity to appeal for votes based on issue positions, rather than clientelist appeals aimed at convincing specific constituencies to deliver their votes to specific candidates. Japan's *yamanote* (suburban) voters (see Weiner, in this volume) and salaried workers (see Miura, in this volume) became a particularly fought-over constituency as this large bloc of floating voters made 'reform' a valence issue. Parties now had to develop a groove that would match this hip-hop beat.

The new electoral system also forced parties to change tactics. Whereas the multi-member-district system had encouraged parties to welcome back victorious independents, the new system made it costly for the party to have two incumbents representing a single-member district. Yet the system also created new opportunities. Prime ministers could use their tighter control of nominations to force party backbenchers to follow their lead, and administrative reforms strengthening the Cabinet Office in the late 1990s created additional levers of power that party leaders could use to position the party to compete in elections.

This change of music was too much for the Socialists. Unable to shift gears from the well-practised moves the party had performed to the sounds of the 1955 System – that is, failing to connect with floating voters or to offer an economic policy alternative to the discredited status quo – the socialists were forced to the perimeter of the dance floor, winning as few as seven seats in recent lower house elections.

The LDP's adjustment was not smooth, either. Reed (in this volume) describes how the party struggled to deal with multiple claimants to single-member-district seats, and how the party failed to reform itself sufficiently, even after Koizumi Jun'ichirou showed it how to thrive in the new electoral environment in the 2005 election. But at least for a while, under Koizumi, the party seemed to find its groove. Both Maclachlan and Toyoda (in this volume) show how Koizumi was able to take full advantage of new leadership powers available to the prime minister to position the party to appeal to voters on the issue of 'reform' during the 2005 'postal' election. Martin (in this volume) describes how Koizumi's decisions to send naval ships to the Indian Ocean and troops to Iraq also helped the party in the 2005 election by attracting voters who found the party's position on security issues preferable to those of the opposition Democratic Party of Japan (DPJ). Finally, Miura (in this volume) also depicts Koizumi as deftly avoiding causing offence to the swing bloc of salaried voters while pursuing labour market reforms. Koizumi is well known for having preferred Elvis, so our musical metaphor does not work perfectly here, but of all of Japan's recent prime ministers, he is the one who seemed to move most adroitly to the sounds of hip hop. Reed predicts the LDP will have to stumble twice (once more, following the 2009 defeat) before it learns to perform the new moves in a consistent way.

Even as the LDP was struggling to adapt, the DPJ managed to push its way onto the dance floor in the 1990s, taking advantage of the Socialists' failure to adapt to the new music. Weiner (in this volume) describes how the DPJ was able to establish a firm base in the suburban parts of major metropolitan areas. Schoppa (in this volume) shows how the party positioned itself strategically to straddle the old cleavage over defence while offering voters a 'reformist' economic policy that promised less corruption and less waste. Finally, Martin (in this volume) reports on the party's recent success in differentiating itself from the LDP on security issues, something which seems to have paid dividends for the party after the obsessive focus on security policy under Koizumi's successors (especially Abe Shinzou) led voters to appreciate the DPJ's moderation on this issue. While the party fell short of victory in most of the elections we discuss, it was much more adept at performing to the new beat than were the Socialists.

The latest phase in the evolutionary dance commenced on 30 August 2009 with the DPJ's landslide victory over the LDP in the lower house election. What happened in that election, and what can it tell us about the dynamics of party system change going forward?

In essence, the LDP, having refused to learn from Koizumi's example, paid the price for failing to adapt to the new music. Looking back at electoral data over the past two decades, it is clear that the LDP had been floundering for a long time. The 2009 result was simply the culmination of trends that had been building since at least 1990 (see Figure 9.1). In the lower house election that year, the LDP won 33.6 per cent of the absolute vote, in large part because 36.6 per cent of voters were members of conservative organizations such as the farmers' cooperatives and local chambers of commerce. Voters belonging to these groups delivered their votes to the LDP in large numbers because, as we saw in the chapters by Toyoda and Maclachlan, these voters were linked to LDP candidates through clientelistic ties that had been cultivated over many years. Given the fact that many voters did not turn out on election day, that the other parties won the support of significantly lower shares of the electorate, and that the LDP earned a seat bonus as the largest party, this 33.6 per cent absolute vote share was sufficient for it to win a single-party majority in 1990 – as it had repeatedly since 1955.

Over the remainder of the decade, however, the LDP's vote share declined steadily, in tandem with the decline in the share of voters who belonged to conservative groups. Farmers were shrinking as a share of the electorate, and young people and urban salaried workers were not joining these groups. Then, after winning ever-smaller shares of the electorate in 1993 and 1996, the LDP was able to stem its vote losses, in large part by compensating for the continued shrinkage in its base constituencies by making a deal with the centrist Koumeitou ahead of the 2000 election. Koumeitou instructed its partisans to vote for the LDP in single-member districts in return for the benefits it achieved through the broader coalition arrangement.

While the deal with Koumeitou helped the LDP stem its loss of absolute vote share, it was only in 2005 that the LDP was able to lift its absolute vote share above this baseline. Koizumi pulled off this feat by winning over a larger share of floating voters by making postal reform a symbol of his effort to push through economic reforms over the objections of the LDP's traditional clients. Not surprisingly, this was not a sustainable strategy. The LDP could not hold onto its organizational vote while also appealing to floating voters by cutting off the

Figure 9.1: LDP and DPJ Vote Shares and Conservative Organized Votes, Lower House Elections, 1990–2009

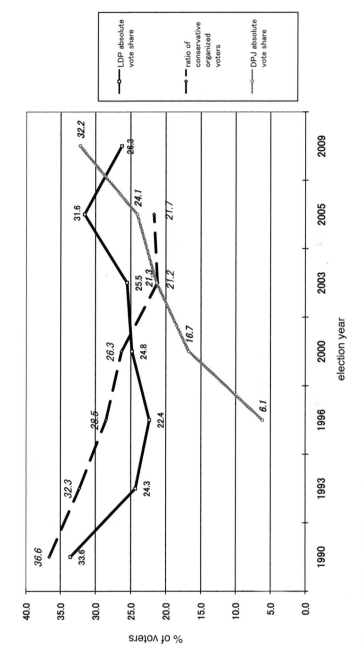

Sources: LDP and DPJ vote shares: Japan, Ministry of Home Affairs / Ministry of Internal Affairs and Communications, *Senkyo Kekka Shirabe*, 1972–2005; *Yomiuri Shimbun*, September 1, 2009; For conservative organized voters, Akarui Senkyo Suishin Kyokai, Nationwide Election Studies, 1972-2005.

flow of government support to its clients. By 2009, as Toyoda describes, Koizumi's successors had tarnished whatever reformist image he had managed to establish by welcoming the 'postal rebels' back into the party. Even this move, however, was not enough to soothe the wounds of all the LDP's traditional supporters, some of whom had switched their support to the DPJ to protest their treatment.

As a result, when the votes were counted on 30 August 2009, the LDP's absolute vote share had reverted roughly to what it had earned in the elections of 2000 and 2003. Of course, the party had held onto power in those years, so to account fully for the DPJ's landslide win in 2009, we now need to change our focus to this other dancer. Even as the LDP was failing to learn the new dance moves that Koizumi had attempted to teach it, the DPJ was steadily improving its rhythmic skills, winning ever-larger absolute shares of the vote (see Figure 9.1). The party received a setback in 2005 in terms of seats, not because it lost votes (it actually gained) but because the LDP earned a huge seat bonus in the single-member districts through its status as the largest party. In 2009, the DPJ simply carried on building its vote share, eclipsing that of the Koumeitou-assisted LDP and winning the big seat bonus the LDP had secured the previous time.

So what happens next? Almost two decades after the music abruptly changed, the two dancers are still struggling to find steady and reliable moves that fit the rhythms of the new electoral system, the new powers of the cabinet, the changing security situation, and an economy that continues to struggle.

The LDP is in deep trouble. By setting the postal system and government financial institutions on the road to privatization, Koizumi's efforts to take on his own party's old guard in order to win over floating voters has made it difficult for the party simply to revert to its old ways. There are not enough traditional voters left for the party to win elections if it is forced to rely primarily on this group, and even if it wanted to appeal to these voters, the economic reforms set in motion by Koizumi (and Hashimoto Ryuutarou before him) make it virtually impossible for it to rely on these old tactics. In the short term, moreover, the LDP's exclusion from office means that it cannot use government subsidies and loans to win votes. But the 2009 election brought defeat to so many 'Koizumi children' (the party lost 177 seats) that it left the party in the hands of a rump group composed primarily of veterans representing the most rural areas of the country. It will be difficult for this group to remake the LDP as a party that appeals to floating voters, and we concur with Reed that this is certainly not likely to happen ahead of the next lower house election.

While the DPJ's landslide win in 2009 puts it in a much stronger position than the LDP going forward, that party, too, faces some major challenges. As a young party, it still does not have much of a farm team: as Weiner shows (in this volume), the DPJ has struggled to find strong challengers to take on LDP incumbents. In 2009, even its weak single-member-district candidates won seats through their shared ranking on the proportional representation lists, so the party will run virtually the same slate of candidates next time, even though some did not go into the 2009 election with strong backgrounds. The farm team is particularly weak at the local level, where the party holds just 15 per cent of prefectural assembly seats.

The DPJ has also struggled to establish a stable position in policy space, with clear and appealing policy differences with its rivals that can attract votes. It achieved initial success with an 'economic reform' agenda calling for less wasted government spending (on infrastructure such as dams and bridges), a smaller and more transparent central government, and an end to the *amakudari* practice of placing retiring bureaucrats in sinecures in public corporations. But when Koizumi outflanked the DPJ with his own brand of reformism, the party began to place more emphasis on social welfare programs. It is still against waste and *amakudari,* but it voted to freeze the privatization of the postal services in late 2009, and its promise to offer every family the equivalent of US$276 a month for each child under age thirteen sounds to some voters like pork-barrel spending in a new guise. With Japan's ratio of debt to gross domestic product now as high as 200 per cent, the party is finding it difficult to strike a balance between these two tendencies. In fact, after budgeting for the first half of the promised child allowance in its first year in power, the party has been forced to postpone funding the second half. Is it the party of social welfare or the party of neoliberal reform?

It is interesting that the DPJ's struggle to establish a distinct issue identity in the area of economic policy has been shared by the LDP. That party, too, moved from 'convoy' social protection under the 1955 System to 'reform with no sacred cows' under Koizumi, and in the 2009 election was back to supporting expanded social welfare programs and aid to small business. As Martin notes, economic growth and welfare are both valence issues – at least in Japan: virtually all voters want more of both. As a result, neither the DPJ nor the LDP is willing to offer a platform that promises just one of these things, and each swings back and forth between stressing growth or welfare, depending on the economic and political climate. These issues are consistently the most important ones for Japanese voters, so the unwillingness of the parties to strike opposing positions on them – or to offer a distinctive policy that credibly promises to restore growth without threatening welfare – suggests that they are likely to continue 'dancing' in this way for some years to come.

As Martin shows, security policy is one area where the parties have established clearer, and more distinct, policy positions. Yet, its first year in office taught the DPJ that this issue can be a vote loser as well as a vote winner. In the 2009 election, it gained votes in part by promising a 'more equal' United States-Japan security partnership and by promising more specifically to reduce the burden of U.S. bases on Okinawa. Having learned that the United States was unwilling to reopen the Okinawa base agreement, the DPJ now faces the loss of votes on both sides. Okinawan protesters and sympathizers in the main islands are upset that Prime Minister Hatoyama Yukio failed to negotiate a new deal and that his successor Kan Naoto also committed to honouring the base agreement. Yet, the DPJ's decision to back down on their promises to Okinawans has done little to mollify voters who want the government to maintain smooth relations with the United States. They are upset that the DPJ caused strains in the alliance for no purpose. As a result, the DPJ is likely to be much more hesitant to campaign for votes on security issues in the future, leaving it to carry on the 'evolutionary dance' in this area as well.

Bibliography

Aldrich, John H., John L. Sullivan, and Eugene Borgida. 1989. 'Foreign Affairs and Issue Voting: Do Candidates "Waltz Before a Blind Audience?"' *American Political Science Review* 83 (1): 123–41.

Amyx, Jennifer A. 2004. *Japan's Financial Crisis*. Princeton, NJ: Princeton University Press.

Amyx, Jennifer A., Harukata Takenaka, and A. Maria Toyoda. 2005. 'The Politics of Postal Savings Reform in Japan.' *Asian Perspective* 29 (1): 23–48.

Aoki, Masahiko, and Hugh Patrick. 1994. *The Japanese Main Bank System*. Oxford: Clarendon Press.

Arai, Hiroyuki. 2003. *Yuubinkyoku wo amerika ni uriwatasuna*. Tokyo: Asuka Shinsha.

Bardi, Luciano. 2004. 'Party Responses to Electoral Dealignment in Italy.' In *Political Parties and Electoral Change*, edited by Peter Mair, Wolfgang C. Muller, and Fritz Plasser. London: Sage Publications.

Belloni, Frank, Mario Caciagli, and Liborio Mattina. 1979. 'The Mass Clientelism Party: The Christian Democratic Party in Catania and Southern Italy.' *European Journal of Political Research* 7 (3): 253–75.

Bessho, Shunichiro, and Hara Hiromi. 2006. 'Kumiaiin no seiji ishiki to touhyou koudou: Dai 19-kai sangiin senkyo wo tsuujite.' In *Suitaka saiseika: Roudou kumiai kasseika e no michi*, edited by Nakamura Keisuke. Tokyo: Keisou Shobou.

Browne, Eric C., and Sunwoong Kim. 2003. 'Factional Rivals and Electoral Competition in a Dominant Party: Inside Japan's Liberal Democratic Party, 1958–1990.' *European Journal of Political Research* 42 (1): 107–34.

Butler, David, and Dennis Kavanaugh. 1999. *The British General Election of 1992*. London: Macmillan.

Calder, Kent E. 1988. *Crisis and Compensation*. Princeton, NJ: Princeton University Press.

– 1995. *Strategic Capitalism*. Princeton, NJ: Princeton University Press.

Cargill, Thomas F., and Naoyuki Yoshino. 2003. *Savings & Fiscal Investment in Japan: The PSS and the FILP*. New York: Oxford University Press.

Carlile, Lonny E. 1998. 'The Politics of Administrative Reform.' In *Is Japan Really Changing Its Ways? Regulatory Reform and the Japanese Economy*, edited by Lonny E. Carlile and Mark C. Tilton. Washington, DC: Brookings Institution.

Carlile, Lonny E., and Mark C. Tilton. 1998. 'Regulatory Reform and the Developmental State.' In *Is Japan Really Changing Its Ways? Regulatory Reform and the Japanese Economy*, edited by Lonny E. Carlile and Mark C. Tilton. Washington, DC: Brookings Institution.

Carlson, Matthew M. 2006. 'Electoral Reform and the Evolution of Informal Norms in Japan.' *Asian Survey* 46 (3): 362–80.

– 2009. 'Japan's Postal Privatization Battle.' *Asian Survey* 48 (4): 603–25.

Carmines, Edward J., and James A. Stimson. 1989. *Issue Evolution: Race and the Transformation of American Politics*. Princeton, NJ: Princeton University Press.

Carpenter, Susan. 2003. *Special Corporations and the Bureaucracy: Why Japan Can't Reform*. New York: Palgrave Macmillan.

Carty, R. Kenneth. 2002. 'The Politics of Tecumseh Corners: Canadian Political Parties as Franchise Organizations.' *Canadian Journal of Political Science* 35 (4): 723–45.

Christensen, Raymond V. 1994. 'Electoral Reform in Japan.' *Asian Survey* 34 (7): 589–605.

– 1998. 'The Effects of Electoral Reform on Campaign Practices in Japan: Putting New Wine into Old Bottles.' *Asian Survey* 38 (10): 986–1004.

Chuujou, Ushio. 2001. 'Yuusei jigyou wo kanzen min'eikashi, jiyuukyousou wo dounyuuseyo.' In *Yuuseimin'eika: Koizumi gen'an*, edited by Mizuno Kiyoshi, Matsubara Satoru, Chuujou Ushio, and Matsuda Makoto. Tokyo: Shogakukan Bunko.

Colignon, Richard A., and Chikako Usui. 2003. *Amukudari: The Hidden Fabric of Japan's Economy*. Ithaca, NY: ILR Press.

Conradt, David P. 1978. *The German Polity*. New York: Longman.

Curtis, Gerald L. 1988. *The Japanese Way of Politics*. New York: Columbia University Press.

– 1999. *The Logic of Japanese Politics: Leaders, Institutions, and the Limits of Change*. New York: Columbia University Press.

Dalton, Russell J., and Martin P. Wattenberg. 2000. *Parties without Partisans*. Oxford: Oxford University Press.

Di Virgilio, Aldo, and Steven R. Reed. 2010. 'Nominating Candidates under New Rules in Italy and Japan: You Cannot Bargain with Resources You Do Not Have.' In *A Natural Experiment on Electoral Law Reform: Evaluating the Long Run Consequences of 1990s Electoral Reform in Italy and Japan,* edited by D. Giannetti and B. Grofman. New York: Springer.

Doi, Takero, and Takeo Hoshi. 2003. 'Paying for the FILP.' In *Structural Impediments to Growth in Japan,* edited by M. Blomstrom et al. Chicago: University of Chicago Press.

Dore, Ronald. 2002. *Stock Market Capitalism: Welfare Capitalism: Japan and Germany versus the Anglo-Saxons.* New York: Oxford University Press.

– 2006. *Dareno tameno kaisha ni suruka.* Tokyo: Iwanami Bunko.

Downs, Anthony. 1957. *An Economic Theory of Democracy.* New York: Harper.

Enloe, Cynthia. 2004. *The Curious Feminist: Searching for Women in a New Age of Empire.* Berkeley: University of California Press.

Estevez-Abe, Margarita. 2006. 'Japan's Shift toward a Westminster System: A Structural Analysis of the 2005 Lower House Election and Its Aftermath.' *Asian Survey* 46 (4): 633–52.

Flanagan, Scott C., Shinsaku Kohei, Ichiro Miyake, Bradley M. Richardson, and Joji Watanuki. 1976. *JABISS: The Japanese Election Study.* Tokyo.

Foote, Daniel. 1996. 'Judicial Creation of Norms in Japanese Labor Law: Activism in the Service – Stability?' *UCLA Law Review* 43 (3): 635–709.

Frühstück, Sabine. 2007. *Uneasy Warriors: Gender, Memory, and Popular Culture in the Japanese Army.* Berkeley: University of California Press.

Garon, Sheldon. 1987. *The State and Labor in Modern Japan.* Berkeley: University of California Press.

Garon, Sheldon, and Mike Mochizuki. 1993. 'Negotiating Social Contracts.' In *Postwar Japan as History,* edited by Andrew Gordon. Berkeley: University of California Press.

Golder, Matt. 2003. 'An Evolutionary Approach to Party System Stability.' Paper presented at the 2003 Midwest Political Science Association Meeting, Chicago, 3–6 April.

Green, Michael. 2000. 'The Challenges of Managing U.S.-Japan Security Relations after the Cold War.' In *New Perspectives on U.S.-Japan Relations,* edited by Gerald L. Curtis. Tokyo: Japan Center for International Exchange.

– 2010. 'Japan's Confused Revolution.' *Washington Quarterly* 33 (1): 3–19.

Hayao, Kenji. 1993. *The Japanese Prime Minister and Public Policy.* Pittsburgh: University of Pittsburgh Press.

Honma, Shuichi. 2003. *Tokutei yuubinkyokuchou ni natta boku no rakudai nikki.* Tokyo: Shinfuusha.

Horiuchi, Yusaku, and Jun Saito. 2003. 'Reapportionment and Redistribution: Consequences of Electoral Reform in Japan.' *American Journal of Political Science* 47 (4): 669–82.

Ikeda, Ken'ichi, Yoshiaki Kobayashi, and Hiroshi Hirano. 2005. *Nationwide Time-Series Survey on Voting Behavior in the Beginning of the 21st Century, 2001–2005.* Tokyo: Japan Election Studies III, Social Science Japan Data Archive.

Ikeo, Aiko. 2003. 'Structural Reforms and the Role of Economists in Japan: From the 1980s to the Present.' Paper presented at the Annual Meeting of the Japanese Society for the History of Economic Thought, Doshisha University, Kyoto, 24–25 May.

Ishibashi, Michihiro, and Steven R. Reed. 1992. 'Hereditary Seats: Second Generation Dietmen and Democracy in Japan.' *Asian Survey* 32 (4): 366–79.

Ishibashi, Natsuyo. 2007. 'The Dispatch of Japan's Self-Defense Forces to Iraq.' *Asian Survey* 47 (5): 766–89.

Ishikawa, Tatsujiro, and Mitsuhide Imashiro. 1998. *The Privatization of Japanese National Railways.* London: Athlone Press.

Itagaki, Eiken. 2008. *Minshutou habatsu kousou shi: minshutou no yukue.* Tokyo: Kyouei Shobou.

Iwamoto, Yasushi. 2002. 'The Fiscal Investment and Loan Program in Transition.' *Journal of the Japanese and International Economies* 16 (4): 583–604.

Japan. 2003. Ministry of Finance. 'The Role of Government and the FILP.' Tokyo. Available online at http://www.mof.go.jp/zaito/English/Za2003-01-01.html.

– 2005. Ministry of Internal Affairs and Communications. Statistics Bureau. *Japan Statistical Yearbook 2006.* Tokyo. Available online at http://www.stat.go.jp/English/data/nenkan1431-11.htm.

– 2009. Prime Minister's Office. 'Jieitai-bouei mondai ni kan suru seiron chousa.' Availble online at http://www8.cao.go.jp/survey/h20/h20-bouei/index.html.

Johnson, Chalmers. 1978. *Japan's Public Policy Companies.* Washington, DC; Stanford, CA: American Enterprise Institute and Hoover Institute.

– 1982. *MITI and the Japanese Miracle: The Growth of Industrial Policy, 1925–1975.* Stanford, CA: Stanford University Press.

Kabashima, Ikuo, Joji Watanuki, Ichiro Miyake, Yoshiaki Kobayashi, and Ken'ichi Ikeda. 1993–96. *Japan Election Study II.* Tokyo.

Kabashima, Ikuo, and Takenaka Yoshihiko. 1996. *Gendai Nihonjin no ideorogi.* Tokyo: Tokyo Daigaku Shuppankai.

Kasai, Yoshiyuki. 2003. *Japanese National Railways: Its Break-up and Privatization.* Folkestone, UK: Global Oriental.

Kataoka, Masaaki. 1994. *Chijishoku o meguru kanryou to seijika: Jimintou no kouhosha senkou seiji.* Tokyo: Bokutakusha.

Kato, Junko, and Michael Laver. 1998. 'Party Policy and Cabinet Portfolios in Japan, 1996.' *Party Politics* 4 (2): 253–60.
– 2003. 'Policy and Party Competition in Japan after the Election of 2000.' *Japanese Journal of Political Science* 4 (1): 121–33.
Kato, Kozo, Tsutomu Shibata, Koichiro Fukui, Aiichiro Mogi, Yuichiro Miwa, Yoshikazi Niwa, Nobuhiko Ichikawa, and Masahiro Furuta. 1994. *Policy-Based Finance* 1 (1): 1–251.
Katz, Richard S., and Peter Mair. 1995. 'Party Organization, Party Democracy, and the Emergence of the Cartel Party.' *Party Politics* 1 (1): 5–28.
Kitschelt, Herbert. 2000. 'Linkages Between Citizens and Politicians in Democratic Polities.' *Comparative Political Studies* 33 (6): 845–79.
Kobayashi, Masayoshi. 2001. *Minna no yuubinbunkashi: Kindai nihon wo sodateta jouhoudentatsu shisutemu.* Tokyo: Nijuuni.
Kohei, Shinsaku, Ichiro Miyake, and Joji Watanuki. 1991. 'Issues and Voting Behavior.' In *The Japanese Voter,* edited by Scott C. Flanagan et al. New Haven, CT: Yale University Press.
Koizumi, Jun'ichirou. 1999. 'Forward.' In *Yuusei mineikaron: Nihon saisei no dai-kaikaku,* edited by Koizumi Jun'ichirou and Matsuzawa Shigefumi. Tokyo: PHP Kenkyuujo.
Kollner, Patrick. 2002. 'Upper House Elections in Japan and the Power of the "Organized Vote."' *Japanese Journal of Political Science* 3 (1): 113–37.
Krauss, Ellis S., and Benjamin Nyblade. 2005. '"Presidentialization" in Japan? The Prime Minister, Media and Elections in Japan.' *British Journal of Political Science* 35 (2): 357–68.
Krauss, Ellis S., and Robert Pekkanen. 2004. 'Explaining Party Adaptation to Electoral Reform: The Discreet Charm of the LDP.' *Journal of Japanese Studies* 30 (1): 1–34.
Kume, Ikuo. 1998. *Disparaged Success: Labor Politics in Postwar Japan.* Ithaca, NY: Cornell University Press.
– 2005. *Roudou seiji.* Tokyo: Chuukou Shinsho.
Laver, Michael, and Kenneth Benoit. 2005. 'Estimating Party Policy Positions: Japan in Comparative Context.' *Japanese Journal of Political Science* 6 (2): 187–209.
Lee, Kap-Yun, Mari Miura, and Robert Weiner. 2005. 'Who Are the DPJ? Policy Positioning and Recruitment Strategy.' *Asian Perspective* 29 (1): 49–77.
Lin, Chao Chi. 2009. 'How Koizumi Won.' In *Political Change in Japan: Electoral Behavior, Party Realignment, and the Koizumi Reforms,* edited by Steven R. Reed, Kenneth Mori McElwain, and Kay Shimizu. Washington, DC: Brookings Institution.
Lipset, Seymour M., and Stein Rokkan. 1967. 'Cleavage Structures, Party Systems, and Voter Alignments: An Introduction.' In *Party Systems and*

Voter Alignments: Cross National Perspectives., edited by Seymour M. Lipset and Stein Rokkan. New York: Free Press.

Luther, Kurt Richard, and Kris Deschouwer, eds. 1999. *Party Elites in Divided Societies: Political Parties in Consociational Democracy.* London: Routledge.

Mackie, Vera. 2003. *Feminism in Modern Japan: Citizenship, Embodiment, and Sexuality.* Cambridge: Cambridge University Press.

Maclachlan, Patricia L. 2004. 'Post Office Politics in Modern Japan: The Postmasters, Iron Triangles, and the Limits of Reform.' *Journal of Japanese Studies* 30 (2): 281–313.

Mair, Peter. 1997. *Party Systems Change: Approaches and Interpretations.* Oxford: Clarendon Press.

Mair, Peter, and Michael Marsh. 2004. 'Political Parties and Electoral Markets in Postwar Ireland.' In *Political Parties and Electoral Change*, edited by Peter Mair, Wolfgang C. Muller, and Fritz Plasser. London: Sage Publications.

Makihara, Izuru. 2005. 'Sengo seiji no soukessan' ga mamonaku owaru: Rekishi kara mita keizai zaisei shimon kaigi to sono shouraizou.' *Ronza* (August): 53–62.

Martin, Sherry L. 2008a. 'Gender, Vote Choice, and the Evolving Security and Defense Debates in Japanese Politics.' Cambridge, MA: Harvard University, Weatherhead Center for International Affairs, Program on U.S.-Japan Relations.

– 2008b. 'Japanese Political Attitudes Against an Evolving Political Landscape.' In *Japan's Political Mess: Abe Failed, Can Fukuda Do Better?*, edited by Mark Mohr. Washington, DC: Woodrow Wilson International Center for Scholars.

Martin, Sherry L., and Gill Steel, eds. 2008. *Democratic Reform in Japan: Assessing the Impact.* Boulder, CO: Lynne Rienner Publishers.

Matsubara, Satoru, ed. 1996. *Gendai no yuusei jigyou.* Tokyo: Nihon Hyouronsha.

– 2001. *Yuuseimineika de kou kawaru: Kokuei shinwa ni wa, mou damasarenai.* Tokyo: Kadokawa.

Mayhew, David R., and R. Douglas Arnold. 2006. *Congress.* 2nd ed. New Haven, CT: Yale University Press.

McKean, Margaret, and Ethan Scheiner. 2000. 'Japan's New Electoral System: la plus ça change.' *Electoral Studies* 19 (4): 447–77.

Mishima, Ko. 1998. 'The Changing Relationship between Japan's LDP and the Bureaucracy: Hashimoto's Administrative Reform Effort and Its Politics.' *Asian Survey* 38 (10): 968–85.

Miura, Mari. 2002. 'Roudou kisei: Atarashi seiji to kyohiken.' In *Ryuudouki no nihon seiji*, edited by Hiwatari Nobuhiro and Miura Mari. Tokyo: Daigaku Shuppankai.

– 2007. 'Koizumi kaikaku to roudou seiji no henyou: "Tasuuha shihaigata" no seisaku katei no shutsugen.' *Nenpou gyousei kenkyuu* 42: 100–22.

– 2008. 'Labor Politics in Japan during "the Lost Fifteen Years": From the Politics of Productivity to the Politics of Consumption.' *Labor History* 49 (2): 161–76.

Miura, Mari, Kap Yun Lee, and Robert Weiner. 2005. 'Who Are the DPJ? Policy Positioning and Recruitment Strategy.' *Asian Perspective* 29 (1): 49–77.

Miyawaki, Atushi. 1993. 'The Fiscal Investment and Loan System towards the 21st Century.' *Japan Research Quarterly* 2: 15–66.

Mizuno, Kiyoshi, Matsubara Satoru, Chuujou Ushio, and Matsuda Makoto. 2001. *Yuusei min'eika: Koizumi gen'an.* Tokyo: Shogakukan Bunko.

Mochizuki, Mike. 1993. 'Public Sector Labor and the Privatization Challenge: The Railway and Telecommunications Unions.' In *Political Dynamics in Contemporary Japan,* edited by Gary D. Allinson and Yasunori Sone. Ithaca, NY: Cornell University Press.

Mulgan, Aurelia George. 2002. *Japan's Failed Revolution: Koizumi and the Politics of Economic Reform.* Canberra: Asia Pacific Press.

Muramatsu, Michio. 1997. *Local Power in the Japanese State.* Berkeley, CA: University of California Press.

Nakakita, Koji. 1999. 'Rengou.' In *Seiji kaikaku 1800-nichi no shinjitsu,* edited by Sasaki Takeshi. Tokyo: Koudansha.

Nakamura, Keisuke, ed. 2005. *Suitai ka saisei ka: Roudou kumiai kasseika e no michi.* Tokyo: Keisou Shobou.

– 2006. *Seikashugi no shinjitsu.* Tokyo: Touyou Keizai Shinpousha.

Neto, Octavio Amorim, and Gary W. Cox. 1997. 'Electoral Institutions, Cleavage Structures, and the Number of Parties.' *American Journal of Political Science* 41 (1): 149–74.

Nihon Keizai Dantai Rengoukai Keiei Roudou Seisaku Iinkai. 1995. *Keiei roudou seisaku iinkai houkoku.* Tokyo.

– 2003. *Keiei roudou seisaku iinkai houkoku.* Tokyo.

Nikkei Business. 2002. *Dare mo shiranai yuusei teikoku.* Tokyo: Nikkei BPsha.

Nikkeiren. 1995. 'Shinjidai no "Nihonteki Keiei": Chousen Subeki Houkou to Sono Gutaisaku.' *Shin Nihonteki Keiei Sisutemu-tou Kenkyuu Purojekuto.* Tokyo.

Nitta, Michio. 2003. *Henka no naka no koyou shisutemu.* Tokyo: Tokyo University Press.

Noble, Gregory W. 2006. 'Front Door, Back Door: The Reform of Postal Savings and Loans in Japan.' *The Japanese Economy* 33 (1): 107–23.

Noguchi, Yukio. 1995. 'The Role of the Fiscal Investment and Loan Program in Postwar Japanese Economic Growth.' In *The Japanese Civil Service and Economic Development,* edited by Hyung-Ki, Kozo Yamamura, Michio Muramastu, and T.J. Pempel. Oxford: Clarendon Press.

Ordeshook, Peter, and Olga Shvetsova. 1994. 'Ethnic Heterogeneity, District Magnitude, and the Number of Parties.' *American Journal of Political Science* 38 (1): 100–23.

Oros, Andrew L. 2007. 'Listening to the People: Japanese Democracy and the New Security Agenda.' The Mansfield Asian Opinion Poll Database. Available online at http://www.mansfieldfdn.org/polls/Commentaries/commentary-07-3.htm.

Otake, Hideo. 1993. 'The Rise and Retreat of a Neoliberal Reform: Controversies over Land Use Policy.' In *Political Dynamics in Contemporary Japan,* edited by Gary Allinson and Yasunori Sone. Ithaca, NY: Cornell University Press.

– 2000. 'Political Realignment and Policy Conflict.' In *Power Shuffles and Policy Processes,* edited by Hideo Otake. Tokyo: Japan Center for International Exchange.

Outa, Hiroko. 2006. *Keizai zaisei shimon kaigi no tatakai.* Tokyo: Touyou Keizai Shinpousha.

Outake, Fumio, and Okudaira Hiroko. 2006. 'Kobetsu Rōshi Funsō no Kettei Youin,' *Nihon Rōdō Kenkyū Zasshi* 548: 4–19.

Ozawa, Ichirou. 1994. *Blueprint for a New Japan.* Tokyo: Koudansha International.

Patterson, Dennis. 1994. 'Electoral Influence and Economic Policy: The Political Origins of Financial Aid to Small Business in Japan.' *Comparative Political Studies* 27 (3): 425–47.

Patzelt, Werner J. 2000. 'What Can an Individual MP Do in German Parliamentary Politics?' In *The Uneasy Relationships between Parliamentary Members and Leaders,* edited by Lawrence D. Longley, and Reuven Y. Hazan. London: Frank Cass.

Pempel, T.J. 1982. *Policy and Politics in Japan: Creative Conservatism.* Philadelphia: Temple University Press.

– 1997. 'Regime Shift: Japanese Politics in a Changing World Economy.' *Journal of Japanese Studies* 23 (2): 333–61.

– 1998. *Regime Shift: Comparative Dynamics of the Japanese Political Economy.* Ithaca, NY: Cornell University Press.

Pempel, T.J., and Keiichi Tsunekawa. 1979. 'Corporatism without Labor?' In *Trends toward Corporatist Intermediation,* edited by Philippe C. Schmitter and Gerhard Lehmbruch. London: Sage Publications.

Pierson, Paul. 2004. *Politics in Time: History, Institutions, and Social Analysis.* Princeton, NJ: Princeton University Press.

Pontusson, Jonas. 2005. 'Varieties and Commonalities of Capitalism.' In *Varieties of Capitalism, Varieties of Approaches,* edited by David Coates. New York: Palgrave Macmillan.

Pyle, Kenneth. 2007. *Japan Rising: The Resurgence of Japanese Power and Purpose.* New York: The Century Foundation.

Quigley, Harold S., and John E. Turner. 1956. *The New Japan.* Minneapolis: University of Minnesota Press.

Reed, Steven R. 2003. *Japanese Electoral Politics: Creating a New Party System.* London: RoutledgeCurzon.

– 2009. 'Party Strategy or Candidate Strategy: How Did the LDP Run the Right Number of Candidates in Japan's Multi-Member Districts?' *Party Politics* 15 (3): 295–314.

– Forthcoming. 'The Liberal Democratic Party: An Explanation of Its Successes and Failures.' *The Routledge Handbook of Japanese Politics.* London: Routledge.

Reed, Steven R., and Ethan Scheiner. 2003. 'Electoral Incentives and Policy Preferences: Mixed Motives behind Party Defections in Japan.' *British Journal of Political Science* 33 (3): 469–90.

Reed, Steven R., Ethan Scheiner, and Michael F. Thies. 2009. 'New Ballgame in Politics.' *The Oriental Economist* 77 (10): 8–9.

Reed, Steven R., and Michael Thies. 2001. 'The Causes of Electoral Reform.' In *Mixed-Member Electoral Systems: The Best of Both Worlds?,* edited by Matthew Shugart and Martin Wattenberg. New York: Oxford University Press.

Rengou 21-seiki e no Chousen Iinkai. 2001. *21-seiki wo kiri hiraku roudou undou: 21-seiki rengou bijon.* Tokyo: Rengou.

Rosenbluth, Frances McCall. 1989. *Financial Politics in Contemporary Japan.* Ithaca, NY: Cornell University Press.

Samuels, Richard J. 2003. 'Leadership and Political Change in Japan: The Case of the Second Rinchou.' *Journal of Japanese Studies* 29 (1): 1–31.

– 2007. *Securing Japan: Tokyo's Grand Strategy and the Future of East Asia.* Ithaca, NY: Cornell University Press.

Sartori, Giovanni. 1968. 'Political Development and Political Engineering.' *Public Policy* 17: 261–98.

Scarrow, Susan E. 1996. *Parties and Their Members: Organizing for Victory in Britain and Germany.* London: Oxford University Press.

– 2004. 'Embracing Dealignment, Combating Realignment: German Parties Respond.' In *Political Parties and Electoral Change: Party Responses to Electoral Markets,* edited by Peter Mair, Wolfgang C. Muller, and Fritz Plasser. London: Sage Publications.

Scheiner, Ethan. 2006. *Democracy without Competition in Japan: Opposition Failure in a One-Party Dominant State.* Cambridge: Cambridge University Press.

Scher, Mark J., and Naoyuki Yoshino. 2004. 'Policy Challenges and the Reform of Postal Savings in Japan.' In *Small Savings Mobilization and Asian*

Economic Development: The Role of Postal Financial Services, edited by Mark Scher and Naoyuki Yoshio. New York: M.E. Sharpe.

Schlesinger, Jacob M. 1999. *Shadow Shoguns: The Rise and Fall of Japan's Postwar Political Machine.* Stanford, CA: Stanford University Press.

Schoppa, Leonard. 2006a. 'Neoliberal Economic Policy Preferences of the "New Left."' In *The Left in the Shaping of Japanese Democracy: Essays in Honour of J.A.A. Stockwin,* edited by Rikki Kersten and David Williams. London: Routledge.

– 2006b. *Race for the Exits: The Unraveling of Japan's System of Social Protection.* Ithaca, NY: Cornell University Press.

Schwartz, Frank J. 1993. 'Of Fairy Cloaks and Familiar Talks: The Politics of Consultation.' In *Political Dynamics in Contemporary Japan,* edited by Gary D. Allinson and Yasunori Sone. Ithaca, NY: Cornell University Press.

– 1998. *Advice and Consent: The Politics of Consultation in Japan.* Cambridge: Cambridge University Press.

Shefter, Martin. 1977. 'Party and Patronage: Germany, England, and Italy.' *Politics and Society* 7 (4): 403–52.

Shinoda, Tomohito. 2007. *Koizumi Diplomacy: Japan's Kantei Approach to Foreign and Defense Affairs.* Seattle: University of Washington Press.

Shiroyama, Hideaki. 2003. 'Seisaku katei ni okeru keizai zaisei shimon kaigi no yakuwari to tokushitsu: Unyou bunseki to kokusai hikaku no kanten-kara.' *Kokusai koukyou kenkyuu* 3: 34–45.

Shugart, Matthew Soberg, and Martin P. Wattenberg, eds. 2001. *Mixed-Member Electoral Systems: The Best of Both Worlds?* Oxford: Oxford University Press.

Solis, Mireya. 2004. *Banking on Multinationals: Public Credit and the Export of Japanese Sunset Industries.* Stanford, CA: Stanford University Press.

Steel, Gill. 2008. 'Policy Preferences and Party Platforms: What Voters Want vs. What Voters Get.' In *Democratic Reform in Japan: Assessing the Impact,* edited by Sherry L. Martin and Gill Steel. Boulder, CO: Lynne Rienner Publishers.

Sugeno, Kazuo. 2000. *Roudouhou,* 5th ed. Tokyo: Kobundo.

Takazato, Suzuyo. 1996. 'The Past and Future of Unai: Sisters in Okinawa.' In *Voices from the Japanese Women's Movement.* Armonk, NY: M.E. Sharpe.

Takenaka, Heizou. 2006. *Kouzou kaikaku no shinjitsu: Takenaka Heizou daijin nikki.* Tokyo: Nihon Keizai Shimbunsha.

Tanaka, Aiji. 1997. 'Seitou shiji nashisou no ishiki kouzou.' *Leviathan* 20: 101–29.

Tanaka, Aiji, and Sherry Martin. 2003. 'The New Independent Voter and the Evolving Japanese Party System.' *Asian Perspective* 27 (3): 21–51.

Thelen, Kathleen. 2004. *How Institutions Evolve: The Political Economy of Skills in Germany, Britain, the United States, and Japan.* Cambridge: Cambridge University Press.

Tiberghien, Yves. 2007. *Entrepreneurial States: Reforming Corporate Governance in France, Japan, and Korea.* Ithaca, NY: Cornell University Press.

Tilton, Mark. 2004. 'Neoliberal Capitalism in the Information Age: Japan and the Politics of Telecommunications Reform.' *JPRI Working Paper* 98. San Francisco: Japan Policy Research Institute.

Toshikawa, Takao, and Richard Katz. 2008. 'Post-election Realignment? Whole Lot of Shakeup Goin' On.' *Oriental Economist Report* 76 (11): 1–3.

Visser, Jelle. 2006. 'Union Membership Statistics in 24 Countries.' *Monthly Labor Review* 129 (1): 38–49.

Vittas, Dmitri, and Akihiko Kawaura. 1995. 'Policy-based Finance, Financial Regulation, and Financial Sector Development in Japan.' World Bank Policy Research Working Paper WPS 1443. Washington, DC: World Bank.

Vogel, Steven K. 1996. *Freer Markets, More Rules.* Ithaca, NY: Cornell University Press.

– 1999. 'Can Japan Disengage? Winners and Losers in Japan's Political Economy, and the Ties that Bind Them.' *Social Science Japan Journal* 2 (1): 3–21.

– 2006. *Japan Remodeled: How Government and Industry Are Reforming Japanese Capitalism.* Ithaca, NY: Cornell University Press.

Watanuki, Joji, Ichiro Miyake, Takashi Inoguchi, and Ikuo Kabashima. *Japan Election Study 1983.* Tokyo.

Weathers, Charles. 2004. 'Temporary Workers, Women and Labour Policymaking in Japan.' *Japan Forum* 16 (3): 423–47.

Weiner, Robert. 2008. 'Prefectural Politics: Party and Electoral Stagnation.' In *Political Reform in Japan: Assessing the Impact,* edited by Sherry Martin and Gill Steel. Boulder, CO: Lynne Rienner Publishers.

Yamamoto, Mari. 2004. *Grassroots Pacifism in Post-War Japan.* New York: RoutledgeCurzon.

Yomiuri Shimbun Seijibu. 2005. *Jiminto wo kowashita otoko: Koizumi seiken sengohyakunichi no shinjitsu.* Tokyo: Yomiuri Shimbunsha.

Zysman, J. 1983. *Governments, Markets and Growth: Finance and the Politics of Industrial Change.* Utica, NY: Cornell University Press.

Contributors

Patricia L. Maclachlan is Associate Professor of Government and Asian Studies at the University of Texas, Austin.

Sherry L. Martin is Associate Professor in the Department of Government and the Program in Feminist, Gender, and Sexuality Studies at Cornell University.

Mari Miura is Professor of Political Science in the Faculty of Law at Sophia University in Tokyo.

Steven R. Reed is Professor of Modern Government at Chuo University in Tokyo.

Leonard J. Schoppa is Professor of Politics at the University of Virginia.

Aiji Tanaka is Professor of Political Science in the Faculty of Political Science and Economics at Waseda University in Tokyo.

A. Maria Toyoda is Associate Professor in the Department of Political Science at Villanova University.

Robert J. Weiner is Assistant Professor in the School of International Graduate Studies at the Naval Postgraduate School, specializing in Japanese and comparative politics.

Index

1955 System, of Japanese parties: collapse of, 27–34; definition of, 4; endurance of, 16, 19–22; politics and policy under, 7–12, 21, 73, 101–2, 205

2000 System, of Japanese parties: 6–9, 12, 14–15, 71; forces shaping emergence of, 27–39

Abe, Shinzou, 59–60, 105, 144, 177, 207
amakudari, 39, 131, 153, 158, 169, 172
Asou, Tarou, 39, 60, 140, 171, 198, 202n9

bank bailouts, 6, 9, 161
Benoit, Kenneth, 15
bubble economy (collapse of), 8, 9, 12

Cabinet Office: formation of, 139, 166, 175n14, 184, 206; role in empowering the prime minister, 159–60, 162, 167, 172
Carmines, Edward, 100, 103, 117n2
catch-all parties, 21, 32, 91

CEFP. *See* Council for Economic and Fiscal Policy
CGP. *See* Koumeitou
child allowances, 7, 39, 117, 211
China, 108–9, 194
Clean Government Party. *See* Koumeitou
clientelism, 24, 44–5, 142, 215
Cold War: 20, 206; as source of major cleavage in the 1955 party system, 4, 19; effects of its sudden end, 9, 30–1, 40, 103–4, 107–8
Communist Party (of Japan). *See* Japan Communist Party
Conservative Party, 5, 14, 64
convoy capitalism, 4, 6–9, 29, 36, 211. *See also* state-led capitalism
corruption, 29, 31, 52–3, 59
Council for Economic and Fiscal Policy: and labour policy, 184–7, 192, 195; central role under Koizumi, 167–8, 171, 199; establishment of, 139–40, 166; Hatoyama disbands it, 200
cow-walking, 30–1, 41n5
critical juncture, 15–16, 107